*PACIFIC*

*OCEAN*

Is.

ma

rianas Is.
pan
m

Truk

NE IS.

ator

· · . Midway Is.

HAWAIIAN· · Oahu
IS.
Pearl
Harbor

· Wake

MARSHALL IS.

Makin

Tarawa     Christmas Is.

Gilbert Is.

Bougainville
SOLOMON IS.
Guadalcanal

Samoa Is.

ral Sea

New
Caledonia

Fiji Is.     Cook Is.

Sydney

*Tasman
Sea*

NEW
ZEALAND

# THE PACIFIC: *Then and Now*

Bruce Bahrenburg

# THE PACIFIC:

## THEN AND NOW

G. P. Putnam's Sons, New York

*To Mickey McMenimen, good friend and managing editor of the Newark* News, *whose interest in the Pacific dating to his service there with the U.S. Marines during World War II made the trip possible*

# Acknowledgments

To Dawn Lospaluto, associate editor of the Newark *News Sunday Magazine,* for her invaluable work on the manuscript; to Frank Dailey, art director of the *Sunday Magazine,* who drew the maps and designed the photograph sections; to Jacqueline Maglione, travel consultant in Pan American's Newark office for arranging the complicated travel schedule in the Pacific; to the information departments of the U.S. Army and Marine Corps in Washington, D.C., for their cooperation in providing combat photographs; to the Monmouth County library in Shrewsbury for its fine collection of World War II histories and its staff which helped me find them; and to William Goldman, who suggested that the series of articles on which this book is based and which first appeared in the Newark *News* could become a book.

# Contents

*Illustrations follow pages 128 and 256.*

# THE PACIFIC: *Then and Now*

# Pearl Harbor

Kolekole Pass lies at the top of a narrow road curving up the side of the mountain from Schofield Barracks. The only sounds there are the metallic humming of the high-tension wires and the muted shushing of the wind-stirred leaves. Occasionally a military car makes its way to the pass, a black shell when it first appears at the bottom of the multicolored valley, but a formidably correct vehicle when it reaches the top and pulls over to the graveled shoulder of the road. An enlisted man quickly gets out of the front seat and snaps open the back door for two middle-aged ladies who alight slowly, without acknowledging his presence, and move cautiously toward the edge of the abutment. Below, the valley is an undulating wave of green and brown squares disrupted by outcroppings of purple spiny ridges. The wind down there is strong enough to slow the flight of birds, momentarily catching and shuttling them upward before their wings take hold. Beyond the valley is the Pacific Ocean, a placid layer of blue shattered at its edge by white-topped waves rushing to shore. The women hold up cameras to the undefined vastness and snap a few pictures without focusing on a specific object. They return to the car, past the driver holding the door open for them. The car proceeds down the southern slope. On the left in a distant field is the skeleton of an abandoned encampment: barrack foundations and stalls of outdoor latrines. There is still the impression of once-used paths in the weeds. On the right side of the road, back up the rocky slope, a huge white cross stands on the dark side of the mountain. At the bottom of the hill, after a slow weaving descent, the car is lost to a thicket of trees edging the plateau on which Schofield Barracks is built, and the pass is again reclaimed by silence.

At 7:55 A.M. on December 7, 1941, Japanese torpedo planes and bombers roared over the pass toward the southern coast of Oahu where, at Pearl Harbor, Hickam and Wheeler fields, and Schofield Barracks, a war began that was to be waged across tiny atolls in the turquoise Pacific and up verdant extinct volcanoes until it was ended more than three and a half years later in the blinding atomic explosions of Hiroshima and Nagasaki.

The war was to circle the globe for five years, and fifty-seven nations became participants. When it was over, the dead among the Allied and Axis military personnel totaled more than 15,000,000. The U.S. battle dead numbered 292,100, of whom 234,874 were soldiers and airmen, 19,733 Marines, and 36,950 sailors. The cost to the United States of mobilizing 12,000,000 men to fight the war, and of supplying her allies, was $350 billion.

Before Pearl Harbor, the United States had been able to stay out of the European war even while overtly supporting Great Britain against Germany and Italy. But she couldn't stay out of the war that began in Hawaii, her major Pacific territory, when 360 Japanese planes took off from six carriers in a task force located several hundred miles north of Oahu and brought crippling destruction to the U.S. Pacific fleet.

This war had become inevitable when the United States, in an act of cooperative retaliation with England and the Netherlands, placed an oil embargo against Japan after she had invaded Indochina. Earlier Japanese acts of aggression in Asia, especially against China, had forced the United States, somewhat belatedly, to impose scrap-iron and steel embargoes. But without oil Japan would be unable to solidify her Greater East Asia Co-Prosperity Sphere which was to include, by either military conquest or economic enslavement, her already-acquired territories of Korea, Manchuria, French Indochina, and parts of China, as well as the soon to be annexed East Indies, Burma, Malaya, and the Philippines.

Japan never seriously considered attacking the mainland of the United States; she didn't have the weapons for it. But to protect her Pacific acquisitions, Japan thought it necessary to establish a defense perimeter that included Wake and the Marshall Islands, two U.S. possessions west of Hawaii. To take them by land troops and to remove any military threat to her Co-Prosperity Sphere, Japan knew she would first have to destroy the U.S. Pacific fleet that was recently assigned to permanent base in Pearl Harbor. Throughout 1941 Japan's best military strategists worked on plans to conduct a sneak attack against Pearl Harbor. There was no doubt among the Japanese warlords it would have to be carried out soon, before the United States turned its industrial power to military preparedness.

When the Japanese attacked Pearl Harbor, their purpose was to destroy the United States Navy of the Pacific. But coming through Kolekole Pass on their way to Pearl Harbor, they splattered the grassy quadrangles and walls of Schofield Barracks with several rounds of ammunition. Though the air strike was brief —a momentary diversion from the main object of the raid—and very few casualties were inflicted, war had come again for the United States.

Schofield Barracks, the site of this first attack, is 35 miles from Honolulu, near the northwest coast of Oahu. The road from Honolulu to Schofield goes through the middle of the island, and the cultivated fields on each side back off to hills topped by irregular cloud formations. The road eventually comes out of the valley into an upland plateau, and the first buildings of the camp, mustard-colored two-story offices off to the left, are partially covered by trees. Despite the network of service stations and cafés outside its entrance, Schofield still seems rustic, attached as it is to the slopes of the Waianae Range with their desolate outcroppings of rocks and stringy bush.

It is very much an Army post of today. Some units going to and from Vietnam are rerouted there for varying lengths of time, while others, after undergoing combat service in the Far East, are permanently reassigned to the base, and the doors and lawns outside their company headquarters are decorated with the symbols and slogans of their service in the Far East.

But, though Schofield's relevance as a collecting station for combat troops supporting the United States' military commitments in Asia is unquestioned, it still resembles in physical detail an institution from the past, and it is this ability to exist in both the present and the past that gives Schofield its quality of timelessness.

Schofield will always be a part of the Great Depression that turned many young Americans to the Army as the only way of surviving economically. Its most famous buildings, the multi-tiered barracks rimming the quadrangles, were built in the 1930's, as were the post library, movie theater, and its unusual sporting arena, dug into the ground, with the spectators' wooden seats circling into the dark pit that forms the sports ring.

Because Schofield was planned when space was not scarce, the buildings sprawl over spacious lawns and are flanked by trees. While not esthetically satisfying, the barracks are functional and, with their pastel colors, do not destroy as much as blend into the lush landscape of northern Oahu. The one-story family housing units for officers and enlisted men on the side streets radiating from the quadrangle barracks are also unobtrusive, and many are covered by caps of waxy leaves growing from the banyan trees.

Everything about Schofield suggests a more leisurely past. Soldiers move unhurriedly down cement walks veining the surface of the camp. Doors to the offices and barracks are not slammed but are allowed to close softly. There are 6,000 men stationed now at Schofield compared with 25,000 soldiers before World War II. The kind of soldiers who were there in the Depression became the 30-year-men who made a career of the Army, and they would become the seasoned cadre of noncommissioned officers during World War II.

If today's soldier is a different breed, there is no difference in the nature of his soldiering. Army barracks don't change and a man's response to them is constant. There are still the uniform rows of cots covered by wool blankets tucked neatly at the corners and the upright dark-green wall lockers spaced evenly down the aisles.

Leisure time is plentiful in an Army camp located outside a war zone, and at Schofield, when the men have no specific duties, they position themselves on the railings of the barracks' balconies and hold endless bull sessions, mostly about sex and fast cars. When a uniformed officer passes, those who bother to direct their attention away from the conversation give him a routine salute, fingers cupped and brought slowly to the eyebrow. Some men make an effort to stay in reasonably good physical shape, and as the sun begins to go down and the humidity diminishes, they strip off their green fatigue shirts and play volleyball or basketball, yelling obscene encouragements to the men bending over and picking up cigarette butts with long sticks in the endless Army ritual of policing the grounds. If there is drilling or marching to be done, it is in the fields behind the barracks at the base of the Waianae Range in an area where, during World War II, divisions of men billeted in tents waited to be shipped to the battlefields of the South Pacific.

When in uniform and on base, the men are restricted by the small regimentations of Army life that require them to be at specific places at specific times to do things of little consequence. Soldiering without a war can become a juvenile charade. At night those who are married can at least return to a home and the semblance of life lived by civilians. The single men, though, must look elsewhere for release from the loneliness of being a man in an all-male society.

For those at Schofield the place to go on weekend pass is still Honolulu, and one of the favorite and more respectable locations for a soldier in civilian clothes with a few dollars in his pocket is Waikiki, a wrinkle of hotels and bars in the coastline up from downtown Honolulu. If there are fewer soldier bars now on the Waikiki strip than there were during World War II, the ones that do exist are noisier with the steady, muffled pounding of drums continuing late into the night. Many of the soldiers in Waikiki are on rest and rehabilitation leave from Vietnam, and as evidence of their country's continued general prosperity, they are often accompanied by wives flown in at their own expense.

A visit may be a disappointment to these young married soldiers. Diamond Head, the imposing massive stone formation at one end of Waikiki Beach, and the island's most famous landmark, is slowly sinking behind a line of tediously commonplace hotels. The view of the beach from the main street is often blocked by this wall of hotels, and inside the buildings electric guitars plunk the music of the islands while overpriced sportswear shops sell aloha shirts that only mainlanders would buy and actually wear. At the end of the day, when the last surfer has rolled up his straw mat and headed for one of the sidewalk bars, the beach is left littered with a blanket of crumpled paper cups and sandwich wrappings.

But a more typical location for the single soldier prowling with his buddies is Hotel Street in downtown Honolulu. At its more impressive end, Hotel Street is the site of the new Hawaiian legislature building, brilliantly designed with an open breezeway on the first floor and a series of fountains surrounding it. The street's distinction quickly dissipates a few blocks away, however, in a clutter of bars and strip joints.

Prostitution has been outlawed in Hawaii since the war, though abortion was recently made legal, and the street girls are forced to operate from so-called legitimate massage parlors which take out newspaper ads to pinpoint their exact location. This has cleaned up the surface of Honolulu, giving it a superficial respectability, but it is always action time on Hotel Street, even during the doldrums of late afternoon just before the offices let out. The street is never without a woman walking aimlessly, stopping to look into a store window until the young man coming from the other direction reaches her. Drinking is an institutionalized divertissement, and it is not uncommon to see a serviceman whip out a pint from his hip pocket, stand unsteadily with his legs apart, and gulp a few swallows before offering the bottle to his new female acquaintance who already is shifting her hip toward the leg of the soldier.

The pursuits of pleasure on Hotel Street seem to be getting more solitary and passive for the serviceman. Liberalized censorship laws have encouraged the growth of pornographic book and film stores, and they now outnumber bars where

women wait out their competition from places offering MALE-
FEMALE SEXANTICS. DOUBLE-BEDROOMANTICS! WHY PAY MORE?
YOU GET MORE IN COLOR. 4 FOR $2.

Where servicemen gather, so do homosexuals, and their trade
is now carried on in popular bars on Hotel Street featuring
stage shows performed by transvestites. Under a café billboard
advertising the revue "Boys Will Be Girls," an incredibly ugly
young man dressed as a woman hustles customers, whispering
seductive greetings and, when his overtures are rebuffed, plead-
ing in a whine to return that night to see the show. Finally he
accepts temporary defeat and walks into the blackness of the
café, his hips swishing from side to side with each exaggerated
step.

If, in the literature of pre-World War II Hawaii, Hotel
Street was romanticized for its swinging brothels, it has now
shifted from lively bars and whores to dirty books and homosexuals. Even so, Hotel Street remains as much a part of Army
life and as important an adjunct to Schofield Barracks as the
parade ground, post exchange and barracks. It is here where
the other side of manliness is tested, the getting of the woman, a
sexual experience to be retold after taps when the lights are out
and the man in the next cot can't tell if your story is a lie.

This was their street before the war, the draftee from New
York, his name picked from a goldfish bowl by a blindfolded
man, and the enlisted man from the coal fields of West Virginia,
who converged with thousands of other young Americans on the
island of Oahu at Schofield Barracks. During the day they dug
gun emplacements in the hills overlooking Waikiki and went
through maneuvers in thick cane fields where the sultry heat
turned a fresh khaki shirt into a damp skin-sticking piece of
cloth. At night or on weekends they would take themselves to
Honolulu and the street where the girls hustled in doorways
and the music resounded from jukeboxes with bubbles of colored water rising in the glass tubes around the speakers. And
then just before getting a taxi to the barracks or one of the
brothels, they would walk along Waikiki Beach, where sand
and water slapped at the main boulevard, and the palm trees,
bent toward the sea, creaked in the forceful offshore breezes.

There was uncertainty for these men, and there was the waiting in the last months of 1941. The United States had been at peace for over two decades, and her steps toward war mobilization seemed hesitant and unreal. Hadn't peace been the trophy she had won in the war to end all wars on the fields of France? Now they said Japan was readying to make its move against the Americans somewhere in the Pacific, a fact established when U.S. Army Intelligence broke the Japanese military code.

One of the men who could confirm the inevitability of the war was Minoru Genda, a thirty-six-year-old commander in the Japanese Imperial Navy. His advocacy of the superiority of aircraft carriers in building up a Japanese navy whose strength would equal that of the United States had at one time made him a pariah in military circles that had rated the battleship as the finest naval weapon. After he was graduated from Eta Jim, Japan's military academy, in 1924, seventeenth in his class, Genda had a variety of minor military assignments, especially during the 1930's when the Japanese were testing the latest aerial bombing tactics on China. He arrived in London in 1939 where he was naval attaché to his country's embassy, and in that city he saw the first German air raids against England. Reassigned to active naval duty, Genda became air officer for the carrier *Kaga* in the fall of 1940, and a few months later was named to draw up plans for a sneak attack on Pearl Harbor. Surprise had brought swift victory to Japanese naval forces in its sea battles against Russia at the turn of the century, and it was a lesson of history the Japanese had not forgotten.

"When I was given the assignment," Genda said many years later, "three elements were most important to the attack. First, the plan had to be kept confidential. Second, a decision had to be made on the course the task force would take to Hawaii. It was agreed it would steer south from Midway. Third, suitable planes had to be selected to do the greatest damage to the ships at Pearl Harbor. Torpedo bombers were among those chosen.

"I made up my first plan in February, 1941. The final one was conceived in November, 1941, after the fleet had left Japan." One of the features of Genda's plan was its reliance on naval aircraft that could come in low over Pearl Harbor and release specially designed torpedo bombs that wouldn't cut straight down through the shallow water and explode harmlessly in the mud. Pilots were trained in simulated low-level bombing raids in the seaport of Kagoshima, where their planes skimmed the tops of buildings that were the height of those to be encountered at Pearl Harbor.

In the task force that sailed on November 26, 1941, were 360 planes, six carriers, two battleships, two heavy cruisers, one light cruiser, three submarines, nine destroyers and eight tankers. The lead attack squadron was on the carrier *Akagi* where Genda was often seen pacing on the bridge. For the attack to be a total success, Genda believed the American Pacific carrier fleet had to be destroyed, and his concern was the hour-to-hour location of the carriers. "Every day . . . every night I worried about every detail of the plan. Everything about it had become very clear. I thought of nothing else but the attack. There were no other considerations. No personal ones. I was a professional soldier and I was doing my job."

At the first grayness of dawn on December 7, 1941, the pilots began to assemble on the flight deck made slippery by the rough seas. One of those awake early that morning was Mitsuo Fuchida, who was to supervise the attack in the first bomber to take off from the *Akagi*. When it was clear the Japanese had taken the enemy by surprise, he was to break radio silence and send the code words *"Tora! Tora! Tora!,"* the Japanese word for "tiger," to show the raid was a success.

"I slept very well the night before the attack. I got up two hours before we were to take off and went to the flight deck. I saw the weather was bad. The carrier was pitching badly and men were clutching onto the planes. If this had been a war maneuver, the flights would have been canceled," Fuchida recalled many years later.

Genda and Fuchida, who was three years older, had attended the military academy together and maintained their close friendship even while Fuchida was accumulating 3,000 flying hours, many of them in the skies over China. When it came time to

pick the man to lead the actual air strike, Genda, without speci-
fying anyone in particular, asked for a man who was "reliable
and an expert in flying." They sent him Fuchida, and that morning they briefly saw each other on the flight deck. "I told Genda
I was going, and he replied, 'Oh! Fucho,' my nickname, very
casually as if I were going down the street to shop.

"It was not a particularly dangerous takeoff, but because of
the radio silence we had no intercommunication among planes
except for hand signals. Once we were airborne, I slid the hood
open so I could look around and try to find a break in the
weather. We flew over the cloud formations at an altitude of
ten thousand feet. At that height the sky was very clear. The
storm was below us. I thought about nothing else but the attack.
I had no time for thoughts about my wife or family.

"I had no particular feeling against Americans, but I did
consider them the enemy. I was a professional soldier. I had no
room for hate, but from my days at the naval academy I had
been taught the United States Navy would be our enemy. I was
very fond of navy life. I was born in 1902, and in school the hero
of my youth was Admiral Togo, who had defeated the Russians
at sea. I joined the naval academy when I was eighteen years
old. All through my naval career I never interfered with politics. It was very important for a naval officer to keep out of politics.

"Just before I was given the assignment to lead the attack, I
met Genda and he said maybe we would have to fight America.
I remembered I was very excited. He hinted I might be the
leader of that attack. I did not question the plans for the attack.
But once we started, I knew it would have to be a successful attack. Nothing else mattered.

"When we reached the coastline of Oahu, the weather broke,
and below us was this very lovely island. I wondered if it would
be possible to bomb such a beautiful place. When we reached
Pearl Harbor, the first thing I saw were the battleships docked
side by side, and I began to count . . . one . . . two . . .
three . . . eight. The information we had was two days old, but
my count confirmed the number of battleships. We had been informed the carriers were gone and I was disappointed. When

we reached the ships, the plane directly behind me, as planned, pulled ahead and released the first bomb."

Ineptitude and self-indulgence by the American military assisted the Japanese, as did the luck of having the weather clear over Oahu just as the invading planes reached the northern shore, and of having the task force undetected as it plowed its

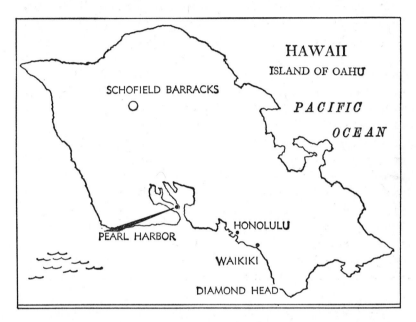

southerly course from Midway. Repeated warnings about the possibility of the Japanese attack and the breaking of the Japanese military code should have alerted the Americans to take precautionary measures. The U.S. fleet, the one military unit that stood in the way of Japan's expansionist plans, was stationed at Pearl Harbor, and an attack here was logical. The U.S. bombers and fighters, the weapons capable of long-range retaliation against the Japanese task force, were grouped on the flight line of Hickam Field. This supposedly protected them from sabotage, but in fact all it did was to leave them vulnerable to air attack. The battleships were in an equally precarious formation, clustered in groups of twos at moorings off Ford Island in the center of Pearl Harbor almost directly in front of the one channel leading to the open sea. The *Nevada* was alone at the head of the line. Behind her paired off were *Vestal,* a repair ship, and *Arizona, West Virginia* and *Tennessee, Oklahoma* and *Maryland,* and somewhat behind, by herself, *California.* The Americans thought this position would protect their battleships from both air and submarine attack. They were unaware of the tediously long hours of training a select group of Japanese pilots had undergone in the special art of low-level torpedo bombings. These planes would sink the battleships on the outer side of this formation, and high-level bombers would then take care of the battleships moored on the Ford Island side of the line.

Below, appearing as a miniature fleet in a bathtub to the Japanese bombers at their altitude of 10,000 feet, everything was in perfect order in accordance with their latest espionage reports about Pearl Harbor. Fuchida, leading his squadron of forty-nine bombers that carried armor-piercing bombs each weighing 1,600 pounds, ordered his plane to cut its speed to permit the bomber behind him to pull ahead and begin the attack. "My target was the *Nevada*," Fuchida said, "and our plane tried to hit it on the first run but we missed. We circled around and this time attacked the *California.*"

The *Nevada* was the one battleship to get away from its moorings, and it foolishly tried to make its way through the narrow channel. If it had been sunk, it would have blocked off the one exit for the ships not sunk or seriously damaged in the attack. In one of the few pieces of luck for the Americans that morning, the *Nevada,* though severely crippled, ran aground in shallow water clear of the channel. The *California,* however, was sunk.

"The Americans were just not prepared for our attack," Fuchida said. "It took at least five minutes for the antiaircraft guns on the ground to begin functioning, and by then the ten groups of planes behind us were in action over Pearl Harbor. From our altitude we could see everything very clearly below, especially the smoke rising from the ships sinking in the harbor and the torpedo planes swooping in for the kill of those that were badly damaged. Once I saw the attack had been successful, I broke radio silence and sent back to our task force the message, '*Tora! Tora! Tora!*' "

Because he was group commander of the attack, Fuchida had to stay above the battle supervising the attack formations. He spent his last seconds over Pearl Harbor taking photographs: "I was most anxious about the results of the attack." When he had photographically confirmed its success, he ordered his lead plane to circle the sky over Pearl to collect those planes out of formation and head them back to the task force. "I didn't feel anything in particular during the attack. I didn't notice any change in my body. There was no special physical reaction to the raid. The attack was everything. It controlled all my thoughts and sensations. There over Pearl Harbor my only concern was that I was doing my job."

There were good times in the last hours of peace for the American serviceman on Hawaii. There was still a liberal policy of passes for the soldiers at Schofield Barracks, and the sailors from the battleships had as little difficulty in getting liberty. Any number of excellent private parties for Army and Navy officers were going on in Waikiki. One of them was at the Royal Hawaiian Hotel, whose twin lights on towers facing the sea were, unknown to the partygoers, being used as location finders by Japanese submarines waiting just below the surface for the morning attack to begin.

Two of the thousands of servicemen stationed on Hawaii that night were Thomas Abruzzo and Earl Bangert. Of the two, Abruzzo was the happier man. Though he was vaguely uncomfortable about world events, his two-year hitch with the Marines was up and he was going home. "Saturday night everyone was in a good mood. The talk was about the peace negotiations going on in Washington, and with all those battleships in the harbor —we'd seen some of them before but never so many at one time —there were parties all over Honolulu."

Bangert was one of those men at Schofield distrusted by the regular Army veterans. He was a draftee and lived with a small detachment apart from the main section of Schofield. "Half the time the regular Army men didn't know we existed. They lived down inside the quadrangle barracks, and the only time we'd see them was when we went down there for some recreation. The sporting rink, movie house and bowling alley were down there, as were the best beer gardens. Schofield was a pretty relaxed place then, even though there was talk about war with Japan. Everyone thought the Philippines was the place that would get hit. Nobody thought it would be Pearl Harbor. We believed what we were told. It was impregnable.

"Everyone was having a good time that night. We'd been on alert for two weeks and had to wear battle gear all the time, and this was the first weekend most of the guys got passes. There was a small café owned by Japanese in the village outside the main gate of Schofield, and some of us went there to celebrate. The Army had decided to release draftees who were over twenty-eight, and a couple of our buddies were going home. After we drank there for a while, we decided to go to Honolulu. The city was mobbed with servicemen. Almost everyone was coming off alert and naturally they headed for Hotel Street. It was so jammed you couldn't move down the sidewalk. You had to go out into the street. We decided to stay overnight in town at the YMCA, but it was completely filled. They even had converted the main ballroom into a dormitory, filling it with cots, and they were all taken. About five thirty A.M. we got a cab to take us back to Schofield. It's a long distance, but there were four of us and the driver charged us a buck each."

Abruzzo was with a detachment of Marines who pulled guard duty at Pearl Harbor, and he lived in one of the ten wooden barracks next to the parade ground. He had just finished mess hall duty shortly before 8 A.M. when he heard a tat-tat-tat sound. He thought it was guns being fired as part of an Army maneuver.

"The mess hall was from three hundred to four hundred feet from battleship row, and a guy was outside blowing a bugle while another one was running up the American flag, and then someone came in yelling the Japs were attacking, and we saw a Jap plane hedgehopping over the battleships. Someone yelled, 'Go get your rifles . . . the Japs are here.'

"We ran back to the barracks and grabbed our rifles. Most of our equipment was packed since we were scheduled to return to the States early in January. From the storeroom we got some ammunition, and guys ran outside and started to fire their weapons at the planes. Some of the men were firing water-cooled machine guns, and because they didn't wear gloves, their hands were soon burnt by the hot steel gun barrels. Me and a Greek friend went to get more ammunition at a place quite far from Pearl, and the man on duty there wouldn't open the ammo room even after we told him the Japs were attacking. Just when we were about to shoot off the lock, a guy came running into the room confirming the Jap attack and the man opened up for us. It was funny. Once the attack began, most of the men didn't ask questions. They began to function like clockwork. Some of the men went up to the roof of the barracks and started firing at the planes. They got one of them, and later we put its right wing in front of our barracks as a souvenir. From where we were, we could see all the ships burning down in the harbor and several of them were already over on their sides. We couldn't believe the Japs could inflict so much damage in so short a time. We were convinced the Japs must have known where the ships were, how many and which ones to attack. We'd been told to expect a Jap attack, but we didn't know where, why or how. And now all around us men were dying; some of them were your buddies. You'd gone out on liberty with them, and there they were fighting back with next to nothing in their hands. These guys were heroes, and heroes are made by instinct. You can't be one if you feel or think about what's around you."

Many men at Schofield were sleeping off drunks when the Japanese planes came through Kolekole Pass and swept over the barracks on their way to Wheeler Field, which is attached to one end of the Schofield military reservation. Bangert said, "Sunday was a day for lying around, and most of us were asleep when the attack started. It woke us up, but the guys with the worst hangovers refused to get up. Everyone thought it was maneuvers. Then some guy came running down the road shouting one of the planes coming in over the pass had a Rising Sun painted on the wing. That scared everyone out of bed. A Japanese plane tried to bomb the water tower at Schofield, but missed it, and down inside the quadrangle barracks some of the guys got machine guns and went on the roof to fire at the planes sweeping low over the barracks' area on the way to Wheeler Field. There was great confusion; guys stumbling around trying to get dressed. No officers were on the base then. The highest ranking noncommissioned officer was a buck sergeant. Finally somebody told us to get down to Honolulu and retrieve guys on weekend pass. I was a truck driver, and after I got dressed, ran outside to the motor pool to get my truck. Was I embarrassed! It wouldn't start."

For the rest of December 7, Abruzzo waited with his Marine buddies for the parachute attack they had been assured would now take place. But no such strike had been planned by the Japanese. Another carrier-based air raid could have been launched, and several naval officers in the Japanese task force wanted to go after military land installations missed in the first assault. But the mysterious whereabouts of the U.S. carriers was the factor that determined there would be no further air strikes against Pearl Harbor. The Japanese could be satisfied with what they had accomplished in one hour and fifty minutes. They had reduced the U.S. Pacific fleet to a maimed giant that would ineffectively operate for the next six months against the surge of Japanese forces through the Philippines, Malaya, the Netherlands East Indies, New Guinea, and the Solomon and Gilbert islands. Of the 96 ships of varying sizes at Pearl Harbor at the moment of attack, 18 were sunk or damaged, and they were important ships. Eight of them were battleships: The *Arizona,* after taking a direct hit to her magazine, blew up and sank off Ford Island, taking with her to the bottom more than 1,200 men; the *Oklahoma* capsized and sank—she was later raised, cleared from the harbor, and resunk off Oahu; the *California* and *West Virginia* were sunk but later raised and repaired; the *Nevada* was also repaired as were the *Pennsylvania, Maryland* and *Tennessee,* all severely damaged, however, and out of action for some time; the target ship *Utah,* formerly a battleship, was sunk almost directly across from the *Arizona* on the other side of Ford Island; the minelayer *Ogala* was sunk. Damaged enough so they never went into action were the destroyers *Cassin* and *Downes.* The cruisers *Helena, Honolulu* and *Raleigh* were all seriously damaged but later repaired and reactivated. Also destroyed, most of them on the ground, were 188 U.S. planes, 92 of them belonging to the Army Air Force, the remainder to the Navy.

The American casualties were appalling. The Navy lost 2,008 men killed and 69 wounded. The Marines lost 109 men killed and 69 wounded. The Army lost 218 men killed and 364 wounded. There were 68 civilians killed and 35 wounded. Of the total number of Americans killed, half died on the *Arizona*.

There were some lapses in the Japanese battle plan that prevented the day from being a complete disaster for the Americans. The carriers were saved, and for some inexplicable reason, the Japanese didn't bomb the oil storage tanks, the military installations or the communication systems inside the defense perimeter of Pearl Harbor. The Japanese also didn't indiscriminately bomb the civilian population of Honolulu, though an occasional strafing by a Japanese plane and the misdirected shells from overzealous American antiaircraft gunners accounted for half a million dollars damage to the city.

The cost to the Japanese attack force was negligible. Shot down or lost at sea were fifteen dive bombers, five torpedo bombers, nine fighters, five midget submarines, and one first-class submarine. The total number of Japanese killed was 185.

This battle, its duration insignificant in the span of a single day, still makes itself felt in Honolulu. A few hours of a nation's trial and the reminders of the agony men were subjected to during it are now bigger tourist attractions than the sands of Waikiki, the multitiered shopping plaza which is reputed to be one of the largest in the world, the hula dancers, the pudgy male singers of banal native songs, and the frigid tomblike pillars that are the modern hotels.

"Everybody keeps talking about Pearl Harbor as if it happened only yesterday," a young Air Force sergeant said. "It's years ago and a different world now, but nobody has forgotten the attack. It still keeps everyone defense-minded." The young man was standing on the lawn outside the Pacific Headquarters building at Hickam Field, a block from the runway where Japanese planes had destroyed rows of U.S. bombers in the first minutes of the attack. The front of the building, an impersonal expanse of white painted cement, is still scarred with the gashes left by bullets from Japanese planes in 1941, and though the building's walls have been repainted many times, the holes still appear fresh.

While he spoke, a stream of white smoke drifted up from the field and a siren sounded near the flagpole by the main hangar. Young officers pushed through the screen door of the headquarters building and walked briskly toward the flight line where jet fighters were being towed by small trucks down an auxiliary runway. It was an exercise simulating a plane crash, and firefighting equipment was being steered among the cumbersome transport planes lumped on the main runway to get to the make-believe stricken craft invisible behind the screen of smoke.

"This goes on all the time," the sergeant said. "It's part of our preparedness program. We have these exercises about once a month."

The military alert at Hickam Field and the seriousness with which officers concentrate on this mock crash almost seemed to be a conscious attempt to correct and amend the deficiencies of those who had been in charge three decades ago.

The most poignant reminder of that disaster is a white marble memorial over the *Arizona's* superstructure. It is hourly invaded by the tourists who stand inside to look down on the *Arizona's* sunken hull, a black wavering shadow just beneath the surface of the clear water.

Open launches leave throughout the day from the mainland side of Pearl Harbor to circle Ford Island, the center of the military base around which are the moorings and piers. There are two types of vessels for this trip. One is for the routine tourist, a plain, functional boat with rows of benches inside. The other, smaller and sleeker, is an official naval launch at the disposal of VIP's, and its departure is flexible, sailing when the guests get to the launching dock. A paneled reception room is there, and on the walls are colored photographs of the Japanese attack, each one having a clarity that makes them suspect. They are, it turns out, still photographs from the movie version of the Pearl Harbor attack, *Tora! Tora! Tora!*

Also available for official guests is a showing of the Pearl Harbor installment of the television series *Victory at Sea*. It runs a half hour less the time taken for commercials when it was shown on a national network. The print is grainy, and actual newsreel footage is intermixed with stock shots from Hollywood war movies, showing Japanese pilots, their lips pushed into brutal snarls, sighting in on American battleships. Kettledrums thump away on the soundtrack, and a monotonously serious voice recounts the litany of treachery committed by the Japanese.

On the tourist launch there is a young sailor in white duty uniform standing next to a map of Pearl Harbor. It is marked with the location of the ships moored there during the attack. In a voice moving with the mechanical swiftness of a record spinning on a turntable, he repeats the story of Pearl Harbor, beginning as a matter of pride by telling what the Japanese failed to do, notably blow up the oil tanks on shore or find the U.S. carriers. As an aside in his narration, the young sailor comments on the age of the ships the Japanese found at Pearl Harbor. "Your Navy then was an antique," he says with less than enthusiasm for this historical fact; it is the closest thing to an emotion his voice betrays during the recitation. One of the antiques of which he speaks so unlovingly is the *Utah,* and the launch passes near where it rests in shallow water off Ford Island, one side sticking out, its wood rotted and metal rusted. A buoy some distance from this exposed side of the sunken ship marks its submerged bow.

For security reasons, the only places where photographs are allowed to be taken inside Pearl Harbor are at the burial sites of the *Utah* and the *Arizona,* and as the launch approaches these places the tourists raise their cameras to their eyes and walk transfixed to the side of the launch closest to the sunken ships, the only visible remains of the attack at Pearl Harbor. Now competing with the young sailor's unbroken commentary is the clicking of camera shutters.

Pearl Harbor is still a major base for the U.S. Navy, and its docks are large enough to accommodate the biggest of today's carriers. But the real strength of the Navy now is its submarine fleet, and Pearl Harbor has its complement of nuclear and con-

ventional submarines. On most mornings some of these submarines are surfaced at the docks and sailors in faded denim pants
and white T-shirts are on the decks and sides scrubbing and
painting. The launch passes these submarines as it circles Ford
Island, which was a Navy air base until 1962, when jet fighters
were introduced, making its short runway obsolete. Several of
the hangars on the island have the dingy, washed-out appearance
of things long unattended, and there are clumps of dried-out
weeds growing from cracks in the surface of the parking strip
alongside the once-usable runway.

The launch's cruise ends at the *Arizona* memorial and guests
are permitted up to six minutes to walk through the monument
and read the names on a metal tablet of those entombed in the
black shadow of the ship below.

Guests from the VIP launch are sometimes taken to the officers' mess at Pearl Harbor, and the conversation invariably returns to the reasons for continued huge expenditures on carriers
and battleships, which most war strategists believe will be ex-
cluded from future wars. "There'll be more conventional wars
like Korea and Vietnam, and you'll need the big Navy ships to
transport men and supplies to the battle zone. Big transport
planes can't do this job alone," says a young officer, slowly turning his Naval Academy ring on his finger.

Inside the club at a corner table sitting stiffly in white dress
uniforms are two Japanese naval officers. Japan today doesn't
officially have a navy—her constitution written by the Americans during their occupation forbids her the use of military
forces—but she does have a home maritime fleet, and these two
officers, always given the courteous treatment afforded visiting
allies, are frequent guests of the U.S. Navy at Pearl Harbor. "I
wonder what they would say if you went up and asked them
about the attack on Pearl Harbor," a U.S. Naval Reserve officer
mused. But nobody at his table took up the challenge, and the
Japanese were left undisturbed to plunge their forks into a
salad of canned vegetables held together by a glutinous paste.

Both Genda and Fuchida have been back to Hawaii, a few
times as official guests of the United States. Genda returned in

1954 and first saw Pearl Harbor from the air. "There were just a few boats in the water. It was very silent down there. It seemed so much smaller than I had thought." But once on land, Genda didn't go to Pearl Harbor, nor has he been there on subsequent trips. And he does travel abroad often on official business. In postwar Japan, Genda became Chief of Air Force Staff and helped organize the present Japanese Self-Defense Force. He was also elected to the upper house of the Japanese Diet in 1965 and is chairman of the National Defense Committee of the ruling Liberal-Democratic Party. For his continued work with the United States on the mutual security pact that keeps U.S. forces in Japan, Genda in 1965 was awarded the U.S. Legion of Merit.

"It is not necessary for Japan to have an army and navy the size she had forty years ago. Today she must cooperate with other countries in a mutual defense force. If Japan tried to take on a large share of the defense of Asia against Red China, other Asian countries would probably misunderstand her action. They remain afraid of Japanese military aggression. It is better that Japan continues to cooperate with the United States in the defense of Asia. The most important task given Japan by heaven is cooperation with the other Asian countries, including Red China, in the economic development of that part of the world," Genda said.

Fuchida visited Honolulu in 1952 and immediately went to the *Arizona* memorial and to Punchbowl Cemetery, the military graveyard on a hilltop across the city of Honolulu from Diamond Head. "I felt sorrow for those men who died in our attack on Pearl Harbor, but I didn't feel any guilt for what I had done. I had acted only as a professional soldier." On this visit he also met an American widow whose son had been born in a Honolulu hospital about the time on December 7 when her husband, a gunnery officer, went down with the *Arizona*. By then Fuchida had been converted to Christianity, and the widow, also a Christian, asked him to pray for her son.

Fuchida was not interested in religion before the war. He had been taught Christians were the enemies of the state and he could be sent to jail for expressing an interest in their religion. "The most anxious problem for me after the war," Fuchida said, "was to understand why I had survived while so many of my friends, including the two officers who were with me on the Pearl Harbor bombing raid, had died. I had made my best effort to fight, yet I had survived. About this time I met an American who had taken part in the raid of Tokyo in 1942 by carrier-based planes led by Colonel James Doolittle. This man had been shot down and taken prisoner. While in jail, he read the Bible and became a serious Christian through this reading experience. After the war this man returned to Japan as a Christian missionary, and he made me interested in reading the Bible. I suddenly realized it was God's will that had been responsible for my survival, and I knew that all the time I had been seeking the God of Christianity." Today, Fuchida is a lay Presbyterian missionary traveling as a Christian circuit rider throughout Japan.

Pearl Harbor remains an event central in the lives of millions of middle-aged Americans. Many can still remember the radio bulletin that interrupted the music of Sammy Kaye, a network program that had gone on the air at 2 P.M.; far fewer are those who were actually at the scene of the attack. "Most of the men stationed there went on to worse war experiences in the Philippines and Okinawa," Bangert said, "but Pearl Harbor sticks with them more than anything else that happened. We have an organization in New Jersey called the Pearl Harbor Survivors Club, and when the guys get together, we talk about the attack as if it were yesterday. Why? Maybe it was the suddennesss of the attack. If we had been at war and knew what was going on and were prepared for it, maybe it wouldn't have been such an overwhelming event—one that stays so vividly in our memories."

Despite its proximity to the scene of the attack, downtown Honolulu is not an ideal place to reflect upon this event. Honolulu has entered its overly flashy middle years, and, like the generation who fought the war in the Pacific, it finds itself no longer very young or innocent. The pleasures of Honolulu, as they are for the middle-aged, are too often high-priced—the frozen seductive smiles of bar girls and the coldly precise words of sympathy by beach boys for aging widows.

Pearl Harbor and the war of the Pacific which occupied America for the next three and a half years remain eternally young events because they happened in the time of one's youth, and the place to recall them is the top of Kolekole Pass.

# Wake Island

*William Bendix, civilian construction worker, dashing around clouds of smoke and sand formed by shells exploding on the glaring flat white beach, ready to put down shovel and take up the machine gun to help drive off the invaders . . . Brian Donlevy, courageous U.S. Marine officer, the landing craft poking through the calm water's surface incapable of making him flinch, his mustache unmoving on his nerveless lip . . . MacDonald Carey, a face so handsomely smooth it seems almost undefined, pilots the last usable aircraft to the runway after doing noble battle with the enemy in the sky, and just after the engines stop, he slumps over dead . . . scenes from the movie Wake Island made in 1942 and repeatedly shown on late night television . . . cinematic perpetuator of the folklore surrounding one of the most glorified, if not militarily significant, battles in the war of the Pacific.*

There is a white speck of coral in the emptiness of the Pacific Ocean, 2,500 miles west of Honolulu, the exposed top of a submerged volcano. Every Sunday about midnight, a Pan American jet touches down on Wake Island, and after a forty-seven-minute stopover to refuel and to allow passengers to stretch their legs in the transient lounge or have a quick drink in the airport bar, it takes off again for Hawaii. On Wednesday morning the Pan American jet returns and, after the same length of time on the ground, proceeds to Guam. These flights provide the only commercial service to Wake Island, which in the first three weeks of the war in the Pacific arrested the attention of the

American public as several hundred U.S. Marines and more than 1,000 civilian construction workers held off a superior Japanese air and naval attack. The defenders, after learning that there would be no relief fleet from Hawaii, were finally overrun by a 1,000-man landing force. But at a period in United States history when her military men were being discredited at Pearl Harbor and the Philippines, this handful of resisters showed that Americans could put up a meaningful fight.

Though its military and commercial significance has been diminished by long-range superjets, Wake Island remains a fueling stop for certain types of medium-range jets flying between Hawaii and the Far East. The airstrip of crushed coral has been lengthened to 9,800 feet and handles up to one thousand flights a month, many of them military transport planes going to Vietnam. The runway is also long enough to accommodate an occasional Boeing 747.

Aside from its nostalgic patriotic appeal, Wake Island has very little to offer a tourist. Even collectors of war relics would have a difficult time finding suitable memorabilia on the sands of Wake. There is still one large Japanese gun on the beach and a few bunkers, but because they are deteriorating rapidly in the corrosive salt sea air, they have been put off limits to tourists. The main task of collecting the weapons of war was awarded to a Japanese scrap iron firm in 1963, and its workers stripped Wake of the few rusted tanks which were the most admired tourist attractions and some small coastal guns.

Wake Island is an atoll made up of three islands shaped into a horseshoe with the open lagoon end tilted to the northwest. The most populated island in the atoll, Peale, is on the north side of the horseshoe. Directly across the lagoon is Wilkes Island, which was the site of the main Japanese landings. It is barren and flat, its highest point only 21 feet. Its sense of desolation is heightened by the vegetation: A few skimpy trees and stunted brush spread across coral sand.

The atoll is 2½ miles in radius, with less than 20 miles of coastline, and because it is practically level with the ocean, it is extremely vulnerable to severe tropical storms. Typhoon Sarah in 1967 sent monstrous waves across it, demolishing most of the buildings erected after the devastating typhoon of 1952. Weather has dictated the architectural style on Wake. Most of the new buildings are one-story concrete slabs supposedly strong enough to survive whatever turbulence blows in from the ocean. The Federal Aviation Agency, which runs the island since almost everyone living on it is connected in some way with aviation, recently put up forty-five single-family units. Pan American also completed a major building program, sinking a half-million dollars in projects, including a dining hall for the eighty-four people who work for the company on Wake.

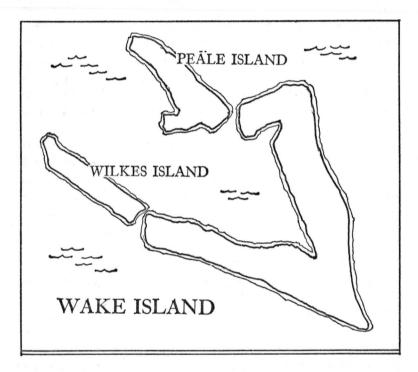

The total population of Wake is about 1,700, of whom 1,000 are civilian employees, and of these at least 70 percent are Filipinos. Some of the men are married, but most are bachelors who have signed up for a tour of duty on Wake of not less than a year. Though its lagoon and offshore waters are fine for sailing, fishing and scuba diving, Wake is no bachelor's paradise since it has no single women, apart from a few unmarried nurses and a half-dozen schoolteachers. For entertainment there is an outdoor cinema, unaffectionately known as the Windy Palace, which shows a different movie each night. There is also the center of Wake's social life: an eight-lane bowling alley with a restaurant and bar, the latter the most patronized institution on the atoll.

The inducement for single men to work on Wake Island is largely financial, though there are those solitary drifters who find their way to the Pacific, propelled by a romanticism that is responsible for their inability to hold down a steady job. Civilian employees on Wake don't pay federal income tax. Food and housing for Pan American employees are free. The FAA and U.S military personnel get a more than adequate housing allowance. Fresh meats and vegetables are weekly flown in from Hawaii and are sold at the FAA-run commissary at very reasonable prices. The Pan American employees, however, draw their food supplies from the company's dining room located near its small air terminal.

"The single Americans on Wake are not very aggressive types with women anyway," a married Pan American official said. "Many of them have been married before and are now more interested in the stock market. Single guys here want to make and save money. They get the *Wall Street Journal* flown in, and they make telephone calls to their brokers in New York once a week. Most of them stay here at least two years, and we know it's time for them to go home when their work gets sloppy from drinking too much or they get emotionally despondent from the loneliness out here."

There is no television on the atoll, a boon for the local library since the tube's absence encourages reading, easily the most popular avocation of Wake Island residents. There is, however, a radio station carrying programs from the Armed Services network which consistently shows great imagination in providing the best in pop and classical music and in old radio serials, among them *Lux Presents Hollywood*, one of the most popular Monday night programs during World War II. The latest Stateside magazines arrive reasonably on time, giving some variety in the reading matter, but the atoll is without a daily newspaper, a deprivation some wives are trying to correct by running off a weekly one-page mimeographed newspaper carrying whatever local gossip is printable.

The worst feature of living so intimately with so few persons on limited acreage, according to the Pan American official, is that "you see the same people all the time and you always hear the same topics of conversation. After a while there isn't any challenge in the social life here. One tends to stop growing or being very interested in much when the range of subjects one is exposed to is so restricted." Schools could aid intellectual stimulation, but there is only one on Wake Island, very small, with two hundred students and eleven teachers, and it stops at ninth grade. When a student reaches that level, he must go elsewhere to attend high school. For many youngsters, this means Honolulu, while others return to the mainland to live with relatives until their parents' tours of duty are up. The Pan American official, whose youngest son will soon be graduated from the local school, plans then to leave Wake. "Life is easy on Wake, and it's pleasant enough for a time, especially if you like fishing and sleeping in the sun. But it does get boring. Children help keep things interesting, but when they get to be teen-agers, they have to leave, and my other two children are already back in the States."

Most of the work on Wake is at the airport, and the activity there is often around the clock because of flight scheduling that must take into account the time change in coming across the International Date Line and the great distances planes must fly between Hawaii and Guam. Pan American services about 200 government-chartered military flights a month, though at the peak of the American involvement in Vietnam the company handled up to 550 flights monthly. The FAA employees provide service for the 800 to 900 U.S. military flights that go through Wake Island each month.

"At the beginning of the Vietnam War, smaller aircraft were carrying men and supplies to the combat zone and this kept us very busy here. But now the planes are much larger and they are capable of taking more men and supplies. This has reduced the number of planes stopping here. Also, a much larger percentage of war materiel is now going to the Far East by ship," the Pan American official said.

To many of the Americans stopping on Wake on their way to Vietnam, a generation that holds most military encounters to be the lowest form of human stupidity, the reason Wake was so valiantly defended in 1941 may seem obscure or even foolish. But for those who followed its defense for three straight weeks in December, 1941, Wake became a legendary battle, an occasion for American fighting men to display what their country considered their innate heroism. Only later was it learned that some of the civilian workers were less than heroic, packing their bags and waiting on the beach for the rescue ships while other civilians and Marines were frantically digging in for the anticipated arrival of the Japanese.

Two decisions made years apart in Tokyo and Washington fated Wake Island to be one of the first Pacific testing arenas of Japan's military strength. Once Japan decided that her Greater East Asia Co-Prosperity Sphere had to be defended on the east by a defense line extending north and south of the Marshall Islands, Wake was doomed since the United States was already there with her Marines and civilian workers pushing to finish construction on an airfield and other military installations.

Wake's importance to Japan was understood by Admiral Husband E. Kimmel, Commander in Chief of the United States Pacific fleet. Stationed at Pearl Harbor, and fated to bear a great share of the responsibility for the December 7 disaster, Kimmel did say eight months before the attack that "one of the initial operations of the Japanese navy may be directed at Wake. If Wake is to be defended, then for the Japanese to reduce it would require extended operations in an area where we might be able to get at naval forces with naval forces."

Wake was considered to have little value to those countries who in the nineteenth century sent their soldiers and adventurers to take islands in the Pacific. As was most of the American territory in the Pacific at the start of the war, Wake had been claimed by the United States in 1899 after the Spanish-American War. Commander E. D. Taussig off the gunboat *Bennington* first deposited the American flag on Wake. He did little else before moving on, leaving the atoll to crews of foreign ships seeking fresh water and to Japanese with the unusual pursuit of searching remote Pacific Islands for birds with feathers suitable for fashion plumage.

Wake became somewhat more important to the United States in 1934 when it was made a transpacific cable station and a stopover for Pan American's first *China Clipper*. Before the military arrived on Wake, Pan American had already set up shop with a seaplane base and hotel on Peale Island. But in the last months of 1941 Wake began to have the appearance of the stationary carrier base Congress envisaged for it when it voted money for the Navy to build submarine and air facilities there and on Midway. Marines, sailors and civilian workers converged in mid-August, 1941, bringing with them heavy machinery to crush coral for the airstrip and coastal and antiaircraft guns for beach fortifications.

Two hours after the Japanese bombed Pearl Harbor, their planes based on the Marshall Islands 600 miles away attacked Wake, destroyed seven of the eight military planes parked on the runway, and blew up two 12,500-gallon aviation fuel tanks. A Pan American clipper seaplane was parked on the lagoon, but though riddled with bullets, it managed to take off after the attack. On the atoll at the time were 70 Pan American employees, 1,100 civilian construction workers, 69 sailors, and 308 combat Marines. The available weapons were six 5-inch guns, twelve 3-inch antiaircraft guns, some machine guns, and 400 rifles. In the first Japanese raid, not only were many Marines and civilians killed and bombers and fighter planes destroyed on the runway, but the hospital was blown up and most of the new Naval Air Station on Peale Island demolished.

The first Japanese invasion fleet of eleven ships, with a landing party of 550 men, appeared off Wake Island four days after Pearl Harbor. As if on a commonplace maneuver in friendly seas, the Japanese began lowering boats, each containing 80 armed men, into the water, an operation that was stopped almost immediately when giant swells began to slam the landing craft against the sides of the ships. Aerial intelligence reports had mistakenly assured the Japanese that the American coastal guns had been put out of action by the daily bombardments, and so, feinting and zigzagging, each movement bringing them closer to shore, four destroyers approached the beach, putting down blistering salvos. The Americans on the beach waited until the destroyers were only 4,500 yards away and then opened fire. When the smoke lifted, one Japanese destroyer had disappeared from the sea, and another was wracked with explosions probably from a fire started by a plane's bomb.

After the invaders were repulsed, a garbled cable message led to the first rallying cry of the war: "Send us more Japs." This was not quite the correct message. The decoder on Wake, acting under orders to throw off the enemy listening in by padding the message with nonsense, had wired: "SEND US STOP NOW IS THE TIME FOR ALL GOOD MEN TO COME TO THE AID OF THEIR PARTY STOP CUNNINGHAM MORE JAPS. . . ." The nonsense was dropped when the message was leaked to reporters, and all that was left was the statement of bravado.

Aware of the enormous interest among Americans in saving the Wake Island garrison, President Roosevelt went on radio to announce that a Wake Relief Expedition would soon be on the way. It was put together in Honolulu on December 13, a flotilla of destroyers and cruisers and the carrier *Saratoga*. It sailed on December 16, but it never reached its destination. Heavy seas prevented refueling of the destroyers at sea, and Rear Admiral Frank Jack Fletcher decided to abandon the attempt to relieve Wake through a daring sea operation.

The island was subjected to daily air raids. Men were repeatedly forced to take cover in foxholes they now had to share with rats shaken loose from their underground homes by the impact of the bombings. There were 20 to 40 planes in the aerial attacks, and when every American fighter plane was destroyed either in sky combat or on the ground, the defenders could do no more than watch the unhindered approach of the Japanese bombers. Only when they came in range of the last few functioning antiaircraft guns could the defenders counterattack, and each time more feebly. And then, suddenly, it was over; and after the last shot was fired the myth making had begun: A Hollywood studio had purchased rights to the name Wake Island.

The real end began on the night of December 22 when the defenders saw on the horizon "a hell of a lot of lights." Off the beach was the Japanese invasion fleet of two light and four heavy cruisers and a number of destroyers. The next morning, simultaneously with a tremendous bomber attack launched from the Marshalls, the Japanese sent ashore at four landing sites more than 1,000 men. In often brutal hand-to-hand fighting, the defenders grudgingly fell back. The prized airfield was overrun in one hour, and after five hours of this intense personal combat the commanders of the garrison realized surrender was the only alternative to the complete slaughter of the men. Throughout the next day, the defenders came out of their foxholes and bush hiding places, tossed aside their small side arms, and walked undefended to their conquerors. Taken prisoner by the Japanese and later sent to internment in China were 470 Marines and sailors and 1,146 civilians. For their victory the Japanese, however, suffered 820 men killed and 33 wounded. Antiaircraft gunners on the ground and Marine pilots in the air also accounted for the destruction of twenty-one planes and four Japanese warships.

"When the survivors of this great fight are liberated and restored to their homes, they will learn that a hundred and thirty millions of their fellow citizens have been inspired to render their own full share of service and sacrifice . . . ," President Roosevelt said of the Marines of the First Defense Battalion.

Before the war was over, American ships returned often to Wake Island and reduced the Japanese fortifications on it to rubble. However, it was deemed unworthy of a land invasion, and Wake Island was bypassed by the island-hopping Americans. Wake was not recaptured until September 4, 1945, when the Japanese on the island surrendered, days after their emperor had asked his countrymen to lay down their arms.

After the Japanese captured Wake, they renamed it Bird Island. One of the first things the Americans did in 1945 was to change the name back.

# Hong Kong

The girls come down early, just after dusk when the lights are turned on in the passenger ferryboats shuttling across the harbor and in the stone homes embedded in the mountainside, and they arrange themselves in straight-backed chairs at bare tables, their short skirts pulled taut over often finger-bruised flesh. Some girls are older than the others. The youngest one is usually chosen first and is steered to a booth in the back of the bar by the palm of a man's hand on her buttock. She leans demurely against his shoulder, her head barely reaching it, entwines her fingers with his, and places the common fist high on his thigh. Amid the stale cigarette smoke and dim lighting of the room, two sailors are pulled to the dance floor by two aging streetwalkers. The male bodies are enveloped by arms of wrinkled flesh decorated with several circles of bracelets and chains, and as meshed units of thighs, groins, breasts and chests, they move over the unswept cement floor, leather shoes making a steady scratching sound. The music is almost indecently slow, a rhythm encouraging bodies to touch, and dancing soon becomes stationary movements of bodies swaying to unsubtle music. Whenever new male customers push through the wooden swinging doors, the untaken girls look up from their drinks with a theatrical stare of sexual delirium on their faces while continuing to stir watered drinks made weaker by melting ice cubes.

The nightclubs on the first floors of the multibalconied buildings in the Wan Chai district of Hong Kong, each advertised by a sign or banner draped over the entrance, are definite about their preference in clientele. Hand-scrawled signs on slate boards in doorways read, WELCOME U.S. SAILORS . . . As if they were bulletin boards in railroad stations, the signs list the names of ships currently docked in Hong Kong. Blue-uniformed American sailors are familiar figures on the three main streets of Wan Chai, walking under the sidewalk arcades, stopping to watch Chinese parents feed their children from a food wagon parked in the gutter, or peeking through an opening in the canvas door of the huge tin auditorium where a Mandarin opera is being performed. These are minor sight-seeing distractions for the sailors, who automatically make their way to the bars and dance halls where instant sin is accompanied by off-key music played by enthusiastic Oriental youngsters.

Nights are long in Wan Chai, and the clubs don't close down so much as shift activity to bedrooms in back alleys after the shutters are locked and the chairs piled on top of the tables. There is no hurry for the girls to find men. If they are rejected by one, there will soon be other sailors and tourists off the ships anchored in the harbor. Men have been coming to Wan Chai for as long as ships have been arriving in Hong Kong.

Wan Chai is the most durable and unchanging section of the city. Its ability to hold out and survive to the last, even in war, was evident on Christmas Day, 1941, when British troops in this section, firing from rooftops and doorways, put up the final resistance to the invading Japanese who had come down through China, quickly overrunning Kowloon before crossing the harbor in open skiffs to attack the outnumbered British garrison.

This is the Hong Kong Edward A. Bull remembers, a city arrested in the history of World War II, not the new Hong Kong —one big air-conditioned discount store and a maze of duty-free shops in ship terminals and hotel lobbies. It is a city of salesmen hawking cheap cameras and suits of the finest British wool made in twenty-four hours—the stitching liable to unravel with the slightest exertion back on boat. Everyone sells below list price, except the whores, and they give Hong Kong a stable reality.

Edward A. Bull came to this British Crown colony in 1937, fought for it through the bleak month of December, 1941, and after it was surrendered to the Japanese on Christmas Day, spent the rest of the war in a prison camp. Now he is finally going home to England. Hong Kong is no longer a city he can comfortably live with.

As have many British, Bull, who is often called John for the obvious reason, has been in the service of his government on foreign soil for most of his adult life, first as a regular army noncommissioned officer in the Middlesex Battalion, and then two decades ago as paymaster for the Hong Kong regiment, a unit comparable in the United States to the National Guard.

"I'm looking forward to going back to England. Many of my friends from here have already returned. But I'm only in my fifties, the age when the British government retires you here, and I'll have to look for another job at home to keep me busy for the next ten years."

Before World War II, Hong Kong's population was just more than half a million. Today it is approaching 4,000,000, the figure swelled by the Chinese refugees who crossed over from the mainland in 1949 after the victory of the Red Chinese over the Nationalist government. The size of the British colony on Hong Kong has remained about 15,000 for years, and though Hong Kong is a haven for refugees all over the Far East—desperate rootless people living in pitifully overcrowded conditions —the British do not seem to suffer a sense of geographical dislocation. Even when filling the colonial bureaucracies in Africa and the Orient, the British know their home always is England. They never leave it even when living abroad, and they bring with them institutions modeled on those they've left behind. In the center of downtown Hong Kong, across the street from the largest Red Chinese bank outside the mainland, is a cricket field and, in the next block, the exclusive Hong Kong Club flying the Union Jack. The technical term for British living outside England is "expatriate," but the word doesn't express the feeling of emotional loyalty the British have for their country. They manage to remain British by banding into restricted social cliques which maintain their familiar life-style, from the ritualistic afternoon tea to a standoffish attitude toward the natives.

Bull has been in Hong Kong thirty-three years, and when asked about current relations between the British and Chinese, he said, "We get along all right. At Christmas we have our Chinese friends into our house and they invite us into theirs on certain holidays. But the British stay pretty much to themselves." How long the remainder of the British stay in Hong Kong is now really up to Red China.

A hilly, arid island, Hong Kong is transformed into something quite lovely by one of the most scenic harbors in the world. But, like Venice, Hong Kong is truly beautiful only if one doesn't look too closely at what's floating on the water. The peasants living on junks tied by the thousands into floating apartments have made the waters of Hong Kong their private sewer, and accumulations of man's daily waste bob freely on the harbor's surface.

Hong Kong has been a British colony since 1841. It was a prize of the opium wars that raged periodically in the early nineteenth century between Chinese and European merchants whose commercial imperialism was often supported by their countries' navies. Added to the British colony in 1860 was the mainland peninsula of Kowloon, 3 square miles in area. This gave Britain control of both sides of the harbor; and in 1898 the New Territories, a tract of land extending 30 miles north of Kowloon and 355 square miles in area, was acquired under a lease with a provision that the New Territories revert to China in 1997. If the government of Peking is still anti-West then, the Chinese could effectively block foreign shipping from entering the port of Hong Kong.

In 1941 Bull knew the Far East was threatened by a militaristic Japan who intended to extend her economic influence southeast even if it meant war with the United States and Great Britain. "But we hadn't a clue the Japanese were actually going to invade Hong Kong." The intentions of the Japanese became evident the morning of December 8, when their artillery on the mainland began shelling British gun emplacements on the island. "I was in a machine-gun battalion, and we had a hundred and twenty-four heavy machine guns in pillboxes on the hills around the harbor, and we managed to keep the harbor open for six days with our fire."

The Japanese, already engaged in a war with China, had been stationed on the border of the New Territories since 1938, and it took them only four days to rout the British army units on the frontier and to move through the jungle of narrow streets of Kowloon to reach the docks from which they could send an in-

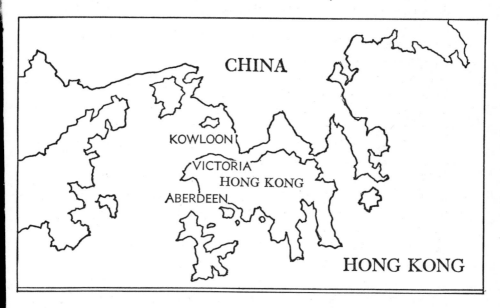

vasion force across the harbor to Hong Kong island. On December 18, the Japanese were finally able to land 7,000 on the main island. Bull's unit was called down from the hills to defend Wan Chai. Crossing the island in the middle, the Japanese reached Repulse Bay, a wealthy residential area with a fine sandy beach, on the other side of the island from the commercial center. Having divided the British, numbering about 10,000 men, the Japanese sent a company into Victoria, the business district of Hong Kong.

"They were pretty good," Bull said. "The Japanese only bombed military installations on the island. The business center was not touched by the fighting, though a few of the fine homes on the hill overlooking the city were destroyed, as were some of the buildings in Wan Chai, during hand-to-hand combat between the Japanese and British." On Christmas Day, hopelessly outnumbered, if not outfought, the British surrendered. In an official history of the battle written almost fifteen years later, the judgment was rendered that "Hong Kong fulfilled its role as outpost of the empire since the duty of an outpost is to delay the enemy and inflict as much damage as possible before being overrun."

Bull, suffering from malnutrition, spent twelve months in a Japanese prison hospital before being sent across the harbor to one of the two prison camps for British soldiers in Kowloon. "The Japanese had their moments," Bull said. "One day they would be giving you cigarettes and the next they would be beating you up. They always hated Americans and British. They seem to have an inferiority complex about their physical size and thought we were always bigger than they."

The war ended for Bull with startling abruptness. One day the Japanese were guarding the prison camp, and the next they weren't, having retreated during the night back up the New Territories into China. The prisoners wandered freely through the streets of Kowloon, greeting Chinese merchants they had not seen for four years, treated by them to pieces of food denied them in captivity, and making their way back by sampans to the island of Hong Kong to seek out family and friends. The British quickly reclaimed Hong Kong as their colony. But after a postwar period of great prosperity made possible by incredibly low business taxes and an influx of tourists to the duty-free shops, Hong Kong is again being tested by an uncertain future.

The colony had rather stable relations with Red China up to 1967 when the Communists, because of reasons having much to do with China's own domestic situation, fomented riots in Hong Kong. The British cracked down with a surprising show of efficient military and police strength. The Red Chinese-inspired disturbances ended quickly. With only a token British military force on the island, Red China could have easily captured Hong Kong. It chose not to, and the most plausible reason is that Hong Kong is too valuable to Red China as an open international port. Hong Kong is a free port; and Red China, with as much right to trade in it as any other country, has taken advantage of this opportunity.

A popular gathering place for Hong Kong tourists today is a square park of tile mosaics and a delicate reflecting pool surrounded by luxury hotels, British clubs and commercial banks on three sides, and across the street on the fourth, the Star Ferry docks. One of the institutions in this park is the Bank of China, which stands between two garishly affluent hotels: the geographic proximity of these buildings a symbol of the peaceful Communist-capitalist commercial coexistence in Hong Kong. One doesn't associate a modern banking institution with a Communist country, but there it is, an inflated, towering stone block with tiers of peephole windows. Guarding the main entrance are statues of two snarling lions, their eyes popping with a frenzied stare. There is a side entrance that leads to an underground garage, and it is watched over by two armed guards sitting on chairs behind a mesh fence. At night the bank is sealed off from the rest of Hong Kong by solid metal doors; the only lights at night shine from one of the building's sixteen floors.

The guards, however, are not cut off from the night life of Hong Kong. Across the street from the back side of the Bank of China is the Hilton Hotel—its parking lot where Bull's barracks were before the war—and music from a cellar discothèque, frequented by middle-aged foreign businessmen, their faces flushed from attempting to do teen-age dances with their Oriental dates, carries raucously to the men in the wire cage.

Inside the Bank of China are steep marble steps leading to the main level of cashiers' cages imprisoning impassive faces. From the middle of the ceiling hangs the familiar Red flag, and surrounding it are pictures of Chairman Mao underlined with his quotations in Chinese script. The customers of the bank are dwarfed by the sheer size of the marble pillars and the height of the ceiling. But the inside can't rid itself, even with the political propaganda, of the conventional stuffiness of most capitalist banks, and the workers tread on the smooth marble floor with the same somnambulant delicacy of ushers at a funeral. The only attentive persons in the bank are the guards in dark-blue work pants and shirts—the dress of the Red Chinese peasant—and they eye suspiciously everyone walking up the stairs.

The Red Chinese have also established a number of their own department stores in Hong Kong, and they almost always undersell the capitalist stores. One of the largest and best stocked of these is on Nathan Road, the main tourist shopping street on the Kowloon side, and the store is easily identified by the picture of Mao in the front window. The store has three floors and no elevators, and on each level there are varied and large inventories of consumer goods from clothing to jade. Prices are remarkably low. A dollar for a worker's shirt. A finely made man's wool scarf for the same price. A raincoat for $10 and a suit for $30. The sales personnel are young and extremely friendly. The clerks wrap each purchase in bright-red print paper, and more than one clerk stops to ask if the customer is an American. When he says yes, the price of the purchase doesn't rise, a sales practice clerks in many capitalist countries should emulate.

The closest a Western visitor can now get to the Red Chinese border is a police station on top of a hill in the village of Lok Ma Chau, about 30 miles north of Kowloon and an hour's ride by bus. The route is along the coast, and it passes the floating colonies of sampans and the high-rise apartments in the suburbs of Kowloon built by the British to accommodate the thousands of Chinese refugees from their country's civil war. The bus finally stops at a road barrier in Lok Ma Chau. Beyond the blockade the road narrows to a footpath over a dirt dike that crosses rice fields and stops at the Shun Chun River. On the other side of the river is a town on a wide, irrigated plain ending at the base of a distant mountain. Its turreted buildings, resembling the Renaissance architecture of Florence, barely rise above the trees growing as a wall in front of them. On the New Territories side of the river there is a high wire fence but very little human activity. The path over the rice paddies is deserted and the doors of the stone houses on the riverbank closed. A boy and a dog walk in a measured circle in front of the fence, and in a watery field on the New Territories side, an old man, bent with ropes around his shoulder that connect him to his oxen, splashes through the irrigation channels.

Life on both sides of the Shun Chun River is observed from the hill by tourists through binoculars. When the tourist buses wind up the hill road to the macadam parking lot next to a trinket and colored-photograph slide stand, old Chinese women press around the visitors, shoving opium pipes and pictures of Mao at the startled passengers. There are also Chinese teen-age girls carrying dirty-faced babies on their backs. The girls ask to have their photos taken by the tourists for a few coins, and if they are refused, the girls stick out their tongues at them.

There is an unreality here in the contrast of the peasant life in the fields below and the blatant commercialism on the hill. From the Berlin Wall to the Arab-Israeli borders, artificial political barriers between nations have been made to pay their way in tourist trade.

The border between Red China and the New Territories is not completely sealed off. A single set of railroad tracks stretches to the frontier, and the Chinese from Hong Kong can get permission to travel to the mainland to visit graves of relatives. They take the train to the border and then walk across the bridge to a train waiting on the Red China side to transport them to the interior in the direction of Canton. Also bridging the border here is a huge black pipe through which most of Hong Kong's water supply is carried in from Red China, another example of the working arrangement for survival negotiated by the British with their potential captors on the mainland.

This frontier, preserved as an ancient wilderness of oxen plows and man-hoed irrigation ditches because it is land separating different political ideologies, is on the tourist circuit but is not a long stopover. The buses stay longer at a roadside teahouse on the way to the border near a floating village. Children, spotting the buses coming around a curve in the hill, race through the dirt parking lot and form a semicircle just as the buses swerve into the lot trailing a stream of brown dust. They stand with hands extended upward, an expression of quiet supplication on their faces. There is no effort by the girl guide on the bus to stop the children's begging; she even suggests a few coins will get the children to pose patiently for pictures.

After five minutes for the tourists on the crest of the hill at the Red China border, the buses are reloaded and driven back by a different route, inland over a hilly road that swings by the new campus of the University of Hong Kong, its boxlike buildings of a washed-out color stacked neatly on terraces, and into Kowloon the back way where rows and rows of tall, squat buildings are jammed into square blocks surrounded by narrow streets. On every balcony flags of white laundry fly, and in tiny one-room flats familes of five and six exist, children sleeping on straw floor mats and mothers cooking on small portable stoves heated by bottled gas.

The bus proceeds to Nathan Road, the traffic moving efficiently in the late afternoon, and the girl guide, who has been somewhat reticent to impart information of interest to the tourists, acknowledges the Red Chinese department stores, as if they would enhance the tour. When the bus stops at the ferry slip, she smiles for the first time and places herself on the steps inside the bus, making it difficult for the tourists to pass her. Some are intimidated by her semibelligerent stance and timidly drop a dollar bill into her hand. It is her right to be tipped, and she takes the money without an appropriate gesture of thanks.

It is dusk, the best time of day to see the outline of Hong Kong from the Kowloon side. It is a city that can never live up to its descriptions in sentimentalized movies, where attractive people are photographed in pleasant surroundings away from the back streets of poverty and near starvation. Tiaras of lights from the tallest buildings in the Victoria district are set off against a constellation of glitterings spaced across the backdrop of black anonymous hills, the highest lights made dimmer by the mist settling on the peaks. On the harbor the new and old glide past the ferry: a U.S. nuclear submarine flying the American flag with a dozen young sailors in white pants standing in a neat row on the wet deck waving at the ferry passengers, and beyond it a sampan steered by one dirty canvas sail. On the bow a mother in a gray mandarin shirt and ballooning slacks braces herself for the child crawling over her shoulder. The junks and sampans are lighted by paper lanterns swaying at the end of poles at the stern, and this illumination is of little assistance to a woman serving a meal in the center of the boat where members of her family squat around a stove fire, picking apart pieces of meat with their fingers, not looking up when the wake from the ferry sets their boat into a sideways rocking motion.

The tourists hasten down the sheltered walk from the ferry to the underground passage leading to the park in front of the Red Chinese bank, then scatter to the hotels flanking the bank and to the shops in the main lobbies. The stores are indistinguishable from one another, and to a foreigner the names on doors all read the same.

"Hong Kong is not as good as it once was," Bull said. "It's not as pleasant. The pace is too fast and the streets too crowded. Before the war it was very quiet, a backwater colony. And the old buildings were more gracious than those built since the war.

"I've had a good life here. But now it is time to go home." It was a voice from the past made uncomfortable by the too-familiar present.

# The Philippines: Defeat

## MANILA

The young Filipino stood on a makeshift platform, and in the stance of an hourglass, his body pinched at the waist, legs wide apart and arms thrust upward in the sign of victory, he waited until the throng in the plaza quieted enough for him to speak. Then he picked up a bullhorn and shouted into it that the Filipino people and not the Americans had liberated their country from the Japanese in 1945. The crowd, estimated at 50,000 people, most of them young, cheered and held over their heads crudely hand-painted anti-American signs.

The mob was passively hostile to anyone who looked as though he might be an American. One stood in their midst, and he was easily identifiable to them because of his freckles, thinning reddish hair and an expensive camera around his neck. When he moved through the crowd, a path was cleared by the curious Filipinos. The American was with a Filipino friend who nervously half pushed the American toward a side street where a detachment of armed police waited.

"We should not be here. You are not wanted," the Filipino said kindly. "Let us go before there is trouble."

Some of the younger Filipinos, no more than children, whispered and pointed at the two men. But no attempt was made to block their way or do them bodily harm. The student organizers of the demonstration had promised there would be no violence. A similar protest a month earlier had ended with several students shot to death in the streets by the police.

This rally was the latest in a series of well-organized student protests against the regime of President Ferdinand Marcos, one of the country's great heroes in the guerrilla resistance to the Japanese in the early 1940's. He was elected to the presidency for an unprecedented second term by a landslide vote in the fall of 1969. When the student demonstrations began in January of 1970, they were primarily aimed at the Filipino government, its alleged corruption and inability to do anything to correct the country's appalling poverty. But these demonstrations had been expanded to include anti-Americanism, a contagious virus in economically have-not countries.

This rally was held in Plaza Miranda, one of the smaller squares in downtown Manila but a strategic one. It is near a number of small technical colleges, a source of vigorous shouters and banner wavers, and a major highway overpass where youths arriving from the suburbs can have the maximum visual effect when they march down a wide ramp into the plaza. Also, the wide steep steps to a bordering church provide elevation for the newspaper reporters and television cameramen who attend every rally in regular expectation of murder. Manila is a city which makes absolutely no attempt to control the sale of small arms.

All roads to Plaza Miranda were sealed off hours before the start of the demonstration at 4 P.M. Owners of shops underneath the arcade surrounding the square had blocked their windows with pieces of plywood and covered their doors with chain gates. Old women who normally sit on street corners cooking chunks of meat over open fires for themselves or hungry passersby had moved their operations into dingy nearby alleyways. No uniformed police were in the square for a very good reason: During a demonstration two weeks earlier in front of Malacanang, the presidential palace, six youths had been shot to death by them, and the charge of police brutality had been picked up by the middle-of-the-road journalists and intellectuals who usually supported President Marcos. After these deaths, late in January, 1970, Malacanang was transformed into an armed fortress. Soldiers were camped on the front lawn, and trees had been cut down to allow a helicopter to land in case there was ever need of an air rescue of the president and his family. For this rally, the soldiers and policemen had been restricted by official order to side streets several blocks away from the plaza. Some of the policemen were armed with pistols, but if the majority of the soldiers had guns, they were not visible. Most of them carried long wooden boards secured to their wrists by leather straps, and throughout the long speeches these soldiers lounged by parked jeeps, smoking and flirting with the passing girls. Periodically they were called to stand in ranks to be inspected by their commanding officers, and they presented, at best, an indifferent formation. The lackadaisical attitude of these men contributed to the surface calm of a city expecting carnage.

Newspaper reporters and television cameramen had posted themselves at the front of the church. Some stood on a platform, the combined weight of the equipment and men making a slight bow in the wooden plank. Others stood on the roof or in the recesses in the front of the church, wrapping their arms around statues to prevent themselves from falling into the mob.

When the classes ended in late afternoon, police had already closed off several boulevards in the center of Manila, redirecting traffic in circles around the city. The students on foot entered the plaza, many of them coming down the long ramp from the highway overpass. Their banners denounced Fascism, police brutality, government corruption, and American imperialism. The students seemed already accustomed to being in the public spotlight. Acknowledging them as if they were old friends, the students smiled at the photographers kneeling in the middle of their parade, then getting up and running backward for several yards before kneeling again, taking the same pictures of students with expressions alternating from surly hatred to youthful boisterousness.

The rituals, language, and even most of the issues have become universal in student demonstrations. Possibly this was why this particular Manila demonstration lacked a sense of urgency or of personally felt rage against economic conditions largely the making of a handful of Filipinos who have sold to foreign interests the limited natural wealth of their country.

"Get out of Vietnam! Student power! End police brutality! End corruption! Give us participation in local government!" the students chanted. These slogans were received warmly if with somewhat less than overwhelming enthusiasm by the students sitting on the pavement before the church. The one issue to arouse them was the anti-Americanism of the main speaker. The fervid harangue by the young man with the bull-horn genuinely stirred the crowd. He charged that an oligarchy of American businesses and a few wealthy Filipino families controlled the economic wealth of their nation, and that this conspiracy of wealth kept the mass of Filipinos in abject poverty.

The students didn't have to be told to stand up. They rose on their own and took up their banners and waved them in rhythm to their stomping feet. "They want you to believe they saved us. They want you to believe we still owe them our country. But we don't. We defeated the Japanese. Our men in the hills did it. Not the Americans."

"Yes! Yes! Yes!" the students roared back, and some of the paper banners ripped when they were too vigorously snapped.

Enough of his country's wealth is either owned outright or is controlled by American-dominated international cartels to give some credence to this young man's argument, and the students only needed to be told something approximating this truth to allow them the luxury of screaming their venom at America. In their schools these students had been taught that a special relationship exists between the Philippines and the United States because of what happened on their soil in World War II. But if, as the speaker argued, the Filipinos had liberated their own country with their own valor and blood, the Philippines no longer owed her soul to the United States, and her liberated children were now free to criticize their foster-parent country.

Not everyone was in Plaza Miranda that night. Some of the wealthy Filipino families, fearing mobs would descend on them to seek a bloody vengeance for the conditions of their servitude, had closed up their palatial homes, leaving them to be tended by fierce dogs, and had moved into the Intercontinental Hotel. Consequently, for the first time since its opening, the hotel was filled, and in the rooftop restaurant all tables were taken and the dance floor was crowded with a select group of Filipino men with their wives or mistresses. It is difficult to see Manila through the restaurant's windows. Reflections of a woman's skirt and a man's shirt blurring into an undefined pattern of dulled colors overlay the panes and block out the buildings and people walking under streetlamps below.

On a television set in the hotel room the rally continues. Lesser speakers inveigh against the United States, and since the rally has gone on too long, the students' response is perfunctory. The cameras cut away from the rally to return to the studio and a commentary on the demonstration. On the panel are intense student radicals, several dutifully serious political economists and a middle-aged female anthropologist, a Filipino version of Margaret Mead. They all agree the students have justification for their demonstrations. There is something wrong with the Filipino government. The Marcos administration had promised so much more than the usual corruption. Above the hotel room, the music from the restaurant continues uninterrupted. The brass voices of two male Australian singers, crushing the intimacy from the lyrics of a ballad, come through the porous walls unhindered, as does the stomping of feet on the dance floor. It is difficult to hear the anthropologist. She seems to be certain of her opinions, however, and that reason will prevail and youth will seek nonviolent redress for their grievances.

And while the rich Filipinos danced and the anthropologist spoke, a girl at the newsstand in the hotel's main lobby idly spun the wire paperback-book rack on top of the cigarette counter and said to the foreigner, "You like it in Manila? It is very nice, isn't it?"

Nothing in the headlines of the English-language newspapers spread over the counter would make one feel secure in her country. Student demonstrations. Charges and countercharges. A provincial mayor from a village north of Manila assassinated, and the Huks, a radical guerrilla band, accused of the crime. The papers, not the Huks, are in effective control of some villages in Luzon, and to keep other rural towns reasonably loyal to the central government, the government has placed them under military administration.

The lobby is fairly empty during the television coverage of the night demonstration. Outside the main lobby on the patio is a pool, and around it a couple walk slowly, their hands together. The pool's underwater lighting system siphons the richness from the water's color until it resembles a bottle of pale-blue mouthwash.

On the television, the demonstration ends. The children of Filipinos who had fought with Americans at Bataan, Corregidor and during the siege of Manila in the last hours of 1941 stand to cheer one last time the anti-Americanism of their youthful spokesman, and then slowly leave the plaza. The rally is over. There has been no violence. No murders. Nobody has forced the crowd to disperse.

"Don't think the actions of the few represent the feelings of most of the Filipinos," the newsstand girl said.

The television cameras remain on Plaza Miranda until it is finally cleared of speakers and protesters and is returned to an old woman hurrying through the deserted square and up the steps of the church. The threat of anarchical acts by Filipino youths who do not have any real sense of national identity has been removed from the plaza. It again belongs to the past and the aged who give any city historical continuity. There was another Manila, not too many years ago, and the old lady lived in it then: It was a city under siege by Japanese.

The Philippines had been the major Pacific acquisition of the United States when it was empire building at the turn of the century. Theodore Roosevelt and his supporters were somehow able to convince a number of otherwise sensible statesmen that his New Nationalism was equated with personal masculinity and carrying the virile American flag to foreign lands was imperative if the country's strength was to be impressed upon other muscle-flexing nations. The Philippines were annexed from Spain in 1898, and the United States, having its Pacific territory, could then compete with England and Germany. For over forty years, without any fervent public displays of acquiescence by the Filipinos, the United States ruled her colony with degrees of civility and human concern. There was a rebellion by the natives, put down ruthlessly by the Americans who introduced the water torture treatment as a method of getting public confessions from prisoners.

Since Magellan landed on the island of Samar in 1521, the Philippines have been subjected to foreign domination in an almost unbroken period of colonization, first by Spain and then by the United States. At the time of her initial experience with European imperialism, the Filipino natives first discovered their will to resist foreign rule, and residents of the island of Cebu killed Magellan. It was a useless gesture of defiance. Several years later Portugal and Spain divided the Pacific into spheres of influence, and though Portugal was to get the Philip-

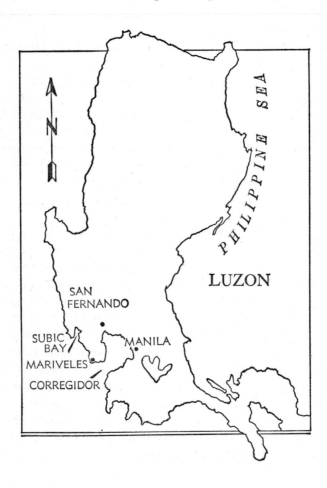

pines, Spain unlawfully took control by the most forceful way: stationing soldiers there. The first permanent Spanish settlement in the Philippines was on Cebu in 1565, and seven years later the island of Luzon was placed under Spanish jurisdiction, an act which ensured the Philippines would remain under the influence of Western European culture.

Filipino nationalism expressed itself in the urge to restore pre-Spanish culture; it eventually ignited a series of rebellions throughout the major islands against Spanish rule in the late 1800's. Although forceably suppressed by a better equipped Spanish army at the cost of the lives of thousands of Filipinos, these civil disturbances created for the Philippines their greatest hero, José Rizal.

A native of the Philippines, Rizal spent much of his adult life abroad in Spain studying to become a doctor. While overseas, he wrote a novel, *Noli Me Tangere,* in which he described the conditions in the Philippines under the oppressive Spanish rule. Though banned in his homeland, the book was smuggled into the country in limited numbers and became the bible for the nationalist revolutionaries. Rizal was arrested on a boat returning to Spain from the Philippines in 1896, imprisoned in Manila's Fort Santiago, and put to death by a firing squad.

The architect of America's entrance as a foreign imperialist in the Philippines was Theodore Roosevelt, then Assistant Secretary of the Navy in 1897. He directed Commodore George Dewey to enter Manila Harbor if war broke out between the United States and Spain and to sink the Spanish warships there. Dewey did this on the morning of May 1, 1898, and ordered the blockade of Manila. Starvation and thirst soon brought the Spaniards within the old walled city to surrender. The insurgent Filipinos, also fighting the Spaniards, considered the arriving American reinforcements as allies, an assumption proved false by the actions of America who, after receiving the surrender of the Spaniards, set about making the Philippines her own colony. Under the provisions of the Treaty of Paris, signed on December 10, 1898, Spain ceded to the United States the Philippines for which she received $20,000,000 and the right to ship goods to the Philippines for ten years.

There was not unanimous support for the treaty in the United States Senate. Before it came up for ratification, however, Filipino rebels began hostilities against their American occupiers, and these acts of insurgency convinced the mildly anti-imperialist American Senators to sign. The treaty passed easily.

It didn't take the Filipinos long to realize the Americans had no intention of giving them freedom. In December, 1898, President William McKinley issued a proclamation that revealed the intentions of the United States to curtail the sovereignty of the Philippines by remaining there as benevolent protectors.

For the next two years Filipinos and Americans engaged in a brutal conflict in which both sides indulged in atrocities. Public hangings were a favorite method. But with the collapse of armed Filipino resistance, the Americans established a military government and inaugurated a policy of Filipinization, bringing into the local administrations friendly natives and giving them some degree of home rule without shifting the real power away from the colonialists. The single most important position in the government was that of governor general, and it was always held by an American. And until the Americans relinquished their imperialistic ambitions in the Philippines, the U.S. Congress retained the right to annul any law passed by the Filipino legislature.

"In forty years Uncle Sam has given them many things, from toilets, neckties, and radios to airplanes, iceboxes and free speech in the English language. They have come a long way since Dewey commenced shooting," an American magazine reported in the early 1940's.

Manila was a charming place to practice colonialism. It was a walled Spanish city of lovely stone cathedrals, gracefully wide streets, and stately homes with sweeping, tree-filled yards. There were always parties at the American Embassy or the Manila Hotel, both on the bay and some distance from downtown Manila where the natives lived in primitive squalor. One of the biggest of these parties was held December 7, 1941, at the Manila Hotel, for Major General Lewis Brereton, commander of the Army Air Force unit stationed on the Philippines.

American domestic problems in the early days of the Depression and increasing sentiment among moderates and liberals for total Filipino independence were responsible for the calling of a constitutional convention in 1934 in which steps leading to Filipino independence were agreed upon: a new constitution, commonwealth status and then full national independence by 1946.

Filipino historians agree there were some benefits from the American occupation of their country. The public school system was expanded and many dread diseases brought under control or eliminated by vaccinations and proper sanitation procedures. The many dialects that had made a chaos of attempts to arrive at one national Filipino language were temporarily overcome by the introduction of English as the official language of school and government. But nothing could rehabilitate the acquired mentality of a subjugated people, the diminution of personal ambition, the psychological dependence on an allegedly superior country, the curtailment of independent thought and action, the acceptance of dutiful imitation as the way to civic advancement.

The actual ruling of the Philippines was to end for the Americans before the official date in 1946. Even though the Americans knew that if war came to the Far East the Philippines would be a major battleground because they lay on the route of conquest Japan would have to take to reach Malaya and the Dutch East Indies, the joint American-Filipino force assigned under the command of General Douglas MacArthur to defend the islands was hardly ready for the task. The size of the force read well on paper—130,000 men—but most of them were badly equipped and ill-trained natives supervised by a cadre of veteran American soldiers. This army was unable to stop the Japanese from successfully landing troops on December 22 at Lingayen Gulf, on the north of Luzon, and on beaches on the southeast coast of Luzon. In a pincer movement, the Japanese closed in on Manila. There was little the Americans could do but to put into operation their contingency plan of desperation: withdrawing their forces into the Bataan Peninsula, hoping to make a stand there until reinforcements came from the United States.

After the Pearl Harbor attack, Clark Field, the largest American air base in the Philippines, located in central Luzon north of Manila, was put on alert and its B-17 Flying Fortress bombers were ordered into the air. But the alert was called off at 11 A.M. on December 8, and the B-17's were parked on the runway next to the P-40 fighter planes when, shortly after noon, Japanese bombers from Formosa attacked. To their amazement, the Japanese pilots found the American planes in a line, waiting for them, and no pursuit planes overhead to protect them. Mac-Arthur had devoutly believed that the American air unit of 277 planes stationed in the Philippines, of which only 35 were B-17's, could stop the Japanese from landing on the island. Blown up by the Japanese at Clark Field were not only 17 B-17's and dozens of P-40's, making it the second humiliating American military defeat suffered in less than twenty-four hours, but also MacArthur's theory that the Philippines could be saved from the air.

MacArthur realized that Manila could not be adequately defended with his force of fighting men, inferior in arms and numbers to the Japanese, and on December 22 he declared Manila an open city to save it from air destruction. The Japanese distrusted the American motives for issuing the unilateral declaration and two days after Christmas, suspecting the Americans were trying to move out supplies and men, resumed bombing of Manila, including residential areas of the old walled city. The streets leading out of the city to the north, the escape route by way of San Fernando to the Bataan Peninsula, were jammed with military vehicles and soldiers on foot. The disorder and confusion of the retreat continued until December 31, when the last Americans withdrew from the city.

In the hours before the entrance of the Japanese, the residents ran wild, looting the stores along the harbor, smashing windows with clubs, and stealing food and household goods. The police who had already surrendered their guns were helpless to prevent the public rioting.

The Japanese marched into Manila on January 2, 1942. In

the first month of the war in the Pacific, the American military establishment in the Philippines had been reduced to the 15,000 American and 65,000 Filipino soldiers on the Bataan Peninsula, a few fighter planes, thirty submarines and some small vessels. The bombers which had escaped destruction at Clark and the smaller Iba Airfield, numbering fourteen, were ordered in mid-December to Australia. MacArthur had already gone across Manila Bay to direct the defense of Bataan from the island of Corregidor, located at the entrance to the bay, a few miles off the southern tip of Bataan.

Filipino leaders were wary of American promises to defend a territory of theirs soon to be freed. President Manuel Quezon even proposed to ask the United States to give immediate independence to the Philippines, which in turn would declare herself neutral in the conflict between Japan and the United States. This would prevent the massacre of many Filipinos and the destruction of their homes. President Roosevelt, concerned by the apparently waning faith of Filipino leaders in the willingness of America to save her colony, rejected Quezon's plan. But he did send a message to the president saying, "so long as the flag of the U.S. flies on Filipino soil . . . it will be defended by our own men to the death. Whatever happens to the present American garrison, we shall not relax our efforts until the forces which are now marshaling outside the Philippine Islands return to the Philippines and drive the last remnant of the invaders from your soil."

Defeat can be as instructive as victory. Just when the Japanese thought they could take the rest of the Philippines without much of a struggle, the surviving American and Filipino soldiers on Bataan, aware that no rescue force would reach them, found their resolve to resist the common enemy. The mop-up of the American-Filipino army which the Japanese thought would take a month took much longer; and in those days, facing common annihilation, Americans and Filipinos shared experiences which became memories that still haunt relations between the two countries.

\*     \*     \*

On the ride from Manila International Airport to the Intercontinental Hotel, the driver, an aging veteran Filipino Army
scout, talked about his love for General MacArthur and the
Americans with whom he fought in the first year of the war
and then later as a guerrilla in the mountains. Seated next to
him in the front seat but separated by a distinctively Asian generation gap was a young Filipino girl who denounced repeatedly American imperialism in the Far East.

The girl, with the annoying self-righteousness that the young
often have about the purity of their moral and political opinions, accused the United States of being responsible for almost
everything wrong with her country. She did not try to connect
her opinions to historical fact; rather she tried to give them
validity through the force with which she hurled them at apolo-
getic strangers. She was a recent graduate of the University of
the Philippines, politically alert and in sympathy with the
student demonstrations against the government of President
Marcos. Her anti-Americanism was a fixed position, but one
that had to be daily compromised since she worked for the hotel
and most of her tourist business was with Americans. At what
expense to her pride did she have to stand outside the custom
lines at the airport waiting for affluent Americans, smiling
meekly at them, offering to help with their luggage, even opening car doors for them while the driver was struggling to put
suitcases in the car trunk? She would never understand the
driver and his loyalty to the memories of the time when the two
countries suffered terrible defeats on Filipino soil. To his generation Americans would always be comrades in arms; to hers
they were the enemy.

The driver slowly steered the car through the early evening
rush-hour traffic, a steady line of private American cars, overaged buses and jeepneys, the most popular public transportation. They are World War II American jeeps with a canvas roof
of bright colors and a hood adorned with leather tassels and
small silver religious statues. When the traffic stopped at inter-
sections, children ran among the cars selling the latest edition
of an English-language paper, calling suspected Americans
"Joe." If unable to make a sale, they leaned against the car
windows with sorrowful expressions on their faces. Some didn't

bother to sell papers but started immediately to beg for American dollars.

The main highway from the airport doesn't go to downtown Manila, fifteen minutes to the north on a road through appalling slums and unpaved side streets littered with decaying food and crumpled newspaper pages. Instead, it passes modern shopping centers, efficient gas stations, the newest luxury hotels and the most exclusive suburban residential sections where hacienda-styled stone houses are surrounded by thick walls and heavy gates marked with BEWARE OF DOGS signs. This highway exists to service the wealthy commuting between airport and home; it was never intended to be used by poor Filipinos who ride on it only when taking public transportation to their jobs at the few factories on this end of the city or to the homes of the wealthy where they are employed as servants or guards.

The highway ends at Quezon City, the new capital of the Philippines, built a few miles outside Manila. It is a collection of government buildings and the University of the Philippines spaced on an empty plain that rolls to the foothills of a mountain range. These official buildings are some distance from private residences and can be easily protected in a revolution, which may have been the intention of the designers of Quezon City.

Even ignoring the fiery rhetoric of the students, there are domestic conditions that suggest a revolution may be coming soon. There are 37,000,000 Filipinos, of whom 90 percent have an average annual income of less than $100. The Philippines has an annual population growth rate of 3.2 percent, the highest of any Asian country. Though it is an agricultural nation, the Philippines has no meaningful land reform program, and most Filipino peasants remain tenants on farms they have no chance of owning. As more rural workers leave the farm for Manila, the country's chronic massive unemployment continues: Of a labor force estimated at 11,200,000, only 8,200,000 are employed. The country's minimum wage is 6 pesos a day, about $1.50, but prices for clothing and food are relatively high in all sections of the city.

The little wealth generated by domestic products comes mostly from the export of copra, rice, and timber products. But

almost half of the major companies in the Philippines are controlled by foreign interests, mostly in the United States, and as
for the Filipino population, only one percent holds the real
economic and political power of the country.

The poverty of the Philippines is magnified to the tourist
by the general tawdriness of Manila. Rebuilt after the war, most
buildings are already decaying and are badly in need of paint
and repair. More than 3,000,000 people live in the city and its
immediate suburbs, many of them in hovels that dip danger-
ously over a sluggishly moving network of garbage-covered
streams. The center of the city is a jumble of second-rate movie
houses—the Philippines is one of the major markets for American movies in Asia—dingy sidewalk food shops invariably selling highly spiced pieces of meat on sticks, run-down department
stores with peeling paint in the front and chunks of wall missing
from corners of the buildings, tourist trinket shops, and dilapidated small apartments with tiny wooden balconies.

The city traffic is intolerable. There are few traffic lights, and
to make any headway taxis and jeepneys swerve into traffic on
the assumption other cars will stop, which most do, though it is
not uncommon to see two cars stalled with locked bumpers.
Running under the city's main intersection is an underpass
continuously filled with slow-moving cars that send up to the
street level a blue haze of polluted air.

The less commercial section of the city with some government buildings, including Congress, is on the other side of the
Pasig River which divides Manila. Here are some of the older,
more prosperous hotels catering to American businessmen and
an almost treeless park of swings and cement paths.

A popular activity on any city street is the black market for
American dollars. The official exchange rate is 3.85 pesos for a
dollar, but on the black market one can get as much as 5.50
pesos. A preferred location for black marketeers is the plaza in
front of Santa Cruz Church. Men stand on the opposite side of
the square, beckoning and whistling to anyone they think may
be an American.

A few blocks from downtown Manila on the waterfront is a
horrendous jungle of cardboard and wooden shacks piled on
each other and separated by dirt footpaths running through it

like clogged veins in an incurably diseased body. The place is
called Tondo, and visitors to Manila are warned never to enter
it. There is no official estimate of how many Filipinos live in
Tondo, but the newspapers contribute to the belief that life in
it is absolutely worthless. There are daily newspaper reports of
murders and of persons missing inside the slum. Police drive
through the few streets open to motor vehicles with windows
rolled up. One of the lethal weapons used by criminals in
Tondo is the poison dart gun, although it is hard to figure out
why such an archaic method is used when guns are so readily
available. It is permissible to carry guns in the Philippines as
long as they are visible, and it is common to see a man swagger-
ing down a mud street in Tondo, a pistol slapping at his thigh.
Some of these gunmen wear T-shirts that reveal tattoos on their
upper arms. Police say these are the trademarks of killers who
have served time in prison.

There is nothing to give a visitor relief from the impact of
abject poverty in Tondo, no park with patches of grass for children or government-financed lower-income housing develop-
ments. Unemployment is a constant problem in the Philippines,
but it is nowhere more visible than in Tondo where able-bodied
men have made an occupation of hanging out, the physical act
of putting themselves in front of public places and watching a
day go by through eyes that never give away recognizable senti-
ments. A detached unemotionalism is the one protective expression for anyone consigned to Tondo. Even death would
have difficulty making the expression change; for it is an
expected visitor, coming in various common disguises but most
frequently as disease and murder.

The social centers and the places of commerce in Tondo are
by necessity on the fringes since few cars can make their way
through the narrow, dirt footpaths. The adult men stand outside the one-room bars, cigarettes enclosed in sealed lips in a
pose from a Humphrey Bogart film. They encourage those who
think they are safe in passing cars to stop and enter. Nearby,
children gather outside huts which become tiny stores when
the wooden shutters are raised. Inside, counters of dirt-smeared
glass jars hold small candies wrapped in colorful papers, while
outside, unattended, naked babies crawl on the filthy paths.

This is the Manila few Americans want or have the opportunity to see. On a visit to Manila, Vice President Spiro Agnew made the more conventional circuit from airport to the Intercontinental Hotel by way of the American Embassy, all places guaranteed to preserve the illusion among Americans who want to believe that conditions are improving in the Philippines with the friendly assistance of American capitalism. But downtown Manila is a dead city, having lost many of its government buildings and business offices to the suburb of Makati.

Some places of old Manila remembered so fondly by American colonialists survive: a few rambling hotels and embassies on the beach side of Roxas Highway; farther along, jagged sections of the wall that once surrounded Manila; and behind the wall, several shells of buildings gutted during the war. But any poignant nostalgia generated by these relics of the past is diminished by the new buildings on Roxas Highway, monotonous, sterile airline offices, flashy nightclubs, and a cultural center whose irrelevance to a poor Filipino says much about the priorities of the Filipino government. The center is a block of drab stone resting on a ribbed neck and extending over Manila Bay. From the water, it resembles a grain silo. The official opening was the social event of several seasons for a few wealthy Filipino families. Even Governor Ronald Reagan of California attended. It is not used every night because of the scarcity of international attractions, but it is kept open daily so that tourists may wander through the auditorium of red seats nailed to a steeply slanted floor. It has not been a popular building with many Filipinos who believe the money could have been better spent on improving social conditions.

It is ironic that the scene of some of the most virulent anti-Americanism is the University of the Philippines in Quezon City, a half-hour drive from downtown Manila. There is a plaque on the administration building noting that most of the university was rebuilt after World War II with American money provided by the U.S. Congress in the Philippines Rehabilitation Act of 1946.

The buildings of the university, designed in an uninspired architectural style somewhat between a functional cellblock and a lavish roadside stand, surround a huge square lawn behind the administration offices. The lawn amphitheater is where noontime student rallies are held. An American being driven to the campus up a paved road through fields where cattle graze is warned not to identify himself as an American and to keep the car windows rolled up.

These anti-American students can't rewrite history, however, and Americans and Filipinos did share defeat and victory in the Philippines between 1941 and 1945. Throughout the city there are reminders of those war years.

There are the walls of Fort Santiago on the bank of the Pasig River near where it enters Manila Bay. It is the oldest fortress in the Philippines, built in the seventeenth century and used as the headquarters of the U.S. Army. During the war the Japanese made it a prisoner-of-war camp, and in its dungeons below sea level Americans and Filipinos were left to drown in the rising tide. Before retreating from Manila in 1945, the Japanese blew up the fort, and all that is left are the outer walls and a concrete block room at the end nearest the bay. Here were found the bodies of six hundred Americans and Filipinos, bodies now buried under a simple memorial stone cross in the center of the fort's flowered main ground.

Fort Santiago is very important in the historical movement of Filipino nationalism. Here the patriot hero, José Rizal, spent his imprisonment before his execution. His actual jail cell was destroyed in the war, but many of his articles of clothing and personal papers are in glass cases in a museum to the right of the memorial cross. Across the quadrangle from the Rizal museum in the more substantial ruin is a stage used for outdoor dramatic productions in the dry season of the year. Most of the plays are American or British and are spoken in English.

In the city there is the University of Santo Tomas, a big, yellowish-brown building set back from the busy main street behind a high iron fence and a spacious lawn on which boys in gym clothes play volleyball and soccer. During the war ten thousand Americans, many of them civilians, were interned there. So notorious was it that, when the city was liberated in 1945, the first American Army units rushed there to release the prisoners.

Outside the city in Makati on the grounds of Fort Bonifacio

is the American Cemetery where 17,206 soldiers are buried on the sloping grassy sides of a small hill. The graves are arranged in a circle around an impressive memorial: upright slabs of marble on which are chiseled the names of the 36,279 Americans and Filipinos missing in action in the Philippines during the war.

The cemetery's simplicity is overwhelming; its design starkly moving. But it isn't in the best location. It is near Forbes Park, the exclusive residential area and inaccessible by public transportation, the only way most Filipinos can afford to travel. The Filipinos find it easier to go to the cathedral of St. Augustin in the old walled city not too far from the American Embassy. The oldest church in Manila, it miraculously escaped destruction in the war, though many buildings around it were reduced to powder by continuous shellings. The cathedral is now a faded gray and pink pastel color. Statues of lions and angels crouch in the dark recesses of the front wall, and an oppressive clammy dampness hangs about its interior passageways.

St. Augustin is prominent in the history of American-Philippines relations. Within its ill-lighted vestry, Americans forced the Spaniards to sign the surrender document in 1898 which effectively made the Philippines a colony of the United States for nearly half a century.

# BATAAN

*We came off the front lines the night before we surrendered to the Japanese on Bataan. We rested that night at Mariveles on the tip of the Bataan Peninsula before starting the march the next day.*

*We didn't know where we were going or how long it would take. There was no food or water, and the men got so thirsty they would drink any kind of water, even the most contaminated. It was so hot the whole time, and the guards kept us standing in the heat. We'd only rest at night when the march was stopped and we were put in compounds behind fences.*

*On the march you'd get so tired you'd just flop down, but if it was the wrong place the guard would just as soon run you through with a bayonet.*

*A lot of men dropped dead of exhaustion along the way. Some of the guys were killed when hit by Jap trucks speeding by, but many others were shot by guards. Some of the Filipinos along the road would pass us food but when the Japs discovered them doing this they'd cut off their fingers and hold them up in the V-sign.*

*When we got to San Fernando, we were packed into railroad cars like cattle to be taken to Camp O'Donnell. Being in those cars unable to move around was almost worse than being on the Death March.*

—*Remembrances of* ALBERT J. SENNA,
*then a twenty-five-year-old U.S. Army private.*

The infamous Death March of World War II took place on a dusty coastal road in Bataan, the mountainous peninsula across the bay from Manila, during ten days of April, 1942. The land along the route is much as it was then, a primitive, rural province of peasants subsisting on tiny farms and in fishing villages, making a living from swampy rice fields, roadside-hut stands, and the choppy sea. To follow the route of the Death March today is to see the agrarian poverty that blights and hinders the growth of the Filipino economy.

The road from the tip of the peninsula to San Fernando in central Luzon is now paved, the one major difference from the time of the Death March. But the peasants along the road live as did their ancestors in one- or two-room straw huts raised off the muddy ground by stilts, or in two-level shanties, the top made of hard Filipino wood and the bottom of cement to keep out water in the rainy season. These huts are grouped into villages called barrios which are spaced at short intervals along the length of the road and are often separated from each other by streams or dense growths of swamp plants. During the day huts fronting the road become stores as their shutters are lifted to reveal three or four shelves of canned goods. There is seldom electricity in the barrio. The sleeping habits of the peasants are determined by the course of the sun: They go to bed at dusk and rise at dawn. The huts have very little furniture, most often only a low bench or a straight-backed chair. The bed is a woven mat on the floor, the stove a pile of stones filled with sand, and the bathroom a hole dug into the ground behind the hut. Water comes from a communal well and is delivered to the peasants through a spigot located in the center of the barrio, usually a square of caked mud. The overflow water is collected in a retaining basin around the spigot and is used by the peasants to bathe and wash their clothes. Pigs also drink from it, as do children.

The peasants use the methods of their ancestors to farm their land and to fish the sea. Boats are still outriggers carved from light wood, seating two persons at most and given balance in the water by poles made of bamboo. The water buffalo, a cumbersome hulk covered with smooth gray skin, is still indispensable, doing most of the cultivation of the rice fields, pulling through the stagnant ditch water a homemade wooden plow to which a man is harnessed by worn leather straps. The water buffalo, an obstinate animal, sometimes lumbers to an unexpected halt, throwing the peasant into a kneeling position in the water. To get the buffalo moving again, the peasant has to get behind it and push against its muddy side.

The green rice sprouts are harvested by hand, a backbreaking job often done by women who must bend over constantly to tug the rice from the ankle-deep water. The harvesters wear hip boots and, if they are women, collect the rice in aprons tied around their waists, or if men, in bags over their shoulders. Modern machinery is available for harvesting rice, but it is too expensive.

Copra, the dried meat of coconuts, is the biggest export of the Philippines. Although the major coconut farms are in other parts of the Philippines, coconuts are grown in Bataan and are collected by barefoot men who use notches carved in the tree trunks to shimmy to the top, yelling words of warning to children below before cutting the fruit which drops to the ground.

Entertainment for the peasants is limited. Cockfights are held on Sunday afternoons in an arena of wood and tin, usually the only building of size and permanency in a settlement. Cockfights are illegal, but this is of no concern to the peasant whose pleasures must of necessity be homemade and cheap. There are a basketball backboard and hoop attached to a tree for the boys and jump ropes from copra twine for the girls. There are also ancient American movies shown in one-room theaters of corrugated-tin roofs and mosquito screens.

This is a desolate peninsula. A mountain range down its spine has reduced the acreage for cultivation, and much of the land is on a swampy plain. An unproductive land retards the growth of modern technology, and the peasants of Bataan are industrial primitives because their land is of marginal value to the economy of the Philippines. There is no rail system linking it with the main part of Luzon, and the bus service is erratic on a road best suited for horse-drawn carts.

The battle fought on Bataan Peninsula for four months in 1942 was the first contact with civilization for many of the peasants; and as quickly as they had come, the mechanized armies departed, but not before the United States underwent another humiliating defeat, one in a string of military disasters that had overtaken the country in the first months of the war.

After their practically casualty-free landings on the coasts of Luzon, the Japanese, expecting the Americans to make their final defense of the Philippines in Manila, dispatched the main body of their troops to the city. The Japanese were unaware, until it was too late, that MacArthur, in a brilliant defensive move, had withdrawn the remnants of his American-Filipino Army to the Bataan Peninsula. Once the Japanese understood MacArthur's ploy, they did send troops to try to cut off the retreat, rushing to Calumpit Bridge to prevent the Americans from blowing up that important crossing. But American tanks in a series of excellent maneuvers fought a rear-guard defensive action until all Army units from Manila had crossed the bridge by late New Year's Day. And then dynamiters sent the two parallel bridges, one of them for a railroad, into the shallow, sluggish river below.

The retreat north on Route 3 continuously threatened to disintegrate into a bedlam of frightened, leaderless men wandering among abandoned trucks and tanks. Any major tie-up would have blocked the retreat, for Route 3 was the only road north capable of accommodating large numbers of men and equipment.

At San Fernando, the road turns west and then south into the Bataan Peninsula. At various lines of defense along its length, the Americans and Filipinos fought gallantly, giving up a position only after food and ammunition ran out, and then retreating a little farther south until the remaining army of 76,000 men, near starvation and fatalistic, were squeezed into the tip of the peninsula near the village of Mariveles. The resistance of the Americans and Filipinos along the road had been so effective that the Japanese military leaders, who had committed overaged troops to Bataan thinking it would be an easy conquest, seriously considered abandoning the Bataan campaign. But on April 9, those Americans and Filipinos unable to get to Corregidor were officially surrendered to the Japanese. By then MacArthur was gone from Corregidor. He had balked at leaving when it was first suggested to him the war effort would be better served if he were not captured. But the decision was taken away from him when he was ordered off the island, and on March 11 a PT boat pulled away from the dock bearing MacArthur, his wife, Jean, and their four-year-old son, Arthur. The boat rendezvoused with a submarine, and the MacArthurs were transferred to it and taken underwater to Australia. Before he left, MacArthur turned to an officer in charge of coastal defenses on Corregidor and reportedly said, "Keep the flag flying. I'm coming back." When his words reached the American public, they had been given greater formality—"I shall return"— making them sound almost Biblical.

The Death March began on April 9 at an abutment of red clay-covered stone in the bend of the road near Mariveles, and for those who survived the ten-day ordeal, it ended 65 miles north in the square in front of the San Fernando town hall where American and Filipino soldiers, hopelessly weakened by malaria, malnutrition and the brutality of their captors, waited in the blazing sun for boxcars to take them to Camp O'Donnell, several miles north of Clark Field in central Luzon.

The Japanese planners of the march never intended it to be an exercise in barbarity. The numbers of those surrendering astonished the Japanese, and they simply didn't have enough vehicles to transport the prisoners. The condition of the prisoners was surprising, too. The Japanese were not prepared to find so many of them near starvation and suffering from the severe chills of malaria. There was not nearly enough food and medicine, and the Japanese knew this when they separated the civilian prisoners from the military and began the forced march up the peninsula. There was some brutality in the beginning. A man was shot when he broke from the line to scoop water from an irrigation ditch next to the road. And there was no food at the start. But the real hardships early in the march were from the searing sun and choking dust. Then, halfway up the coast, all discipline among the Japanese guards broke down, and individual Japanese, never under orders by the commanders of the march, began beating and killing the prisoners, sadistically torturing some, beheading others, denying water to men slowly dying from dehydration.

Of the 72,000 Americans and Filipinos who began the Death March, between 7,000 and 10,000 died, of whom an estimated 2,600 were Americans. The impact of the Death March on the American public was enormous when the story began to unfold in the newspapers and on radio. It was as if people had forgotten how cruel men could be to one another. At Wake Island, the Americans who died did so while fighting the enemy. In the Death March, men died who had finished their fighting, lost and surrendered to the enemy, expecting treatment as established by international conventions based on commonly accepted ideas of humanity and justice. But civilized behavior among men who have become enemies can perish under the stress of battle, and the Japanese guards acted with uncommon barbarity. Torture and legalized murder practiced during a war by the victors on the defeated is an affront to the rules of the game; it seems to become permissible only when there is a distance between the aggressors and the victims, as in an air raid.

Those who died in Bataan are remembered probably more vividly than those who died in other battles because they, more than most others killed in the war, seemed to be innocent victims of baser human emotions. And one thinks of them, the victims, as he is driven over the bumpy road the length of the Death March.

Bataan is so very close in miles to Manila, but so excruciat-

ingly far in travel time. The simplest way of getting there
would be to take a fast boat across Manila Bay to the tip of the
peninsula, a distance of some 30 miles, and then drive north by
car the 65-mile route of the Death March. The easiest is often
the most impossible, however, in countries where the tourist
business is rudimentary. There is no rent-a-car business at
Mariveles or adequate bus service to take a tourist up the
peninsula and back within a reasonable time. The only sure
way of getting to Bataan is to rent a car and guide in Manila
and follow the road of the American retreat up Route 3 to San
Fernando and then south on the Bataan Peninsula to Mariveles.

Getting a driver-guide is not difficult. Any of the hotels servicing tourists has one, but finding a driver who speaks English
well enough to make the long trip educational and pleasant is
hard. English is required in the Philippine public schools. It is
also the language used on street signs. But many of the middle-
aged drivers in the tourist business didn't go to school or, if
they did, didn't stay long enough to learn English. They disguise their inability by learning to put together a few basic
English sentences that make most Americans believe they can
fluently converse in the language. They succeed at their job by
using these until the passenger finds the driver repeating "it's
a nice day" to the question: "What town is this?"

The young clerks in the official government tourist office on
the ground floor of the Intercontinental Hotel claimed this
particular Filipino driver was a prize for any American. The
driver spoke English, they said, and as a bonus for someone
interested in the history of the Bataan campaign, he had fought
there as a scout.

The trip up Luzon began at dawn, an hour late. The driver
had overslept, and he tried to make up the lost time by going
at excessive speeds up Route 3, which is wide enough only for
two-lane traffic. To pass cars, he swerved his off the pavement,
onto the graveled shoulder, sending up a trail of powdery dust
and pebbles while struggling with the wheel to keep the car
from tipping over until he could spin it back onto the pavement. He was finally induced to stop the vehicle on the other
side of the Calumpit Bridge, but only grudgingly and after it had

been explained to him that the bridge had great military significance. The American pointed to the concrete foundations of one of the bridges which had been blown up by the retreating Americans. The driver shrugged his shoulder. The American thought it was an unusual gesture, not yet realizing the extent of the driver's lack of English. Impatiently puffing on a cigarette, the driver lingered by his car as the American walked back to the bridge and leaned over the railing to take a photograph of native boys pushing water buffalos through the eddies of brown muddy water.

The stop concluded, the driver once more resumed the fast speed, weaving around trucks, cutting off small passenger cars, edging the right-side wheels into the gravel, and spraying the hood of the car behind him with pebbles. North of the Calumpit Bridge, off in a field, was an American soft-drink bottling company, and on a wire fence in front of it men were hanging signs made from bed sheets. The plant was being struck by native workers, an almost unheard of act of insubordination by men used to blindly accepting orders from bosses. Cases of empty bottles were stacked to the side of a driveway now closed off by a fence locked with a chain. A few workers paraded in front of the fence with signs wrapped around their bodies, the words on them denouncing management and low wages. This slight and tentative disruption of the accepted way of life in the Philippines was in the back country, away from the mass of Filipino workers, and thus not an immediate threat to the general stability of relations between laborers and management— a stability based almost entirely on the workers' servility to those who control the available jobs in a country plagued with massive unemployment.

After reaching San Fernando, the driver was asked to continue north to Clark Field rather than to turn left and begin the descent into the Bataan Peninsula. Clark Field is the largest American air base outside the United States, and the presence of so many American servicemen in central Luzon is often used by student revolutionaries to stir up crowds. Clark Field is a few miles outside Angeles City, one of the most notorious towns in the Philippines. It is in a part of the country that has been under siege from the Huks, the insurgent left-wing guerrillas, since the end of the war. Every week there are newspaper accounts of elected officials in villages of central Luzon being shot down in public. One day a mayor attending a Sunday afternoon cockfight is killed while making a bet, and a few days later, another mayor is shot to death while being escorted by armed guards in a busy street. Each crime is attributed to the Huks. Because Huk activity is extensive around Angeles City, it has been under military rule for some time.

The city itself is a miserable collection of dumpy hotels with names such as Pentagon and Liberty. Prostitutes, known to the American servicemen as Blue Ladies, work their trade from doorways, and dingy shops specialize in a profitable black market trade in American camera film. Many streets remain unpaved, and cars must crawl over them to avoid open sewer ditches and piles of rocks.

Clark Field's main gate is at the end of a corridor of straw hut bars which bring to the gates of the American fortress the accepted pleasures of military camps around the world: booze and prostitutes. For Filipinos to enter the base, they must have special permits. The driver assured the American he had one and presented a wrinkled official-looking document to the MP on guard, who said it was not valid. The driver protested. The MP, treating the driver as a slightly dense child, held the paper close to the driver's face and pointed to the permit's expiration date. It had been invalid for over a month. The driver ceased protesting. The MP considerately assured the American there was really nothing to see at Clark Field. The runway on which so many B-17 Flying Fortresses had been destroyed in 1941 was now used by B-52's and because of security was closed to visitors. Though he could probably get the American authorization to enter Clark Field, the MP said it would be futile without transportation since the facilities open to guests were scattered around the base and not within walking distance of each other.

The MP gave a rigid hand salute to the civilian, a gratuitously nice gesture to a fellow American. Behind him a B-52 effortlessly lifted itself above a row of hangars and in a slow ascent followed a path over the mountains. The distance was visually compressed, and it appeared as if the belly of the giant bomber barely cleared the mountain peaks.

The Filipino drove next to San Fernando and the railroad station across the street from the town hall. It was noon and only one person stood on the benchless platform alongside the single line of railroad tracks. The sun was without clouds, and its light removed the distinctive coloring from the buildings and vehicles in the street, casting all of them in a neutral silvery glow. The grass in front of the town hall was also drained of life, reduced to withered, dust-covered blades. Here survivors of the Death March had waited for the boxcars that were to take them north of Clark Field to Camp O'Donnell, which is now an empty field of rugged weeds.

From San Fernando to Mariveles there is nothing visible of the war: no planes or rusted tanks or bent artillery guns. There are only signposts placed every kilometer (.6 miles), and on them painted in black, three stumbling soldiers, each trying to help the other, and over the top of these silhouettes the exact mileage of the Death March at that point. But at least half of these signs are missing from the posts, some having fallen off and others having been removed by tourists.

For the first half of the journey down the peninsula, the road goes through a plain of rice paddies on land between the sea and the mountains. The fields are cut up into sections by the barrios, and along the length of town and field, scenes are repeated: water buffalo trudging through the muck; women sitting on mats stripping leaves from cabbage plants; children sleeping curled under coconut trees; men chipping away with crude mallets at pieces of wood; and harvesters stopping to stretch aching arms, standing in the shallow water of the paddies.

The barrios soon lose their individuality. Same huts, stores and mud squares. Nothing distinguishes one from the other; even the barrio south of the Balantay River, which was the defensive position in the Bataan retreat known as the Abucay line, carries no distinction. If anything, this barrio is a little smaller than most, constructed as it is along a river with no defined banks. Thick, wide-leafed plants have grown to the water's edge, their leaves dipping into the stream and hiding the place where the river ends and the bank should begin. A bridge over the river is covered with a film of chalk dust. Barefoot children sit on the wall of the bridge fishing while the elders of the village squat in the square by the church and draw patterns in the dirt with sticks. On a sandbar women bend over freshly river-washed clothes, pounding them with flat paddles.

A few miles south of the Abucay line, the road becomes crowded with walkers. Cars are bunched and move in a slow line, weaving through pedestrians. A fair is being held at a barrio church, and around the base of its stone walls women have set up boards on which are nailed religious articles. Other women have spread mats on the ground and are displaying handmade toys and the omnipresent meat cooked over open fires. There are also women at the entrance to the church selling lighted candles to the few faithful entering the dark interior. Men wander through the crowd, their fists holding strings attached to colored balloons.

These fairs are called fiestas and are exciting semiannual events in the life of the barrio. They are also a basic way for the church to raise money.

The next important town on the peninsula is Lamao at the end of the plain where the road begins to wind up a fairly steep hill. On the outskirts there is an ESSO refinery which gives work to some men of the village, but not to all of them because it does not have enough jobs. During the day many men go to the beach to mend nets or patch the sides of their thatched fishing boats.

Asked about the cut-off road to Lamao, the driver denies such a town exists. He is told it is where General Edward King, Jr., surrendered the men of Bataan to Japanese General Masaharu Homma. The driver finally accepts its existence when the American shows him its location on a road map.

The exact site of the surrender ceremony is marked by a stone monument in the center of the village. There is a footpath leading to it and on each side patches of dead grass are in evidence. The monument is surrounded by a chain fence and is obviously rarely visited by the villagers. On the other side of the square is an outdoor basketball court, and at noon young-

sters from a school on a hill overlooking the village come down
to play the favorite sport of the Philippines.

Little commerce exists in the village apart from fishing, although there is a wood-carver's shop at the main dock. Against
the wall of his building that faces the sea he has placed a rack of
shelves filled with his carvings, most of them religious in theme.
There are also a few wooden, shuttered, one-room grocery
stores. But the center of the village is deserted at noon, except
for the boys playing basketball, the fishermen on the beach, and
a young nurse in a clinic across the street from the basketball
court giving vaccinations to the children. She said health conditions have greatly improved in the village since the war but
that dysentery, which often puts its victim to bed for weeks, is
still uncontrollable, even with modern medicine. Her clinic is
not well stocked. Most of her supplies and medical equipment
are contained on three shelves in a glass case behind a desk in the
corner of the room. There is no hospital in Lamao. Few villages
in Bataan have one. If a villager is very sick, he must be taken
to Manila either by boat over the short water route or the much
longer way, by road around the bay.

Below Lamao the terrain becomes rugged, and the road
passes through upland sugarcane fields recently burned off,
leaving a pungent smell of smoke in the air.

There are many curves in this mountain road, and around
the bend of one of the steepest the road abruptly stops its ascent
and drops dramatically toward a deep valley. The valley begins
where the mountains cluster at the tip of Bataan and ends at
the village of Mariveles, consisting mostly of fishing shacks supported over the water by long thin poles. In the last bend of the
valley road before it straightens and enters Mariveles is a
memorial to the Death March. Embedded into the side of the
hill across the road from the memorial is a metal plaque designating where the Death March began. On a point of land jutting
toward the water, a U.S. Army rifle is secured in a cement block,
and fitted to the gun's butt is a soldier's metal helmet. Few
tourists ever get to Mariveles, and the road to it is paved only
with ruts and holes. Seeing an American standing at the memorial with his camera, the children of the village rush up the

street toward him, thrusting their hands out for coins even before they reach him. "Hey, Joe! Give me money." To many these are the only words of English they know, taught to them by parents who had dealt with American soldiers during the war. One girl, carrying an infant tied to her back by a dirty rag, didn't use words to plead. Her eyes rolled dramatically, and when the American ignored her, she muttered, "bastard."

The driver had pulled the car over to the shoulder of the road under the protective edge of the rock and walked back across the street, past the children, to the memorial. He stood with his hands shading his eyes, looking to the island three miles off the coast of Mariveles. It is Corregidor and the Filipino had been there before. For the first time in this journey to Bataan, he seemed certain where he was and how he got there. When he looked back to the American, he was once more puzzled, not at being there at the same time as the American, but at what separated them still, the begging children, the poverty in the barrios, the misunderstandings because of the language barrier. All he could do then was turn away, light another cigarette and stare toward Corregidor. The memories of the war could not hold them together. They had become strangers in his country.

# CORREGIDOR

The whistle from the boat edging into the harbor—a clear, piercing, sustained note—sounded like an air raid siren in an old war movie, and the young men on the dock, soldiers of another war, stopped what they were doing to listen and to watch the excursion boat turn sideways and slide across the still water toward its pilings. They were American servicemen on rest and rehabilitation leave from Vietnam, and their small cruise ship, which had been taking them along the northern coast of Luzon, was tied up at the one pier on the island of Corregidor.

On the top deck of the excursion boat, now bumping gently against the mat-covered pilings, a pretty young American girl stepped from under the canvas awning, tying a scarf over her head, aware instantly without looking at them that the young men were flirting casually and ignoring the fact that the man next to her was probably her husband. "Where're you from?" one of the young men shouted over the last backfire from the engine before it was turned off.

"Anybody from Peoria?" another youth yelled. When he didn't get an answer from the few Americans on the excursion boat, he continued excitedly, "I'm a short-timer. I've only got forty-five more days and I go home."

He was interrupted by a third young man. "I've only got eighteen days before I leave."

One of the young Americans stood by himself at the end of the pier, and when a Filipino crewman tossed him the docking rope, he had to move quickly to his side, a maneuver made difficult on legs scarred badly by wounds received in Vietnam. But at the last moment, by stretching as far as he could after locking his legs in a wobbly, widespread stance, he caught the edge of the rope and securely wrapped it around a piling. It was a very small triumph, but one of many necessary for his recovery, and his walk back to his friends almost became a swagger.

The Americans had brought to this section of the concrete pier—patched and resurfaced since it underwent constant bombings throughout the first months of 1942—something of the youthful energy and life-style of Americans wherever they gather. A portable barbecue was set up on the pier next to the boat. Hamburgers and hot dogs were being cooked by an Army nurse, and the tangy smell of the food woke several men who had been sleeping barechested on the ship's deck.

Around the boat the calm of the green-blue harbor water was continuously disrupted by bare backs, snorkel-topped heads and feet in black webbed flippers popping through the surface, and around these skin divers a small outboard motorboat, steered by a Filipino, towed a water skier. Other men in bathing suits sunned on the dock, occasionally raising themselves on their elbows to sip from bottles of Filipino beer.

There were a number of women with the soldiers. Some were nurses, others were wives who could afford to pay their fare to the Philippines, and some were Filipino girlfriends brought along for predictable purposes. While most of the young men were eating and resting at the dock, two soldiers with their Filipino dates made their way toward the bushes at the base of the hill behind the beach. The hand of one soldier slipped from the girl's waist to her buttocks, propelling the girl's body forward at a faster speed than she had expected, almost tripping her as her shoe heels caught in the gravel.

There is an almost innocent eagerness in Americans when abroad to be noticed and liked, and this leads many to be overly friendly, often persisting at it long enough to make the trait obnoxious. But, curiously, while these Americans want to be loved, they also do things to elicit a different response from the natives. Here, when they had finished their lunch, the young Americans systematically littered the surface of what appeared to be very clean harbor water with napkins, dirty paper plates and empty beer bottles. These items resisted sinking and were eventually washed up on shore.

These young Americans also seemed more interested in eating and resting than in touring the historic island. Only a few of the soldiers chose to investigate the skeletons of buildings lining the road that circles to the highest hill on the island.

To another generation, Corregidor remains a legendary feat of incredible valor accomplished by a handful of Americans and Filipinos in the worst days of World War II. But these young men had not been born when Corregidor was under siege in the winter and spring of 1942, and if they knew about it at all, it was from a cursory reading of high school history books or in stories told them by their fathers.

The young girl on the excursion boat knew even less about Corregidor. She was an airline hostess, and because of the greatly reduced fares for airline personnel when they fly with other companies, she was able to come to Manila to visit her boyfriend who was stationed at Clark Field. That morning the two of them had boarded the excursion boat at a pier at the end of a park close to the American Embassy in Manila. From the same location, MacArthur had left for Corregidor in December, 1941, to direct the defense of the Philippines.

The trip across Manila Bay can take from one to three hours, depending on the speed of the boat. The tour boat that leaves from the park off Roxas Highway several times a week is hardly luxurious. There is a second-deck salon with plastic furniture and card tables secured to the floor, and a dining room of long, plain tables also anchored to the floor in case of rough seas. Present also is a nauseatingly strong smell of disinfectants sprinkled liberally in latrines and passageways. Since the weather is invariably muggy on the crossing, passengers prefer to sit on the open stern deck sheltered from the sun by an awning. But the tour boat is rarely filled, though the company goes out of its way to make the voyage pleasant, serving a plentiful meal of meat and fish.

The Philippines, even with their battle sites from the war in the Pacific, are not a popular stop for American tourists. Only 55,000 came to the Philippines in 1969, and this figure is not expected to increase greatly considering the growth of anti-Americanism there. The trip to Corregidor is uneventful, across water overlayed with a chalky smog that erases the distinctive lines of the coasts on each side of Manila Bay, making them wavering dark blurs on the horizon.

The airline hostess is noticeably bored during the trip. She accompanied her boyfriend to Corregidor only on his insistence, knowing nothing about the battle or unwilling to listen to his account of it. To her the trip means one less day of shopping for bargains in Manila.

Three miles off the coast of Bataan Peninsula, Corregidor is the natural defender of Manila Bay. The island is tadpole-shaped with two prominent hills: The higher, 650 feet, faces the China Sea and the lower, in the middle of the island, connects with a chain of barren rocks barely out of the water's surface at the tail end of the island that points toward Manila.

Corregidor's place in the war was guaranteed the moment the Japanese decided to attack the Americans at Pearl Harbor and then land forces on the Philippines. It stands in the way of an invasion of Manila from the sea, and the city is a principal objective of any conquering army since it has the best port facilities in the Philippines. Any massive movement of supplies and reinforcements by sea must come past Corregidor. Its geographic position determined it would be the headquarters of the American-Filipino Army if that Army had to be moved from Manila, and from December, 1941, through March, 1942, when he was ordered by President Roosevelt to go to Australia, MacArthur was on Corregidor planning the strategy for the defensive action on Bataan.

Corregidor was subjected to almost daily bombings from December 29, 1941, until the first week of May, 1942, when the Japanese were finally able to move barges across the water separating Bataan from Corregidor. This final crossing was made easy by the saturation bombing which knocked out most of the long-range artillery guns that had prevented the Japanese from mounting an earlier invasion by water.

There were 11,000 Americans and Filipinos on the island after Bataan fell, a number of them American nurses, and at the critical moment of their ordeal, when Japanese barges were banging against the rocks on the north coast, a radiograph from President Roosevelt was decoded, and it read: "During recent weeks we have been following with growing admiration the day-by-day accounts of your heroic stand against the mounting intensity of bombardment by enemy planes and heavy siege guns.

"In spite of all the handicaps of complete isolation, lack of food and ammunition, you have given the world a shining example of patriotic fortitude and self-sacrifice.

"The American people ask no finer example of tenacity, resourcefulness, and steadfast courage. The calm determination of your personal leadership in a desperate situation sets a standard of duty for our soldiers throughout the world.

"In every camp and on every naval vessel soldiers, sailors, and Marines are inspired by the gallant struggle of their comrades in the Philippines. The workmen in our shipyards and munitions plants redouble their efforts because of your example.

"You and your devoted followers have become the living symbols of our war aims and the guarantee of victory."

The message was received by General Jonathan Wainwright on May 4. There were five days left for the defenders, and one of those who remembers the last hours before the death of Cor-

regidor is Austin Patrizio, then a twenty-five-year-old U.S. Army
tech sergeant. He had been stationed on Corregidor two years.
"We tend to remember only the good times," he said, "and duty
was good on Corregidor in those days before the war. The climate was fine and Manila was only thirty miles away across the
bay.

"I was supply sergeant for the harbor defense units on the
rock. When General MacArthur arrived on the island, he took
over our supply headquarters building on the main hill, and he
used it for a couple of months until it was destroyed in a bombing raid."

During the air raids and the shellings from Japanese artillery
batteries on Bataan, Patrizio shuttled between his supply room
and beach defenses, often stumbling and crawling around fresh
bomb holes. "I had to go about my job. The men on the line
had to get clothes and supplies."

Morale was sustained by the innate ability of man to avoid an-
ticipating his own death. They could hope for a sea rescue from
Australia or the skies to become filled one day with American
fighter planes: permissible daydreaming, the substance of survival when confronting the inevitable. But eventually the men
and women of Corregidor admitted no help was coming. "After
the Japs hit the beach in the first week of May and were not
driven off, we knew the battle was over," Patrizio said.

It raged for a few days more, however, as the Americans retreated into Malinta Tunnel, a complex underground fortifica-
tion. The main tunnel is 912 feet long with twenty-four lateral
tunnels off it. These served during the siege as a one-thousand-
bed hospital and living quarters of both MacArthur and Filipino
President Quezon, who was sworn into office for a second term
at the entrance to Malinta Tunnel on December 30, 1941.

With the fresh water supply from Bataan cut off, the medicine gone, and little food and ammunition left, Wainwright had
no choice but to surrender the garrison. "Everyone was living in
Malinta Tunnel at the end, and before the official surrender
there were rumors General Wainwright was negotiating with
the Japanese to surrender. Most of the men were disappointed.
I even saw one guy kneel down and start crying," Patrizio said.

"I was in the tunnel when the surrender came, and when we marched out, the Japanese told us to lift our hands over our heads so we could be photographed in the position of surrender. We stayed on Corregidor for a week before being moved off. Other than having no food or water, we weren't mistreated by the Japanese guards. That came later in our internment."

The surrender ceremony took place on flat ground a few feet from a pier that extends from a cove on the southern shore of the island. There is a square of white stone, and attached to it is a plaque with a brief description of the events taking place on Corregidor in early 1942. To the right of this monument, up a short curved road, is the entrance to Malinta Tunnel, and the Japanese had advanced to within 50 yards of it before the Americans surrendered.

Except for the activity of the young Americans that day, the island was now deserted and awesomely framed by the mountains of Bataan behind it. In 1947 the United States turned over Corregidor to the Filipino government, and it was made into a national park. The only persons living on it now are caretakers and security guards. There is an overnight guesthouse on a knoll above the pier. It only has a few rooms, but, then, not many tourists stay on Corregidor.

There is a bus on the island for the tourists, and it waits for them at the end of the pier. The guide is a Filipino who speaks fluent English, and before the bus pulls away, he points to a stretch of beach to the right of the pier and to a large boulder half in the water. It was the officer's beach before the war, and from it MacArthur and his family waded into the surf to reach the PT boat, the beginning of their journey to safety in Australia.

Most of the tourist attractions are along the winding road up the island's biggest hill. A dense foliage of leaves and bushes half conceals the walls of decimated buildings. "This was the largest barrack for soldiers on the island before the war," says the guide.

About 95 percent of the island's vegetation was destroyed in the two battles for the island. (Corregidor was recaptured by the Americans in February, 1945, after a bloody eleven-day battle in which thousands of Japanese committed suicide in Malinta Tunnel.) The Americans reforested the hills of Corregidor, and the growth is now very thick, covering over many ruins.

On the top of the main hill several shore battery guns are still sunk in the wells of concrete gun emplacements, and one of them is still turned toward the open sea. The most important gun emplacement on Corregidor was Battery Geary. It had eight 12-inch mortars. On May 2, 1942, Japanese bombs ignited the battery's ammunition dump, and the explosion tore loose the guns, tossing one 150 yards. Several of these mortars are there today under the collapsed roof of the concrete bunker. Across the road a huge gun barrel lies in the ditch where it landed after the explosion.

Also on top of the hill is a ghost town of military buildings reduced to skeletal walls. Here was the center of the island's activities: the movie house, golf course, another enlisted men's barracks and MacArthur's headquarters. There is nothing inside the buildings now except weeds, pieces of twisted metal and chunks of stone.

Back down the hill, the tourist bus, which the guide informs the Americans was made in Japan, enters Malinta Tunnel. The center of the main tunnel is shored with scaffolding and the road has sections of its pavement missing. But it is still open to small cars, and the minibus goes the whole length, veering around the workers' wooden platforms, stopping at the other end of the tunnel closed off by a fence. The driver backs his bus to the middle of the tunnel and stops. From here the tourists can enter the musty-smelling, totally black laterals. There is no electricity and a flashlight or a torch is needed. The guide provides both, and he moves ahead into the blackness, followed by the tourists walking on each other's toes, seeking security through personal contact. Each lateral has a sign telling what it was during the siege: MacArthur's office, Quezon's living quarters, the mess hall, kitchen, hospital, and one which is still barred by a wooden gate —the nurses' quarters. At the end of one lateral, the guide directs the beam of his flashlight on a wall and part of the ceiling. "This is where the Japanese crowded together when the Americans recaptured Corregidor. They refused to surrender. The Americans drove their tanks right to the entrance," he says, nodding his head toward the dim natural light from a slight aperture behind him. "They fired their guns point-blank into the Japanese." The light uncovers strips of cement that had been peeled off the roof and ceiling by the shell explosions. There are also stains on the wall, as if human blood had been absorbed into the exposed sections of dirt and pebble.

"Several weeks ago," the guide says, "two American nurses who had been captured on Corregidor and interned at Santo Tomas in Manila for the duration of the war returned for their first visit to Corregidor. They stood right here where they had been stationed during the battle." It was not the terrifyingly dark laterals or the claustrophobic fear of being enclosed in a tomb that they remembered, he says, "but it was the feeling during the daily bombardments that they were living inside a drum with someone pounding on the sides continuously."

For the first time in the tour, the airline hostess became authentically animated, clutching her boyfriend's hand in the darkness, keeping a running commentary going about senseless things, her talisman against the darkness and the stagnant smell.

"The Japanese got this far," the driver says as the bus comes out of the tunnel and thuds to a halt a few feet into the daylight. There is nothing on either side of the weed-infested roadway to indicate the precise location of the farthest Japanese advance. There is nothing but pale-green bushes and insects fluttering in small circles before landing on the dust-coated leaves.

The tour ends at the Pacific War Memorial built behind the derelict buildings on top of the highest hill. Its commanding feature is a marble dome with a hole in the center of the top. Under the hole is a plain stone monument, and once a year when the sun is directly over the hole, the light shines through, briefly turning the white monument to gold. Several hundred yards away from the dome is a statue made of bits of metal molded into the shape of a cathedral spire. Between the dome and the statue is a walkway with a pool down the center. On the sides of the path are stone walls on which are inscribed the names of the battles that took place in the Pacific during the war.

The water in the pool is supposed to be circulated by machinery to give it a rippling effect as it courses down the levels of its terraced bottom. But the machinery isn't working, and the water is a turgid pea-green color with cigarette wrappings floating on top. An empty American beer can lies on its side in a flower bed next to the pool.

The most impressive memorial on Corregidor is not the official one which cost the American government more than a million dollars and is seen by so few tourists. It is a simple wooden cross stuck by Japanese Christians into the ground near where the shore artillery gun points to the sea. The words on the cross are in English and Japanese and read: "May the souls of the dead soldiers of the Philippines, the U.S. and Japan rest in peace."

There was nobody on the pier when the bus returned from the memorial on the hill. The servicemen's cruise ship was gone. The airline hostess, who had been preparing to receive their casual flirtations, seemed deflated by the disappearance of the young men. There was now a retrenchment in the width of her bosom, as if it automatically resumed a normal position when it was no longer being stared at. She went to the upper deck on the excursion boat and stretched out on a hard bench. Before the boat was much out of the cove, she was asleep and drops of perspiration were already slipping into her hair, matting it against her pale forehead. She was asleep when the boat drifted into the opaque haze that separated Corregidor from its mountainous Bataan background, making it a dark lump adrift on a still sea.

Corregidor. How many men had died defending it? Historians now say probably no more than 5,000 Americans and Filipinos were actually killed in the battle for the Philippines in the first six months of the war in the Pacific. But how many more died from starvation and disease? Thousands! And as a reminder of this human sacrifice, what is left on Corregidor? Walls of gutted buildings. Unused artillery guns. An expensive memorial. An empty beach.

The airline hostess slept on as Corregidor vanished into the haze, gone as a page of a book when it is turned.

# Midway

Pearl Harbor, Wake Island, Bataan, and still more defeats for America and her allies in the first six months of the war in the Pacific. Guam, the American territory in the Marianas and an important naval base, was bombed by the Japanese on December 8, 1941, and two days later the Japanese put ashore between 5,000 and 6,000 men. The island defenders consisted of 365 U.S. Marines and 300 Chamorro natives, and they were no opposition for the Japanese. After a token resistance during which a few guns were fired in the town square, the men surrendered. The next month, the Australian garrison of 1,400 men at Rabaul, a magnificent port in New Britain, was overwhelmed by 5,000 Japanese soldiers. Some of the Australians, after surrendering, were massacred. Others made their way through the jungle, escaping to New Guinea from the southwest coast of New Britain. But New Guinea was no longer safe, and in March the Japanese landed on Lae in eastern New Guinea. Five days later they invaded the Solomon Islands, having already captured the major atolls in the Gilbert Islands. Then came the capitulation of the American-Filipino Army.

The Japanese losses up to May 1, 1942, were staggeringly slight considering the size of the territory their army and navy had captured. Twenty-three naval ships had been sunk, none larger than a destroyer. Sixty-seven merchant ships and transports were lost. A few hundred airplanes shot down. The human casualties were also minimal: a few thousand sailors and soldiers killed.

In the midst of these shattering defeats, the United States reorganized its military forces in the Pacific war zone. MacArthur was named supreme commander, Southwest Pacific area. It would include the Netherlands East Indies (less Sumatra), Australia, the Philippines—MacArthur was obsessed with recapturing that country since his military reputation had been badly damaged there—the Solomon Islands, and the Bismarck archipelago. Appointed commander in chief, Pacific Ocean area, which took in practically the rest of the Pacific, was Admiral Chester W. Nimitz, and his command was divided into three zones: the North Pacific, including the Aleutians; the Central Pacific (Hawaii, the Marianas and Marshall islands—also taken by the Japanese early in the war—the northern Gilberts and the Palaus); and the South Pacific (New Zealand, New Caledonia, the southern Gilberts, Fiji and Samoa).

The Japanese had hoped their initial success would bring the United States to a quick military surrender in the Pacific, or at least to her recognition of Japan's territories acquired by force. Instead, the Americans launched a number of carrier-based air attacks against the Marshalls and Wake in February, 1942, and on April 18, 1942, led by Lieutenant Colonel James H. Doolittle, sent sixteen U.S. Army B-25's from the carrier *Hornet* to bomb Tokyo, a raid with almost no military value but one with incalculable propaganda significance for an American public conditioned suddenly to be losers in a world war. Throughout the spring of 1942, the United States continued to build up her forces in Australia. The United States had signed an agreement with her allies in March, 1942, to take on the responsibility for the defense of the entire Pacific, including New Zealand and Australia.

The Japanese battle strategy now was quite simple. The rest of the U.S. Pacific fleet had to be smashed in 1942 before America's industrial manpower could produce the ships to bolster the fleet in the Pacific. In the week her officers accepted the surrender of the remnants of the American-Filipino Army on Corregidor, Japan sent her troop-loaded ships from Rabaul to take by sea Port Moresby on the southern coast of Papua in New Guinea. Port Moresby, only a short distance from Australia across the Coral Sea, was being enlarged as a major air base from which to conduct the defense of Australia.

In the same first week of May, 1942, the U.S. fleet was sent into the Coral Sea. Both navies were now on a collision course, the Japanese coming south from Rabaul, and the Americans, with their carriers *Lexington* and *Yorktown,* heading northwest after launching a carrier-based air strike against Tulagi in the Solomon Islands.

The battle of the Coral Sea began on May 7, when Japanese carrier-based planes sank one U.S. destroyer with three 500-pound bombs and an oiler. The sinking of these ships was a break for the Americans. It drew off Japanese scouting planes from locating the main U.S. fleet. On the same day planes from the carriers *Lexington* and *Yorktown* sank the Japanese carrier *Soho* and one cruiser.

The battle resumed the next day when carrier planes from both sides crisscrossed in air to seek out the enemy. The Americans had 122 planes and the Japanese 121 committed to the attacks that day. The initial American sorties against the Japanese carriers were not successful. The American pilots, being tested in their first battle of the war, released their torpedo bombs too soon, so some missed the carriers while others failed to explode on impact. Only two hits were scored on Japanese ships by Americans. A much larger air strike was made by the Japanese against the *Yorktown* and *Lexington*. About 70 planes participated, and from altitudes of only 50 to 200 feet the torpedo bombers swept low, their explosives slamming repeatedly into the *Lexington* in a run that lasted less than fifteen minutes.

By the end of May 8 the Japanese had lost one light carrier, a destroyer and several minecrafts. One large carrier had to be retired from the battle and sent home for repairs. The U.S. losses included one destroyer and an oiler, with two large carriers damaged.

On May 9 the *Lexington* went down with the bodies of 216 men and the damaged remains of 36 planes. Because she took so long to die, other ships were able to rescue 2,735 men from the carrier, and 19 of her planes were taken aboard the *Yorktown*.

Japan, however, lost so many planes in the four-day battle that adequate air protection could no longer be given to her fleet, and though she might have pressed the attack and finished off the *Yorktown,* she withdrew her ships toward Rabaul.

The Coral Sea was the first major engagement for the U.S. Navy in the Pacific War, and if the result was not an offensive victory, it did have benefits for the Allies. Port Moresby was temporarily saved. Never again would the Japanese send a fleet to try to take it from the sea. The next assault on Port Moresby would come through the Owen Stanley Range. While the Coral Sea could be called a strategic victory for the Americans, it was a tactical one for the Japanese, their planes having inflicted the greater damage by sinking the *Lexington.* Also, the Coral Sea was the first naval battle in modern warfare fought entirely by planes from carriers which never caught sight of one another.

Today there is no strip of land in the Coral Sea on which to land a commercial plane. It is now, as it was then, a water passageway between New Guinea and the northern coast of Australia. From the air the sea that claimed the *Lexington* and her dead sailors is a pale green-tinged blue, the name of the sea coming not from its color but from the miniscule pieces of coral breaking its surface. From the air the sea reveals none of the terror it must have held for those men forced to leap from the burning carrier deck into the shark-filled water.

In May, 1942, the Japanese pressed to consolidate their defensive perimeter on its easternmost line 1,350 miles west of Hawaii. The objective was Midway, an atoll 6 miles in diameter which geologists estimate rose from the sea 25,000,000 years ago. It now consists of two islands: Sand, less than 2 miles long, and Eastern, little more than a mile long, both devoid of significant tropical vegetation. The Japanese plan was to invade Midway, draw out the numerically inferior American fleet, destroy it, and then land an army of 5,000 men on the atoll, a final insult to American pride that would hopefully make the United States sue for peace.

From the sea, the initial sight of Midway is a barrier reef several feet in height which forms a breakwater around the atoll. It was first spotted by an American ship in 1859 at a time when many American sailing masters were claiming Pacific islands as fueling stops for their country's merchant fleet. But it was never formally possessed by the United States until August 28, 1867. The United States planned to make it a coaling depot, and in 1869 Congress appropriated $50,000 to dredge a channel between Sand and Eastern islands. The project took seven months, and when the money ran out, the channel was deep enough only for flat-bottom boats to cross in calm water. For the next half century few Americans arrived to bother Japanese feather hunters on their periodic visits to Midway. Finally, in 1903, President Theodore Roosevelt decided to put the island under the control of the U.S. Navy, intending to make Midway a connecting link in the Hawaii-Luzon cable network. The few Japanese hunters on the atoll were scared off on June 3, 1903, by men from the USS *Iroquois.* The Navy's investment in the atoll was a lighthouse on Sand Island, the cable itself and a station house, all protected by a garrison of twenty U.S. Marines. For the first quarter of the century Midway was also used as a fueling stop for U.S. destroyers.

With the start of transpacific air service in the mid-1930's, Midway assumed a greater importance. Pan American made it an official passenger stop in 1936, building an airport and seaplane ramp on Sand Island and, on the lagoon side of it, erecting a small hotel for passengers forced to spend the night there. This passenger service, which continued until the war, was resumed in 1945 but discontinued permanently in 1950.

In 1940 the U.S. Navy began to erect a major air and submarine base on Midway. Before the start of the war, a detachment of several hundred Marines and construction workers had completed a 5,300-foot airstrip on Eastern Island.

Midway did not escape December 7, 1941. Two Japanese destroyers steered close to shore and shelled the installations, destroying one Catalina patrol plane, knocking out the Pan American radio direction finder, and setting afire the roof of the seaplane hangar. The human toll was four killed and ten wounded.

The Japanese decision to invade the atoll was made in the spring of 1942. In the last days of May, the Japanese assembled an armada of four heavy carriers, three light carriers, two seaplane carriers, eleven battleships, fifteen cruisers, forty-four destroyers, fifteen submarines, and a variety of smaller craft. Some of these ships, however, were to be diverted for an attack on the Aleutian Islands at the tip of Alaska.

With the carrier *Lexington* at the bottom of the Coral Sea and the *Yorktown* docked at Pearl Harbor for extensive repairs, the U.S. fleet, which consisted of only three heavy carriers, eight cruisers, eighteen destroyers, and nineteen submarines, was badly mismatched for the battle. But the United States had several advantages. She had radar. The Japanese didn't. She had 115 land-based bombers and fighters. The Japanese had none. Also, the Japanese fleet was scattered over miles, and at critical moments in the battle, her ships would be out of contact with one another.

If the attack on Midway was to be a success, it depended, much as had Pearl Harbor and, far earlier, the battle at Port Arthur in Manchuria against the Russians, on the element of surprise. But in a small cluttered room at Pearl Harbor, the Navy's Combat Intelligence Unit headquarters, the Japanese secret code was broken. Knowing the Japanese now planned to invade Midway, the Navy began a massive buildup of the island's defense. By June 4, 1942, there were 141 officers and 2,886 enlisted men on Midway, many of them on round-the-clock guard duty in foxholes dug in the sand around impenetrable pieces of coral.

In an uncensored letter to his family, one of the young American pilots stationed on Midway wrote, "We have history in the palm of our hands during the next week or so. If we are able to keep our presence unknown to the enemy and surprise them with a vicious attack on her carriers, the U.S. Navy should once more be supreme in the Pacific. But if the Japanese see us first and attack us with their overwhelming number of planes, knock us out of the picture, and then walk in to take Midway, Pearl will be almost neutralized and in dire danger—I can say no more—there is too much tension with me—the fate of our nation is in our hands."

The Japanese didn't anticipate a great concentration of U.S. naval vessels at Midway. They knew the *Lexington* was sunk and believed the *Yorktown* out of action. This latter assumption proved to be false. By working around the clock, civilian electricians and welders, joining with skilled naval machinists, patched up the *Yorktown* in two days instead of the anticipated three months, and it was dispatched to Midway along with the carriers *Enterprise* and *Hornet*.

The only prebattle casualty was Admiral William F. "Bull" Halsey, who came down, probably owing to an attack of nerves, with a disabling body rash. Placed in command of the naval defense of Midway was Rear Admiral Raymond A. Spruance.

An American fighter pilot first sighted the enemy on June 3 at 9 A.M., and thinking it was the main Japanese fleet—it was probably transports carrying the Japanese landing force through preinvasion maneuvers—he radioed for an air strike. A high-altitude run was made by B-17's against these ships late in the day without any appreciable success. The pilots dropped their bombs and didn't sink one Japanese ship. Much of this early battle inaccuracy by American pilots was attributable to their inexperience. Many of them had just been rushed through flight school, and for almost every man, it was his first battle.

The next morning the carrier *Enterprise* received a radio message that enemy carriers had been spotted by American pilots. Within a few hours a Japanese air strike force was over Midway: 36 torpedo planes, 36 dive bombers and 36 fighter planes launched from ships 240 miles away. The raid lasted only twenty minutes, but it provided twenty minutes of hell and panic for those men on the ground. The Marine command post and mess hall were destroyed, the powerhouse on Eastern Island badly damaged. Many American fighter planes were demolished on the runway. But in the air action, American pilots downed 30 Japanese planes while losing only 17, and their stout defensive action prevented the wrecking of the airfield on Midway. At 6:50 A.M. on June 4, the air raid was over. Never again was Midway to be subjected to a Japanese attack from the sky.

Up to this point in the battle, the American land-based aircraft had been ineffectual against the Japanese fleet, and in the first minutes of attack by the American carrier-based craft, the torpedo planes were equally powerless. But then the Dauntless dive bombers were sent in, and in just a few minutes fifty-four young American pilots turned around the war in the Pacific.

Their bombs ripped through four Japanese carriers: *Akagi, Soru, Kaga,* and *Hiryu.* By noon on June 4 three of the carriers were fatally stricken and eventually sunk. The fourth, abandoned, was sunk the next day by a Japanese submarine in a naval mercy killing. After this, the Japanese were left in desperate condition while the American naval force was intact. Without their carriers, the Japanese could no longer hope to press the attack against the Americans.

In retaliation, the Japanese sent ten torpedo bombers and six fighters against the *Yorktown.* Bomb after bomb crashed into her sides, and she began to list badly. A salvage crew went aboard and reported she was hopelessly damaged, but could be saved if there were tugs to tow her to port. There were none and 2,270 of her crew were ordered to abandon ship. Effortlessly, without explosions violently shaking her sides, she sank on June 7.

Midway, like the Coral Sea, was a battle in which the damage was done by carrier planes without the opposing fleets coming in sight of each other. The Japanese had inflicted some damage on American carrier planes. The *Enterprise* lost 14 of her 37 dive bombers, 10 of her 14 torpedo bombers; the *Hornet* lost all of her torpedo bombers and 12 Wildcats; the *Yorktown* lost all but one of her torpedo bombers. But with the sinking of four of their carriers, the Japanese decided to withdraw. By nightfall on June 6 the Battle of Midway was over and the turning point of the war in the Pacific had been reached. The Japanese had suffered their first defeat and it was a devastating one. Japan's carrier-based air force had been irreparably crippled. About 250 carrier planes had been shot down and with them Japan's best fighter pilots. Never again in the war would Japan's carrier aircraft be a major threat to United States armed might in the Pacific. The U.S. losses were comparatively slight: the *Yorktown,* one destroyer, 151 planes, and ninety pilots.

There were some consolations for the Japanese. Her fleet, even without the carriers and one cruiser sunk at Midway, was fairly intact; and her ships had carried an invasion force to the Aleutians, where her soldiers occupied Kiska and Attu, thus fulfilling at least one objective in sending Japan's greatest armada to

Midway. On the return of the fleet to the ports outside Tokyo, the Japanese newspapers claimed a great victory. But the truth was known to her war leaders: An almost unbearable reversal of fortune had been handed Japan.

In the decades since American and Japanese carriers fought the single most important naval battle of World War II, Midway has lost much of its geographical significance because of the advent of long-range jet planes. It exists now principally as a refueling station for U.S. Navy ships. It is also a convenient meeting place for the United States and her Far East allies whenever they find it necessary to discuss American commitments in that area of the world. President Richard Nixon and South Vietnam's President Nguyen Van Thieu conferred there for a day, using a small room with avocado-green carpets and gold-painted walls on the naval base.

About the only post-World War II excitement on Midway was the battle between the humans and the gooneys. "Gooney bird" is the slang name for the Laysan albatross, and at their procreative postwar peak more than a million of them made the island their Pacific home base. Midway was then being used as a refueling stop for planes going between San Francisco and the Philippines, and the birds had developed a habit of zooming head on into the planes. In one month about 538 birds were killed by military planes at an estimated $256,000 in damage to the aircraft. The Navy tried everything to convince the birds to resettle elsewhere, the sailors even setting off firecrackers to scare them away. Then the men tried to catch the birds by hand and crate them off to uninhabited Kure Island 65 miles away. Finally the Navy ordered the birds killed and the sailors went after them with clubs. But one of the hunters happened to be a member of the Audubon Society, and his complaints to Washington against the massacre brought orders for it to stop. Unable to decide what to do with the birds, the Navy's decision was made by time and technology. The widespread use of jets did away with the need to maintain Midway as a major plane-refueling stop, and the birds were allowed to settle into a domestic truce with the Americans. The bird population still outnumbers the human. There are only a total of 2,250 people on Midway, of whom more than half are Navy personnel, the remainder being military dependents and civilian workers.

Though Midway is not officially in the tropics, its average annual temperature is between 69 and 81 degrees, making it ideal for those who enjoy water sports, and the blue lagoon between Eastern and Sand is the best location for sailing and scuba diving. For Midway residents unmoved by beautiful water, there are organized softball, volleyball and bowling leagues and an 8,000-volume library, extremely popular with the residents who borrow on the average of 1,500 books a month. In the room where presidents Nixon and Thieu conferred, movies are shown nightly, bingo games held almost as often.

There are very few automobiles on the island and this posed a problem during Nixon's visit. There were only three official cars and a handful of trucks here, so the Navy had to import sedans for the distinguished visitors. Those forced to live here year round find bicycles the most common form of transportation, and there are more than two thousand bikes registered.

Even with American military commitments in the Far East and an armed conflict there now, Midway has not been able to regain anything resembling the strategic value she had in World War II. She remains a U.S. possession, not part of a state, though she is considered the western end of the Hawaiian archipelago. Ships still refuel at Midway, and from it the Navy provides search and rescue service for ships in the more than 1,500,000 square miles of the Pacific Ocean around her.

But the island is probably of more consequence now to the albatross, safe again as it was before man and his wars disrupted its ancient way of life.

# Guadalcanal

"Sure. There's not much to do here at night. And there aren't many girls. Most of these that are here are natives. But after a while you don't notice the color of the skin. The girls all look alike in the dark. Anyway, I got me a pommy bird," the young Australian said.

"A what?" the American replied, trying not to appear stupid.

"Pommy bird!"

"Do you keep your pet in a cage?"

"No." He laughed. It wasn't a body-shaking one—he was of British ancestry with all those centuries of personal reserve inhibiting him—but a chuckle that put temporary frown lines in his cheeks and on the bridge of his nose. "A bird's a girl," he explained patiently, "and a pommy is an English person. It's Australian slang. She's a nurse from London. Been at the hospital in Honiara a few years. Most of them over from London don't stay too long. It gets to them here, and they go back. Some crack, though, before they leave."

The two men were standing on the apex of Bloody Ridge rising like a broken nose on the flat profile of the land around Henderson Field, and years after the American Marines battled one thousand Japanese for its possession one night in 1942, it now stands at the end of a winding weed-clogged dirt road.

The Australian was Paul Wright, the twenty-three-year-old son of the postmaster of Guadalcanal. Wright had come here with his family in 1957 and was now an assistant manager of the travel agency in Honiara, the capital of Guadalcanal in the Solomon Islands.

Extremely lean and tall, his body made more angular by being stretched over a long frame, and his hair curled on the back of his neck, the young man was appropriately dressed for the march to the ridge, one that he takes when the occasional visitor comes to Guadalcanal to seek it out, but more often by himself to search through the grass for war souvenirs. He wore a short-sleeved shirt open at the neck, walking shorts, a hat for protection from the brutal sun, thick laced boots and wool socks ending in a double fold just below the knees.

The road to the ridge, which begins at the end of the Henderson Field runway, coming off the main road from Honiara that parallels the beach, is really only two worn tire tracks in a field of dense, high weeds. The Australian, his vision almost continuously blocked by weeds falling over the car's windshield, kept looking out the side window, ducking quickly back into the car when a low-lying branch or bush slapped at its side. Up ahead in the middle of the road a house loomed. "I don't know why they let him build this in the middle of the road," he said, referring to an anonymous native who had constructed a very efficient one-room roadblock. "There's only one way to get around this," and he wrenched the wheel so the car spun off sharply into the field, its top disappearing immediately under the growth. A choking cloud of dust and weed fruit rushed through the window. The car, without any reduction in speed, bumped over ruts and dried-up drainage ditches. "You used to be able to get right to the top of Bloody Ridge on this road." He steered the car in a half circle, ending up back on the road, which became impassable at the base of the ridge, near the empty bunker used by General Alexander Vandegrift, commander of the First Marine Division. The bunker is on the first of a series of small hills that cover the side of the ridge. It is now partly hidden by the tall stalks. Twirls of rusted steel poke from the space where chunks are missing, having been torn away by exploding shells. From this bunker Vandegrift directed the battle for the heights near Henderson Field, and it still offers the best panoramic view of the long coral and cement airstrip at the edge of a coconut plantation.

A few yards up on the next plateau is the foundation of what used to be the Marine engine repair shop. From here to the top of the ridge is a short distance but an arduous walk up a fairly steep footpath. A center island of weeds, taller than the height of most men, forms a canopy over the tracks worn by trucks moving up the hill years ago to bring supplies to Marines from the First Raider Battalion and First Parachute Battalion who had fought it out with the Japanese on the night of September 14, 1942.

"Any snakes around here . . . the poisonous kind?" the American said, unable to conceal his fear.

"Nah," the Australian replied, dodging nimbly off the footpath into the weeds, disappearing from sight to look for empty rifle shells left from the battle. His movement sent aloft a covey of insects in a frenzied flight.

A violent battle ended here in hand-to-hand combat, and most of the large pieces of battle evidence—guns and tanks—had long ago been cleared, mostly by natives who carted off the metal to be sold for scrap and by the few tourists who made it up the ridge and took back most of the empty shell cartridges. But not everything is gone. There are old glass soda bottles scattered in the weeds, and at the side of the ridge down from the engine shop, half buried in the jungle growth, is a large rusted Coke machine.

The ridge is but one of the sites of the struggle that took place around Henderson Field from August, 1942, until February, 1943, when, after losing more than 20,000 men, the Japanese finally evacuated Guadalcanal and President Franklin Roosevelt could tell the American public, "It would seem the turning point in the war has been reached."

Henderson Field is much the same as it was in World War II. The airstrip, originally made of crushed coral, has been paved with cement and lengthened to handle medium-range jet aircraft. But the airport terminal is roughly the same size, partitioned now into a waiting room and a customs area where natives in British colonial dress—the Solomon Islands are still a colonial possession of Great Britain—lethargically go through luggage, if it inspires them to do so, and politely ask their visitor to fill out a formal entrance card. (One needs a visa from the British government to enter Guadalcanal. It can be easily obtained and without much wait from any consulate in the United States.)

Also very much as it was then is the aircraft tower for fighter planes in the field a few hundred yards away from the terminal. "I was responsible for getting them to repair these steps," Wright said, taking two of them in a bound. The steps may have been repaired but the railing wasn't. It swayed with the slightest change of air current, and heavy footfalls sent it reverberating crazily. The American stayed on the first level of the tower, gulping for air that wasn't humidity-soaked. "I guess I'm about the only one who comes here regularly," Wright continued. The wind was his only companion at the top of the tower, and it carried his words away from the American, leaving the Australian's mouth moving with no words coming out. He bounded back down the stairs with the same athletic stride, and he struck out for the thickest bush. "Here's an American bunker. Probably used during air raids." The bunker was a mound of grass-covered dirt shaped like a mole-made furrow in a lawn. Some rusted GI mess kits and engine piping were embedded in the earth of the partially hidden underground entrance.

Most of the intense fighting on Guadalcanal took place on a very small section of the island, which is 90 miles long and 30 miles wide. The Marine campaign for several months was encompassed on a 7-mile beachhead extending 4 miles inland. The island's geography determined pretty much where the battle would be fought. Much of the land is mountainous and blanketed with an almost impenetrable jungle. But on both sides of the mountain plains sweep to the sea, and on this flat ground coconut plantations were built before the war. The growth under the trees had to be kept clear for the harvesting of the coconuts, and this was advantageous to the Marines who, when they landed, had practically a clear run from the beach to Henderson Field.

Why was Guadalcanal chosen for the first land offensive by American forces in the Pacific?

The mission assigned to MacArthur and Nimitz, the two ranking officers responsible for the defense of the Pacific, was to hold the islands between the mainland of the United States and

Australia that were not yet in Japanese hands. They were also to prepare for major amphibious operations in the Southwest Pacific. Immediately there arose a conflict in strategy between MacArthur and Nimitz, having really to do with their conceptions of warfare based on the service branch they represented. MacArthur wanted to use air and ground forces in the Solomon Islands and New Guinea to capture airfields. Nimitz wanted to bypass these islands and go directly to Rabaul with a combined air and naval attack on Japan's mightiest military outpost in the South Pacific. MacArthur won. He had a convincing argument for his planned invasion of the Solomons. The Japanese had just completed building a 3,778-foot airstrip on Guadalcanal, and it could be effectively used to harass Allied shipping throughout the whole South Pacific.

The Solomons, a British protectorate since 1893, had fallen early in the war, taken by a relatively small Japanese force in May, 1942. Not all the British fled. Some took to the hills with native guides to set up clandestine spying on Japanese ship movements. Because many maps of these islands were out of date, the information supplied by the coastal watchers was invaluable, as to not only the ships but the terrain in Guadalcanal. These watchers had reliable comrades in the natives, a gentle, humorous people of Melanesian stock who were under constant threat of torture and death by the Japanese to force them to betray the coastal watchers. There was not, however, one authenticated case of a native committing treason for the Japanese.

Some of the preinvasion intelligence given the Americans was not correct. The estimated strength of the Japanese on Guadalcanal was inflated. Expecting 8,000 men, the Americans found only about 3,000 when they landed at Red Beach on August 7, 1942. Also, some of the rivers feeding into the sea from the swampy ground near Henderson Field were misnamed on maps, notably the Tenaru, the site of one of the first and bloodiest engagements. Most of these errors were made in the misreading of aerial photographs taken by two Marine Corps officers a month before the invasion.

The American invasion fleet for Guadalcanal grouped 400

miles southeast of Fiji. Aboard the nineteen large transports were 19,000 men, most of them having had jungle training in field exercises at New River, North Carolina, and Solomons Island, Maryland, before being shipped to Fiji. The invasion

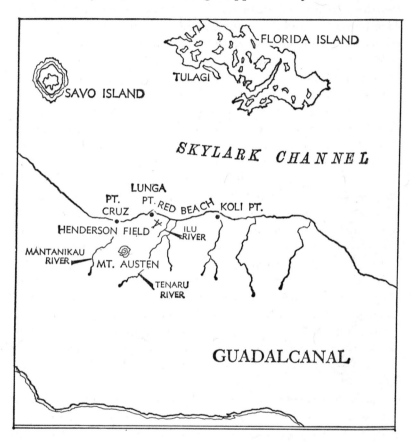

force totaled eighty-two ships, including five cruisers and six destroyers that were sent close to shore for several hours before the landing to lay down bombardment. Forty-four planes also pounded the coastal defenses on Guadalcanal and Tulagi, the small island headquarters of the Japanese located directly across a narrow strait from Guadalcanal. After the air support was completed, the Marines, each carrying two canteens of fresh water and a roll of mosquito netting, went over the sides of the transports, climbing hand over hand down rope ladders to the landing crafts bobbing on the water. The first Marines went ashore at 9:10 A.M. on a 1,600-yard front. There were no Japanese on the beach to meet the invaders, and by 2 P.M. that day 10,000 Marines had landed. A detachment of 3,000 Marines was then sent to Tulagi. In the preinvasion ship and air bombardment, none of the cave defenses was hit, and the Japanese waited for the Americans in these underground fortifications. Tulagi was to be only a footnote to the major invasion on Red Beach across the strait; but, while no Americans lost their lives in combat the first day on Guadalcanal, 36 died on Tulagi. Of the Japanese garrison of 1,500 men there, 4 escaped, 3 surrendered, and the rest were killed before Tulagi was officially declared secured.

The first day on Red Beach is remembered by Harry Way. He was then an eighteen-year-old private in the U.S. Marines.

"I was in the first wave to come ashore. I'm small in size and the water was up to my neck. I kept wondering whether I was going to drown. My clearest memory of that day is not having to go into the water, or the fear of being fired upon; it was of having to go on an enforced march through the jungle once I was ashore, and of sleeping that first night on a mudbank."

Today Red Beach is a strip of finely grained sand bordered by coconut trees. Across the strait, called the Slot, Tulagi rises in the early morning mist as a purple turtleback curved on a blue-black sea. Red Beach has been reclaimed by serenity. Native women come in the early morning to wash their clothes and to bathe. All that remains of the invasion are a half-dozen landing barges in the bush back up from the beach. They stand in an orderly row, a proper position for military war machines sentenced to endure abandonment.

"There used to be some tanks back in here, but one of the salvaging companies took them away a couple of years ago," the Australian said.

Farther down the beach nearer Henderson Field, where the coast curves inland, there is a brown stain on the surface of the sea; the muddy, sluggishly flowing river called the Tenaru enters it here. The Tenaru passes through a private coconut plantation, one that is well guarded by hired men in jeeps patroling on a dirt road outside the barbed-wire fence surrounding the stately, withered coconut trees.

"They're mean. They don't like anyone going on their property," the Australian said, holding apart the barbed wire for the American to crawl through. The floor of the plantation was a soft mat of dead palms, footprints in it quickly filling with foul-smelling water.

"Watch out for falling coconuts," he said. His warning heralded the thud of a coconut splattering on the watery mat behind them. "You should wear a hat in here."

The Tenaru is very narrow where it empties into the sea, and its black mudbanks are used by crocodiles for sunning. At the juncture of the river and the sea, a narrow bridge lying almost on top of the water has been constructed. "Look out for the crocodiles in this part," the Australian said, having led the American to another barbed-wire fence along the mudbank. "See what I mean . . . over there." He pointed to a brown object floating toward the bank, the hump on its back appearing ominously in the water. Another coconut in the distance hit the ground with a splat.

After the Americans landed on Red Beach, they moved quickly inland to take their main objective, Henderson Field. Not only did it have an airstrip equipped to handle sixty planes, but around it were two large radio stations, two electric-light plants, machine shops, an air-compressor plant for torpedoes, and huge quantities of canned vegetables, rice, soybean sauce and beer. Within two weeks of the invasion, Henderson Field held twenty-four serviceable or repairable B-26's and thirty-three B-17's. Now the Americans could bomb Rabaul, only 675 air miles from Guadalcanal.

Recovering from a temporary military paralysis, the Japanese sent planes low over Red Beach the day after the invasion, strafing and bombing men in the foxholes and the piles of supplies dropped carelessly over the beach. There was hardly any American air coverage, and once the men were ashore, many boats from the invasion fleet had been called back, permitting the Japanese to move freely down the Slot and bring troop reinforcements ashore northwest of Red Beach on Lunga Point. By October the troop strength between the combatants was fairly equal: The Japanese had 22,000 men, the Americans 23,000. But in naval action in the Slot, the Americans lost the carrier *Wasp.*

"Our first real contact with the Japanese was on the north bank of the Tenaru River," Way said.

On the night of August 21 the Japanese reinforcements had reached the Tenaru. At low tide a sandbar emerges and the river can be crossed on foot. But the Marines had blocked the sandbar with barbed wire. In frantic, disorganized waves, the Japanese tried to cross it, completely vulnerable to American fire.

"It was a good moonlit night and we could see them crossing the river. They were silhouettes against the sky, and these images came alive, shouting and yelling, and because they weren't distinct, we had to fire into the noise, and when we did, we could hear their screams," Way said.

Their advance was finally stopped at the machine gun emplacement of Al Schmid, a young Marine from Philadelphia, who, though blinded by a grenade, continued to fire into the Japanese until the attack ended. All there was in the shallow, bloody water were bodies of dead Japanese soldiers. In this battle, lasting only a few hours, 871 Japanese were killed, and 34 Marines lost their lives.

Between the Tenaru River and Henderson Field is Hell's Point, a few acres of ground covered with small mounds and separated from the main road by a barbed-wire fence. These mounds are live-ammunition dumps left from the battle, and each day native laborers go into the field and carefully open another mound, removing shells and placing them in a small red truck with letterings on its back and sides: DANGER, HIGH EXPLOSIVES.

There is another live-ammunition dump on the beach south of the Tenaru. Rusted shells have been placed in pyramid-shaped piles here, the top of them level with the wire fence, so the Australian could lean over it, pick off one at the apex, and recklessly toss it back and forth in his hands.

From Hell's Point through the sparse vegetation of stunted trees and scraggy bushes, Henderson Field terminal appears to be squatting in the brush, with only the upper parts of the windows and the roof clearly visible. Throughout the opening months of the Guadalcanal campaign, the airstrip was daily bombed, and in October it was put out of use for a month for heavy and medium bombers. This airstrip was protected on each side by two smaller fighter strips and trenches of men armed with automatic weapons. After it was disabled, Seebees, working through the air raids, constructed a grass strip for lighter aircraft parallel to the main runway at Henderson.

For the first two months, most of the fighting on Guadalcanal was between small forces, mostly patrols in fencing maneuvers against one another's defensive lines. The Japanese objective was the recapture of Henderson, and it was to achieve this end that they sent 2,000 men to take Bloody Ridge. When the attack was over at dawn, the Americans walked through the weeds and counted 600 Japanese dead. In another counterattack on Henderson Field on October 23 and 24, 2,000 Japanese were killed, their bodies scattered on the approaches to the runway. The fierceness of their attack was to no avail against the incredible defense put up by the Americans dug in around Henderson Field. The Japanese were never able to get closer than one mile to the fighter strips at Henderson.

"The things I remember in those first months were that we had no air force to protect us and the Japanese bombed us at will," said Way, "and the second thing was the three or four days we were shelled by Japanese ships. I'd rather be bombed from the air. At least you can see the planes and have an idea where the bombs are going to fall. But with shells from the ships, you can't hear the whistle from them until they are past you, and you don't know where they're going to land. It is very frightening to sit in the midst of a naval bombardment."

In November, 1942, a Japanese convoy tried to get through the Slot to land 10,000 men on Guadalcanal, but they were met by an American fleet of battleships. After a close-range night battle, the Japanese lost two battleships, one heavy cruiser and three destroyers. Of their troops, only 4,000 landed safely, but even those were without enough supplies and rations to sustain them in a major offensive against the by now well-entrenched Americans. The American naval losses in this engagement were also severe: one light cruiser, two light antiaircraft cruisers and seven destroyers.

Guadalcanal was a brutal campaign. Malaria and heat exhaustion took almost as great a toll as Japanese bullets and bombs. By November hard ground fighting by Vandegrift's forces, now totaling 39,000, backed by U.S. Army reinforcements, had secured Lunga Point, which stretched the American beachhead almost the whole length of the coast. But the casualties from illness and wounds continued to mount. By December, of the 10,635 First Marine Division casualties, 1,472 were from gunshot wounds and 5,794 from malaria. Almost everyone had lost weight from an inadequate diet, and secondary anemia was a common illness.

Still the Japanese fought on, almost insanely in what was now a losing cause, for by December the Americans had 40,000 men on Guadalcanal compared with a Japanese force of 25,000.

Way said, "We were in a reserve battalion at the Matanikau River and were called in to plug up a hole in our line made by a Japanese counterattack. It took some time to get there. We were pinned down in open terrain by Japanese bombers, and when we got to the river the next morning, the Japanese had already been driven back across it.

"A few days later we were called out on company patrol and were ambushed and pinned down for eight hours. When we finally got back to our bivouac area, we were told it was our turn to be stationed on the banks of the river and we were sent back.

"The next morning we woke up and saw five or six Japanese transports off the coast, and through binoculars we watched the soldiers climbing down the rope ladders.

"The Japanese made three drives to get across the river. I got it on the second drive. It was about ten P.M. on October twenty-third, and my left leg took an almost direct hit from a mortar. I yelled to my buddy next to me that I was hit, and he tried to

drag me back from the river. I got hit again, this time in the
right leg from machine gun bullets.

"We couldn't get out until the next morning. I was carried
on a stretcher a mile to the base hospital. The doctors said gas
gangrene was throughout my body and they had to amputate
my left leg to save my life. I was flown to New Hebrides where
the operation took place. The doctors managed to save my right
leg, though it was shattered."

The war was over for Harry Way, and less than two months
later the First Marine Division was withdrawn from Guadalcanal, its place taken over by two regimental combat teams of
the U.S. Americal division and most of a separate U.S. Army
infantry regiment.

There is no natural harbor on Guadalcanal, and sections of
the coast are protected by offshore coral reefs. Since supplies
had to come ashore, the Americans built a port on a lean finger
of land hooked into the sea eight miles around a peninsula from
Henderson Field. It was called Point Cruz and before the war
had been a coconut plantation. When the Americans left
Guadalcanal, returning control of it to the British, this port became the town of Honiara, now the capital of the British Solomon Islands with a population of 9,000. Since the war the commercial section of Honiara has expanded for a mile along the
waterfront. The residential area, mostly for Europeans who run
the government and the island's economy, is on a hillside with a
magnificent view of the harbor and the islands in the distant
sea.

Along the main road in Honiara and on the sides of the hill
are many small wooden markers designating where battles were
fought late in the campaign by the U.S. Army. Other remains
of the war in Honiara are a rusted shore gun at the Guadalcanal
Club, a social institution for the European settlement—the gun
is on the beach facing the sea and is located several feet away
from a swimming pool for the Europeans (the ocean is filled
with sharks and bathing in it is prohibited)—and the fuselage
of an American plane. Stripped of its wings, engines and cockpit, it is in a clearing of a coconut grove across the street from
the police station. A faded star on the side of the plane is barely

visible. Most of the paint on the fuselage has been scratched away by persons carving their names into the metal. Inside the fuselage is the rank smell of stale urine.

Across the street from the Guadalcanal Club is the recently opened Solomon Islands Museum, and on the grass behind it are several weapons. One is a small Japanese cannon, and placed on each side of it are American machine guns, the three weapons joined now in peaceful neutrality.

The young Australian's war tour for the American ended on the hill overlooking Honiara. It was high noon and the heat was stifling. He had driven the agency's car by a back way, showing the American new apartment housing for the colonialists and some two-room residential homes for the native workers —on the door of one outhouse was posted a colored picture of Queen Elizabeth. Parking at the top of the hill, the Australian got out, opened the door for the American, and together they half slid and stumbled down the side of the hill through the burnt weeds until they bumped into a dead tree trunk.

"There should be some here." The Australian knelt on the ground, and with the expert sight of one used to finding four-leaf clovers in fields of grass, he uncovered a cache of empty rifle and pistol shells, both Japanese and American. They were together where they had fallen in a face-to-face confrontation of the enemy. One of the Japanese shell cartridges had a jagged hole in it made by an American shell.

"Here, take them," he said, "before they're all gone."

The battle for Guadalcanal was over in February, 1943, when the Japanese evacuated 13,000 soldiers to Rabaul. A total of 60,000 U.S. soldiers and Marines had participated in what was the first amphibious operation conducted by U.S. military forces since 1898. The American casualties were 1,600 killed and 4,245 wounded. The U.S. naval losses were two heavy carriers, six heavy cruisers, two light cruisers and fourteen destroyers. Of the Japanese force on Guadalcanal, 14,800 were killed or missing in action, 9,000 died of disease, and 1,000 were taken prisoner. The military hardware lost by the Japanese were 600 planes, 2 battleships, 1 light carrier, 3 heavy cruisers, 1 light cruiser, 11 destroyers, and 6 submarines.

Back from the hill, the Australian stopped off at his office, where the American paid him in dollars. Not knowing the tipping habits in the South Pacific, the American hesitatingly offered him $5 more.

"You must be kidding, mate. We've already overcharged you for the tour around the battlefield." The morning tour had cost $14. But the American insisted, telling the Australian he must have gone out of his way to take him to places other tourists never get to see: the banks of the Tenaru, the Red Beach landing site, the hill where the shells had been found.

"If you insist," he said outside the air-conditioned office on a sidewalk broiling in the sun, "you can buy me something." He led the American to a bookshop in the center of Honiara and permitted him to make a gift of a paperback copy of James Jones' *The Thin Red Line,* a fictionalized account of the battle for Guadalcanal.

The Fiji Islands are where the journey to Guadalcanal begins, and since there are no split-second connecting flights for the air traveler coming into the South Pacific from Hawaii, there is invariably a night stopover at Nandi, where the international airport of Fiji is located. Air service is very infrequent to the Solomons, two flights a week with two stops in the New Hebrides, and it is very costly. Air fares in the South Pacific are the most expensive per mile in the world.

The airport is outside the village of Nandi on a plateau scraped off one of the several hills cut by a stream coursing over a finely pebbled bed. There are two modern motels near the airport with the conveniences expected by jaded travelers: private bath, or at least a shower with hot and cold water, air conditioning, though the nights on Fiji are pleasantly mild, and by the headboard of the bed a dial controlling the selection and the volume of canned American music played without commercial interruptions. Several nights a week at one of the airport motels, Fiji men and women perform traditional native dances on a yard of cropped waxy grass within the motel compound. The dancers have enough naked flesh showing to make their dress seem authentic. The men wear nothing on their chest, grass skirts, trinkets of wood around their necks and wild lines painted on their face. The women wear skirts of colorful material, wrapped tightly around their waist and falling to their ankles, and cloth stretched tautly across their bosom. In the flickering orange light from torches stuck in the ground along the edge of the lawn, the dancers grunt and chant, rushing with their spears in front of them toward the tourists sitting in rows of chairs at the end of the lawn. Their movement is done in a series of leaps, and after each one the men land on flat feet so that their progress across the lawn is heavy and abrupt.

The only quick transportation for a tourist to Nandi is by taxi, and the fare for the several-mile trip is reasonable, about five dollars. The Hindus, imported to Fiji by the British in the nineteenth century to do the manual labor, have resisted integration within the community of the black-skinned Fiji natives. But they have taken over the places of commerce, and many of the drivers standing by cabs outside the airport are Hindus. They are very self-effacing to visitors, chattering in a soft whine that grates on the ears and offering pieces of information when none is asked for.

The center of Nandi resembles the outskirts of any one of many American towns built around an Army base. The stores of tin and loosely held together cinder blocks give the appearance of places that can be quickly dismantled and be reassembled where the troops stop. Most of the stores are discount houses, advertising in their windows bargains for the tourists who usually have very little time to shop in Nandi.

The interesting activity on that Sunday night was a Hindu fair, on the banks of a stream at the edge of town. It was a religious revival for the pious combined with what amounted to a gambling den, with those not interested in praying or betting sitting on the stone floor under a tin roof eating highly spiced food cooked in open stoves near the water. The penitents, few in number, proceeded with hands in front of their faces, fingers touching at the tips, toward a gold altar enveloped by incense. Candles were being lighted and placed in an upright urn at the side of the altar. Behind it, standing in a field denuded of grass by the wear of footfalls, a woman chanted a prayer. Hundreds of women, sitting with legs crossed on the floor, held bowls in the folds of their saris, scooping up the food with their hands. Outside, under a huge, multilimbed tree, men were gambling at a long table, betting money on the spin of a wheel. There were many drunks stumbling through the mud, pushing the penitents out of the way at the altar, going off into the empty field to urinate. A fight broke out between the most boisterous of the drunks and the dealer who was spinning the wheel. Though few joined in the ineffectual struggle, the crowd formed a circle around the battlers, swaying and pushing with each punch until the ranks broke and it became a mass of individuals tripping to get away from the table.

"It is best to leave the fairground now," the driver said in his feminine whine. "Liquor is too freely sold here."

The brawl was now out of hand and policemen had to be called. They made their entrance into the fairground, slipping on the sheen of mud, one of them going to his knee.

The company servicing the Solomon Islands is Fiji Airways. It is sufficiently solvent to have recently spent a great deal of money on several medium-range two-engine jet passenger planes for its flights up the Solomons to New Britain and New Guinea. Small by the standards of those on regular runs in the United States and Europe, these jets are comfortable, two seats to each side, and the scarcity of customers on any one flight allows most travelers to have a row to themselves. The two hostesses on the flight, clothed in native dress of wrap-around skirts and blouses of the same bolt of material, kept the passengers' paper cups filled with fruit juices.

The flight is long and monotonous over this stretch of the Pacific. The first native airport at Efate in the New Hebrides is a novelty, however. This runway and the one at Espiritu Santo, also in the New Hebrides, are made of modern materials and were constructed during the war when the Americans used the New Hebrides as a staging area for troops island-hopping toward Japan. Its terminal was rudimentary, nothing more than a one-room hut large enough for customs officers to stand behind a wooden plank luggage rack. The New Hebrides are coadministered by the French and British, but at Efate the customs men, brought to the shack in an open government truck down an unpaved road, spoke only French, as did the merchant in a thatched-roof hut next to the terminal. He sold drinks kept cool by chunks of ice in a metal drum on the floor.

One of his customers was a young man from Espiritu Santo. An exile from an Eastern European country, he had emigrated with his family to Australia and married a New Hebrides native girl whom he had met there. Her father set him up in a meat-cutting business. He was pleased by life in the South Pacific, its relaxed pace and the opportunities for advancement in an embryonic economy, and he had no desire to return to Europe, though he enjoyed his yearly trips to Sydney to visit his parents.

At Espiritu Santo Airport, as charmingly primitive as the one at Efate, the young man was met by his brown-skinned wife. She held their infant son, who was more interested in the curl of dark hair on his mother's forehead than in the arrival of his father.

The approach to Henderson Field is over the mountainous center of Guadalcanal, and from 20,000 feet, the jungle covering keeps changing its shade of green. It rains often during the day, a steamy barrage of enormous drops splattering loudly when they hit the sidewalk. At Henderson, a violent tropical storm had just departed, and the runway and the stone terrace at the entrance to the terminal were covered with puddles already beginning to dry up swiftly in the blazing sun.

A new invasion of the Solomons is now taking place by young engineers, mineral explorers and adventurers, and their entrance is through the Henderson Field airport. Most of these men come from Australia and New Zealand, and for them the South Pacific is one of the last great unexplored and underdeveloped areas in the world. Geologists believe it may also be a land containing a variety of wealth-producing minerals. Up to now the major commercial export from Guadalcanal has been copra. But hopefully for the economy, the island may also have exportable minerals.

The Japanese and Americans are also back on Guadalcanal in limited numbers, and their purpose for being here is another kind of struggle men have engaged in along with their wars. It is economic exploitation, and American and Japanese companies recently staked claims to explore the island for minerals.

Young men living here have to accept conditions of primitiveness since most of their work is in uninhabited sections of the mountainous jungle. Other than working with the natives in the excavations, there is nothing for men to do in the bush except read, and there is a shortage of both paperbacks and electricity on the island. Outside of Honiara most of the light comes from kerosene lamps unless a hut has that rarity, a generator.

For half the year the island is in the torrents of a rainy season, and the daily downpours loosen the soil, causing dangerous landslides. Not too long ago four men were killed and dozens were injured during a rockslide at a mining camp on Bougainville, a large Solomon island northwest of Guadalcanal. The benefits for living this rugged life are almost all financial. The worker gets a good overseas living allowance, a tax break on his income, and a salary accumulating back home in a bank.

Much of the traffic in the two major hotels in Honiara is provided by these young men coming home from leave in Wellington or Sydney and going back to islands farther up the chain. On any afternoon the humidity and the rain keep most of them in their air-conditioned rooms on lumpy mattresses watching the progress of insects up the bare walls. When evening begins to fall over the hills west of Honiara, the men head to the bar.

One of the two hotels is owned by Chinese and is called the Honiara Hotel. The only thing Chinese about it is the pagoda-shaped sign over the entrance and the menu of rice, fish and chicken dishes prepared and served all in the same thick sauce. The hotel has a small pool, and the water is refreshing for a few hours in the morning until the sun slowly broils it. The sides of the pool under the water are covered by a green fungus.

The tourist business just hasn't materialized in Guadalcanal. There are no beaches or resorts to keep the guest entertained. The few Americans showing up periodically are most often middle-aged men who had fought here and, now that they have made their money, return with their families to where their youth was spent. Even if there were an influx of tourists, the island would not have enough air-conditioned hotel rooms to accommodate them. The oppressive humidity is a factor in determining the length of one's stay on Guadalcanal. For the nonnative, a brief walk in the morning sun can become a physical ordeal. The air is not only wet but leadened, warming the skin with a steady outbreak of hot beads of perspiration. Nonnatives, who number about 700 of Guadalcanal's total population of 50,000 and are mostly British and Australians, wear shorts and long knee socks to the office. The native men are more practical. They wear sarongs and go barechested. The women are equally pragmatic. When the sun is at its brightest at high noon, native women walk through town under umbrellas. The British and Australian women, conscious of their tans, rarely carry them.

Compared with living conditions in the jungle interior, Honiara is a paradise, but one with limited attractions. The social headquarters for whites is the Guadalcanal Club, and the favorite pastime is drinking at night on the open stone patio where breezes off the sea are funneled through the bar and the dining room. This is really a womanless society. The men are mostly young and bored at the club and are without women unless they are married and have brought their wives to Guadalcanal for their two-year tour of duty. Interracial dating is not approved, but the practices of young Australians and British of taking native girls to the outer islands for long weekends of skin diving and sex are condoned as an acceptable alternative to enforced celibacy.

Honiara has one movie house, a converted Quonset hut, and the films shown are older than the war fought on the site years ago. The library is poorly stocked and open only at odd hours. There is a secular bookstore with an inadequate supply of paperbacks, but the largest bookstore is run by fundamentalist Protestants and contains nothing but religious tracts.

Guadalcanal's food supply comes frozen from Australia. Though the quality of the meat and vegetables available in the stores and restaurants is excellent, something of the taste gets lost in being too long in refrigeration, and there is little difference between eating a piece of steak and a breast of chicken. Fresh eggs and milk are nonexistent.

Immediately after World War II newly arrived Chinese merchants built a one-street Chinatown at one end of Honiara on the road to the airport. The Chinese stores are very cluttered. With space at a premium, clothes are hung from the ceiling on long poles, and most of the floor is covered with everything from rolled bed mattresses to piles of shiny metal buckets. Unlike those owned by non-Asians in the center of town, which close promptly at 5 P.M., these Chinese stores stay open every evening until 9 and 10 o'clock.

The best restaurant on Guadalcanal, the Lantern, is also owned by Chinese. Built on stilts over the Mendana River at the end of Chinatown, it has walls of woven palm leaves which retain the day's humidity late into evening. The only moving air comes from whirling overhead fans. The menu is almost exclusively Chinese, and dining is a leisurely, charming experience until one hears the toilets being flushed and the waste pouring from open pipes into the river.

The British no longer have an empire, but the remaining colonialists on Guadalcanal have taken their reduction in power with equanimity and are administering the Solomons with a good deal of common sense. The British have expanded the school system and put up well-designed and ventilated schools on the coast road to the airport. Nearby is a maritime academy for native boys, graduates of it getting berths on merchant ships plying the South Pacific. The British also administer a fairly large general hospital, as well as a mental hospital which is ominously hidden behind a hand-painted NO TRESPASSING sign and a barricade of thick shrubs.

The most vital of the government-run corporations is the radio station, broadcasting daily a limited schedule of news programs from London and Sydney and pop music from America. Some of the news for the benefit of the natives is read in pidgin English, a melodically singsong bastardization of the English language.

The Solomon Islands' natives are mostly dark-skinned, fuzzy-haired Melanesians, though there are some Polynesians here, a lighter-skinned people who are from Hawaii and Samoa.

The night life of Honiara is compressed into the few hours

after dusk when everyone is walking the main street, the numbers of pedestrians forcing the cars to move slowly. The Guadalcanal Club is packed with families eating in the dining room
and loud young men standing in groups at the bar rail, talking
about the comparative prices of motorcycles on the island and
the best places to take girls on weekends. Suddenly it comes to
an end. The streets are empty, except for a native woman hurrying in the gutter of the road and balancing on her head a basket
of wash for a European family. In the distance there is a roar of
a motorbike and a car door slamming. Night is then taken over
by the sounds of the jungle, pressing down from the hills to the
edge of the road. At first the noise is almost soothing because it
is even-pitched and constant. But then there is the shriek of a
bird to disrupt the pleasant tranquility, and soon every sound
becomes a threat: the rustle of leaves possibly a deadly snake,
the flapping in the sky a bird of prey.

These were the sounds heard by the American soldiers and
Marines during their nights of war on Guadalcanal, and because of the enemy around them, the sounds were then even
more hostile and threatening. This is what one remembers of
Guadalcanal, the night noises, harbingers of future danger to
those who fought there and those who hear them now. They
remain with the listeners long after leaving Guadalcanal, and
eventually all the young go, first the Americans and then the
young colonialists, back to Australia or England after their two-
year tours of duty are up in the mines, banks and government
offices. Only the native young remain, walking alone down the
dark night streets of Honiara.

Paul Wright will be among those leaving eventually, the
paths in the battlefields already too familiar to him, their mys-
teries no longer hidden. At night in his bedroom he lies awake
thinking about his chances of getting to southern California
and of the endless beaches of pretty blondes in bikinis. This is
his America, if not exactly the one of the men who fought for
Guadalcanal.

# Guadalcanal to Rabaul: A Journey

The DC-3 has been a two-engine plane of great functional skill in its many years of commercial service since the end of World War II. Insignificant in size compared with the oversized jet passenger planes of today, it is still in regular use up the Solomon Islands chain from Guadalcanal to Rabaul in New Britain. Instantly sensitive to air turbulence outside, it shudders and dips with every sudden change in air currents, and forced to cruise at much lower altitudes than the jets, it barely skims over the jungle mountains.

The first major landing of the DC-3 after leaving Guadalcanal was Mundo in the Solomons, but before arriving there, it had come in low over shallow pale-blue water, with clouds of black coral formations outlined below the surface, and had touched down on a grass airstrip at a private coconut plantation to take aboard a man and his wife who were waiting in the shade of a thatched lean-to. Two native men pushed a portable stairway across the rough-surfaced field and stood beside it, almost at attention, until the white couple climbed aboard.

Mundo airport is similar to almost every other one in remote Pacific islands. There is a cement-covered coral strip on the fringe of the jungle near the coast. If it becomes necessary for a plane to crash-land—planes in this area of the Pacific only fly in daylight since the airports do not have the lights to handle night flights—chances of survival are still better in the surf than in the tree-crowded jungle.

Several natives inside the Mundo terminal—a cool, dark room—had displayed their wood carvings on racks along one wall: death masks of warrior faces, sublime, courageous, but dead, and miniature sharks, teeth covered, reducing their fierceness to a muted anger. The carvings are quite reasonable. Even the largest ones, up to ten inches in length, are sold for under ten American dollars. But because Australian customs officers in Rabaul—New Britain is administered by the Australian government—are very strict about imports from the outer islands, the natives must laboriously write out a description of the purchase and its cost on an official customs form.

The plane takes on more white passengers and lifts off the runway, just clearing the tops of a row of palm trees before rising on a straight path for Bougainville, the largest island in the Solomons and the scene of fighting as bloody as that on Guadalcanal, though the number of troops involved was fewer. The air corridor for this flight is directly over the Slot. On each side of the plane, 10,000 feet below, are broken lines of islands, some longer than others but all dark green in color. In the interior of the islands natives have cleared patches on the sides of the hills, leaving a field of bare tree stumps around straw huts. One native settlement of a half-dozen huts is at the base of a beautiful slender waterfall, the velocity of it creating puffs of white foam where it smacks into a rocky pool.

The Bougainville air terminal is parallel to the coastline, separated from the water by a few hundred yards of rocks and stubby grass. There is solemn activity outside the terminal while, inside, Australian customs officers laboriously weigh every piece of luggage taken off the plane, a requirement that seems foolish since the luggage was weighed at Guadalcanal before it was loaded. This tedious procedure does distract the passengers milling in the terminal from seeing what is taking place outside.

Behind the customs building, two natives lift a plain crate box, drop it on a handcart, and tug it around the side of the terminal to the front where the plane is parked. The box has been kept apart from the other freight being sent to Rabaul on the DC-3, and it is left aside until all the other baggage is loaded into the plane's belly.

The passengers are requested to return to the plane, and when they have adjusted their seat belts in preparation for the takeoff, the young Australian hostess—the plane is owned by a domestic Australian airline—asks if they would mind having the crate in the center aisle for the remainder of the flight to Rabaul. The passengers appear unconcerned; inconveniences are expected by air travelers in this part of the world.

"You see," she says shyly, "it's the body of one of the workers killed in the landslide at the mining camp last week."

Death as a possible air companion for these passengers makes them restless, and they cast furtive glances at strangers in the next seats.

"The man was cut in half." This, she obviously thought, would appease those curious about the size of the box. It could not possibly have contained the body of a normal-sized human.

The only thing left on the parking ramp is the orange-tinted crate. The natives have backed away from it. The customs officials huddle with the pilot in the aisle at the front of the passenger compartment. The concern is over the weight of the box since the plane's present load is precariously close to the danger point for a satisfactory takeoff. A decision is finally made, and the customs men leave, taking the ramp steps two at a time. With a visible sigh of relief, the hostess slams the door from inside. Almost immediately, the plane's engines turn over, the brakes are released, and with a slight jolt, the plane moves to the main runway, taxies to one end, turns and races down its length for the lift-off.

Death is on the mind of many passengers. By looking back through the window, they can see the crate on the ramp, the natives still standing some distance from it in the shade of the terminal.

Directly in front of the runway is a high rounded mountain, and rather than veering sharply to the right for a course over the water to miss the peak—this maneuver could possibly cause a reduction in power and the engines would stall—the plane proceeds toward the mountain, all the time lifting gradually, seemingly not fast enough or at a steep enough angle. Apprehension, a noticeable lightening of color, is on the faces of many passengers who find themselves automatically shifting their weight, lifting upward by pressing their hands down on the

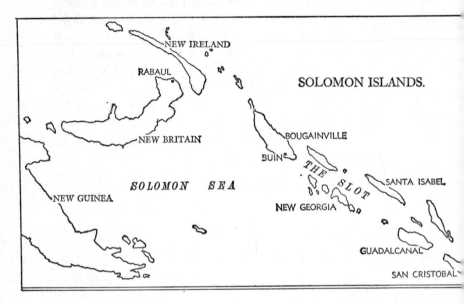

armrests, straining until their movement is stopped by the seat belt. One passenger, the nails of his fingers putting white ridges into the palms of his hands, mutters, "Jesus Christ . . . he's going to crash this plane into the mountain." He looks to the hostess, the one person on a plane to observe for indications of serious trouble. She has been taught to show no emotion and seems unconcerned. Still strapped into her bucket seat attached to the wall next to the door, she is filing her nails.

Everything on the side of the hill suddenly has wonderful clarity: the center vein in the gigantic leaves flowering from the top of coconut trees, the fires outside the native huts. The plane stays with its struggle to lift clear of the mountaintop, but the ground looms closer, the objects below there to be touched. The hostess still doesn't look up. She is now slowly adjusting

Now a tranquil scene, Kolekole Pass on Oahu, Hawaii, on the morning of December 7, 1941, echoed to the roar of Japanese bombers on their way to Pearl Harbor, Hickam and Wheeler fields to begin a war that would claim nearly 300,000 American lives before it was over.

"Day of Infamy": *(above)* the U.S. battleship *Arizona* sinks under Japanese fire. Today the marble memorial below marks the spot where she went down, taking more than 1,000 men with her to their death. More destruction: *(above right)* planes burning at Hickam Field; *(below right)* smoke rising from the harbor after the attack.

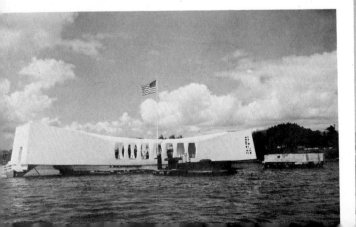

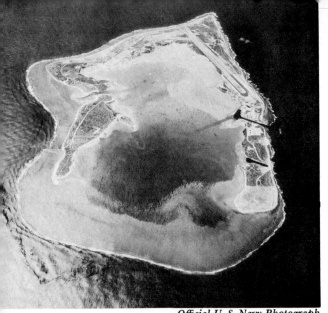

Wake Island.

Midway, 1942: the Japar

Smoke rises from bombs dropped on Manila in December, 1941. One month later, the Japanese occupied the city without resistance.

at was a turning point in the war.

Bataan: a memorial marks the beginning of the infamous Death March of April, 1942. In the distance, the island of Corregidor.

United States forces surrendering to the Japanese on Corregidor.

*Above:* live-ammunition depot stands today near the Guadalcanal invasion beach. *Right:* a Marine squadron warms up before strike at Henderson Field in December, 1942.

Guadalcanal: From August, 1942, to February, 1943, 16,000 U.S. Marines battled 24,000 Japanese in an effort to capture Henderson Field. *Left:* part of a Marine camp on the island in 1944. *Below:* the Honiara Hotel, one of the few public places on Guadalcanal today.

*Defense Department Photo*

An American B-25 strafes Japanese
dugouts in Rabaul, New Britain
*(above)*. Once a lovely South Pacific town, Rabaul lost 90 percent
of its buildings in two years of air
attacks. *Right:* a Japanese crane
still sits where it was hit by American bombs.

*Left:* a native family walks the Kokoda Trail, the route taken by the Australian defenders of Port Moresby in New Guinea. *Below:* the city's Australian military cemetery.

THEIR NAME LIVETH FOR EVERMORE

*U. S. Army Photograph*

*Upper left:* a view of Port Moresby as it appeared in May, 1943, after it had been secured from the Japanese. *Left:* American and Australian Allies read copies of *Guinea Gold* in December, 1943.

*U. S. Army Photograph*

The brief but bloody battle for Tarawa in November, 1943: *(upper left)* the Marines' Sixth Regiment lands on West Beach; *(upper right)* a Marine tank as it stalled attempting to climb the seawall; *(lower left)* Marine reinforcements wade ashore beside latrine stalls, aerial photos of which had enabled the Americans, using a unique calculation, to determine the size of the Japanese force on the island; *(lower right)* the reinforced concrete structure that had held the Japanese High Command on Tarawa.

Scenes of Tarawa today: *(top)* a rusted gun on the beachhead; *(center)* Tarawa airport; *(bottom)* a graveyard for Australian and New Zealand coastal watchers killed by the Japanese.

*Defense Department Photo*

Marines attempt to flush out remaining Japanese soldiers from Saipan caves with flamethrowers in July, 1944. *Below:* American tourists today stand near Suicide Cliff where Japanese soldiers jumped to their death on the rocks below.

Banzai Cliff, Saipan: When the Americans looked down, they saw so many Japanese corpses a small naval vessel was unable to steer through them.

In wartime a landing site, now a Saipan garbage dump.

July 25, 1944: U.S. Marines wade ashore at Tinian in what was probably the most successful amphibious landing of the war.

From this Tinian loading site, the U.S. bomber *Enola Gay* left to deliver an atomic bomb to Hiroshima, thus closing one chapter in history while beginning another. *Right:* Herman T. Palacios, the author's guide around the island.

*Top:* a Japanese memorial stands in Tinian Town more than two decades after American artillery fire reduced it to rubble before the July, 1944, invasion. Tinian also provided the Americans with their first target for napalm fire bombs. *Above:* the Tinian landing site from the sea.

the buttons on her uniform. And then the plane is over the top of the mountain and there is nothing in front but the blueness of the Pacific and another green-humped island in the distance.

The last stop before Rabaul was an airport at the tip of Bougainville. From above, the land surrounding it was alive with signs of the leisured class: sailing, fishing and scuba diving, and ranch-styled homes with shutters and Spanish-tiled roofs at the end of private docks, giving the area the appearance of Miami Beach. The air terminal itself was partitioned into a number of sections, one of them containing a magazine rack of already-dated publications. Most of the people inside waiting for the plane's arrival or to see people off were white. But outside at one end of the terminal two native women, their breasts bare and voluptuously tipping downward with the weight of their fullness, peeked around the corner and gave tentative waves toward two young white Australians walking across the pavement to board the plane. The men didn't acknowledge this recognition. They wouldn't want whites who were strangers to suspect they had slept with these black women.

The most gregarious passenger in the terminal was a handsome man of an age which had given his face enough lines and a slackening of the skin under the eyes to make one suspect he was living well and intensely in the years of early middle age. His clothes were more youthful than his physical appearance. He was fashionably modish: wide-striped shirt opened at the neck showing off a religious medal secured by a chain and lying flat on his chest hairs, moderately tight pants and loafers. He seemed to be saying farewell to many persons without really centering his attention on one in particular. The subjects of his conversation were two: an unconsummated business deal and an abortive plane trip.

He had intended to fly farther down the islands, possibly to Mundo, but a foul-up in plane reservations had left him without a seat on the plane that went down the day before, and his trip had terminated at this airport. When he boarded the plane to Rabaul, the only seat left was next to an American, and he greeted him with a "hi," affecting a casualness that didn't come off because of his thick European accent, probably German or Eastern European.

"How about a beer?" again said with an American-inspired openness.

"I didn't know you could buy them on the plane," the American replied, his stomach sour from the quantities of fruit juice consumed on the trip up.

"Australian. As good as any you can buy in the world." He slipped into an accent approximating the roughness of English spoken by Australians, but failed to disguise an English learned by a European in Britain. It was quite theatrical without an amusing touch of cynicism.

After the second bottle of beer, drunk as quickly as the first one, he said, "She's dying to go out with me."

"Who?"

"Her. The hostess. I've already got a date with her. Saw her in the airport, and, like that—" He snapped his fingers. "Maybe she knew who I am."

In the telling of his life story in the sky over the sea between Bougainville and Rabaul, he was many persons, first a German youth escaping with his parents from the Nazis, and then, when his age was questioned for such a daring feat, he said it was from East Germany with the Communists on their heels. He did spend some time in London, the reason he had acquired a king's English accent which the American was smart to detect so rapidly, and then he sailed on a merchant boat for the Middle East, jumping ship in Cairo. There was a period of his life in which he wandered through the deserts of Arabia. His arrival in Australia came in an astonishing jump in time sequence which further reduced the credibility of his narrative, the escape from Arabia being what the listener wanted to hear about, even if the story wasn't true. There was a succession of dull jobs in Sydney and Melbourne, none of them acceptable for a German with ambition. There may have been a wife, possibly a child, but they too disappeared into the complexity of his narrative and were never mentioned again, offered only as a reference point to his heterosexuality, already presumably estab-

lished by his pursuit of the hostess—bachelors traveling alone
must often give indications, some more rudely than others,
about their sexual proclivities.

"Do you like fish?"

"Love it," the diet-conscious American replied.

"I just opened a restaurant and a small motel about ten miles
up the coast from Rabaul. It's a great place. Quiet. Relaxing.
Good food."

"I'm already booked into a motel near the airport in Rabaul," the American lied, made wary by the loose ends of his
companion's story.

"You can call from the airport. Break the reservation. Stay at
our place. We have a dozen units, though only a few are opened
now."

"Do you have air conditioning?"

"It's not necessary. The room opens to the sea and there's always a breeze coming off it at night. Anyway, when you get done
eating and drinking, you won't notice the weather."

It would be fun to stay at his motel, even if the American
was no longer certain the place existed—the ability to make
dreams triumph over reality being the power of romantic adventurers in the South Pacific.

The more he drank, the more his youthful high spirits became irrepressible, but the flush in his cheeks, rather than
giving them a healthy redness, turned them to a pasty color. If
he were not such an animated, exuberant person, he could have
been thought ill.

There was a descending motion to the plane with an accom-
panying increase in pressure on the eardrums of the passengers.
The hostess, who had been up front with the pilots for an in-
ordinately long time, came out of the cockpit and asked the
passengers to adjust their seat belts for the landing at Rabaul.
She made her way down the center aisle, having to climb because of the pitch of the plane now, and was almost past him
without even giving him the slightest sign of recognition. His
hand shot out and his fist tightly encircled her wrist, a desper-
ately harsh movement. "About tonight," he asked sternly.

"I'm terribly sorry. We're not staying long in Rabaul. We're going on to Port Moresby."

"You're lying. It'll be dark before a plane can take off to Moresby and planes don't fly at night."

"Look. I really am sorry, but something else has come up."

The American remembered the length of her stay in the cockpit, and he felt embarrassed, not wanting to see another man rebuked publicly by a woman.

The man was silent for a few minutes and then said without preparing his hearer for the urgency of the pronouncement: "I have cancer. They thought it could be cured by an operation, but—"

The American was at first stunned, then surprised the impact didn't remain longer, possibly because he thought it just might be another fiction added to a life story already burdened by the unexpected and the improbable.

"Cancer . . ."

The plane came in over the bay of Rabaul past an extinct volcano, one side of it dirt brown where the vegetation had slid down to its base.

The man said nothing until they were in the terminal, mobbed with natives moving in frantic motions of welcome until it became obvious they were in the terminal not to greet passengers from the plane but to pass the time of days long and without any significant purpose.

"Are you coming?"

Embarrassed, uncomfortable, the American didn't answer. There had been too many intimations of death for one day. The fields around Henderson where so many Japanese and Americans had died. The corpse in the orange crate. A man with cancer. He turned his back, fumbled in his pocket for a coin, acting as if he were going to telephone to check his hotel reservation, not even knowing how to use the phone.

The man didn't have any luggage, and he walked past the American out into the sun and down a line of parked taxicabs, not taking any one but walking beyond them into the blinding light.

# Rabaul

She was used to having her acts of kindness paid off in ways other than financial, and she would wait for the American to kiss her cheek, knowing she would never see him again.

"Ta-ta . . . ," she called to a Catholic priest also leaving that day but in a different direction, southeast to the Solomon Islands and his jungle mission station. "Don't forget the Christmas card and put a note in it this year. Let us know what you're doing there." The priest waved back to her. Behind him was a young Australian girl whose devotion to Christianity, an instance of allegiance in an age of disbelief, had motivated her to volunteer to live at the priest's mission for two years to work at the medical clinic.

"Oh, well, another one gone," the woman said, deflated by yet one more departure. Her life had become a series of greetings and farewells at the airport. She would probably have been there by habit that day even if her friends weren't leaving Rabaul. Her compulsive drive to be in the thick of travel came from the fact so many others were sentenced to short times on New Britain while she would be there all her life, away from her native Australia, with only increasingly infrequent trips back, and those not really worthwhile since so many friends had moved on or died.

"You should really read Han Suyin if you're going to Hong Kong. What was the name of her last book, not the one about the Eurasian who had a love affair with an English correspondent, but the one where the heroine goes home to Red China. . . ."

Her view of reality had been fashioned by an imagination fed by books and movies, not actual experiences, and Hong Kong for her was a beautiful, intelligent woman doctor running up a hill to meet her handsome Englishman and being pressed into the fresh, damp grass to make romantic, asexual love. This woman was not too old to have these dreams of escape, though the puffiness under her eyes, rather than being from a lack of sleep, was an indication of her age, somewhere in her early forties, when these releases through flights of the imagination can become critical to survival.

Though she didn't need the money—her husband had a good, well-paying job at the country club—she worked part time as a driver-guide for a tourist agency, thus giving her more contact with travelers. The day before she had driven the American and a much-younger Australian male student, her only passengers, to an incredibly lovely beach around from one of the many mountains surrounding Rabaul. She drove fast, swerving with professional skill to miss a flock of chickens scurrying across her path, never interrupting her descriptions of the life of colonialists in New Britain.

The entrance to the beach was in the forest at the top of a hill, and the road here became a series of impassable rain-carved ruts blocked by a fallen log. "We'll have to walk from here," she said, climbing without assistance over the log, her skirt rising to plump, attractive thighs.

It was a beach made in the mythology of the South Pacific: uninhabited, pristine, dazzlingly white sand, translucent blue water. The only person there was a native man mending his fishing net, and when he finished, he waded into the ocean. It is extremely shallow for several hundred yards before the coral shelf ends abruptly and the coast drops off into fathomless purple-black water. The man moved parallel to the beach, pulling the net underwater and stopping often to lift it up and count the number of fish trapped in it.

Around the bend in the beach, behind a rock with a pathway worn through it by natural erosion, there is an enormous cave.

It was used during the war by the Japanese as a submarine base. The Japanese would sail their submarines to the coral reef, have them lifted over it by cranes and placed in the protective cave where they couldn't be spotted from the air.

"Why don't you go swimming here?" she encouragingly asked the two males. "It's a beautiful spot."

"We don't have bathing suits," the American answered.

"What's the difference? You can go in without them. There's nobody here."

The fisherman had progressed around the bend in the coast and disappeared behind the submarine cave.

"I won't look," she said with anxiety in her voice. "I'll go on back to the car." She started up the rutted road.

"I bet she peeks," the Australian said, dropping his pants and underwear.

"Maybe," answered the American, his word muffled as his mouth was covered by the undershirt being pulled over his head.

They slipped into the warm water, naked, letting their bodies drift with the gentle movement of the tides, and they became shadows wavering in the water as their bodies passed over the coral bottom.

Not having towels, they put their clothes on over their wet bodies and scrambled back up the hill to the car. She was in the front seat and her composure had returned. "Nice swim?" she inquired.

Later, when the American told an experienced scuba diver he met at the hotel where he was staying about the paradise he had been taken to at the Japanese submarine cave, the diver acknowledged it was a wonderful place to go swimming except for the sharks that came very close to the reef, some of them even getting over it to attack swimmers, and the deadly poisonous small gray snakes that moved in schools in the cave.

Rabaul, the place most Americans fighting in the South Pacific expected to see but never did. Rabaul, a city doomed to die naturally.

Rabaul is precariously built at the base of five volcanoes on the shores of a natural harbor. Of the volcanoes around the city, only the smallest near the airport is known to be active. The last major volcanic activity in Rabaul until recently was in 1937 when a new volcano erupted from the bay, rising almost 1,000 feet above the surface.

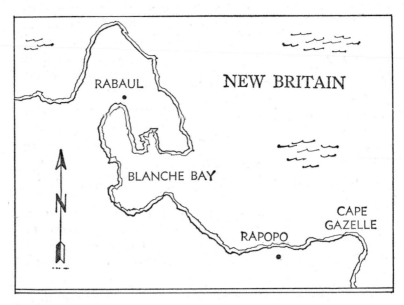

For all the elaborate seismographical equipment in a laboratory on top of one of Rabaul's mountains, scientists were surprised in early 1970 when Mount Uluwum, 70 miles down the coast, sent up a blast of red flame and smoke, and it continued to erupt daily for weeks. There was time enough, however, to order the evacuation of natives from within a mile radius of the base of the volcano. The eruption provided a nightly spectacular. It could be seen from any of Rabaul's mountains, a flickering red stain on the night sky often compressed between layers of dark clouds, so the redness ran like a river through the whole sky.

There is a discomforting theory among some geologists studying the future of Rabaul that it was once a mountain city built on the comb of a volcano and that it is slowly sinking into the sea. But it never seemed more substantial than it did in the first two years of the war in the Pacific when it was central in the strategic thinking of every American military officer.

Rabaul was captured by the Japanese in January, 1942, and they turned it into an almost impregnable air and naval base, building four airfields around the town and surrounding them with 376 antiaircraft guns. On the harbor the Japanese also constructed seven wharves, and into the mountains a fantastic system of tunnels to which they moved when the Allied raids began on Rabaul. From this base, the Japanese sent their troops to the Solomon and Gilbert islands and their ships to the Coral Sea.

By July, 1942, American strategists had designated Rabaul their prime target in the South Pacific, and amphibious landings were planned. But it would have been suicidal. There are now military estimates the Americans would have lost up to half a million men trying to take Rabaul from the more than 100,000 Japanese stationed there.

American air attacks on Rabaul began on January 25, 1942, most of them by B-24 bombers escorted by P-38 fighters. In October the Americans conducted their largest raid against Rabaul and claimed to have destroyed 100 planes on the ground, badly damaged 51 others, and shot down 26 in air battles. The shipping losses in the harbor were three large merchant vessels, three destroyers and dozens of harbor ships. When the United States finally adopted the policy of island-hopping to the mainland of Japan, capturing a few of the more important ones through amphibious landings, it was decided Rabaul would be bypassed and left to wither on the vine. But the air attacks were continued. In the month of January, 1944, heavy bombers flew 263 sorties against Rabaul. By March 17, 1944, it was estimated that 67 percent of the 1,400 buildings in Rabaul had been destroyed, and by April 20 that year all but some 120 had been flattened or burned.

The Allies eventually landed troops on New Britain. U.S. Marines invaded Cape Gloucester on December 26, 1943, and by the 30th had captured the airstrip there. In the spring of 1944, the Marines had moved halfway to Rabaul, taking Talesa, but still making no effort to capture Rabaul by land. It was a wise decision. After the war, the Australians, who had administered New Britain since World War I, returned and transported to Japan the force that had surrendered: 140,000 men.

Those who had lived in Rabaul before the war said it was the loveliest town in the South Pacific. Colonized by the Germans before World War I, Rabaul, built to conform to the architectural and city planning then popular in Europe, was filled with gingerbread homes trimmed with gables and long porches set back from big squares and sweeping avenues. But the daily bombings wiped out that Rabaul. On their return, the Australians found all that remained of the original downtown shopping street was the side walls of one department store and the completely intact New Guinea Club, an exclusive white colonialist institution.

Rabaul today has the look of something improvised from the recent past. Many of the stores on the main street are put together with war surplus building materials, and more than one is in the shape of a Quonset hut, its prior existence given away by the curved, ribbed tin roof. But it is still one of the most attractive settlements in the South Pacific and a pleasant place to visit, even though the tropical sun in early afternoon presses an unbearable humidity down on anyone foolish enough to try window-shopping.

The leading hotel is frequented by airline pilots and hostesses—a sure giveaway about whether it has the modern conveniences of a private bath, air conditioning and bar where the unattached can meet. It is located at the end of the main street nearest Lakunai Airport and can be reached rather inexpensively by taxi. The social activity is around the pool, where the Australian airline hostesses gather in late afternoon, wearing the extremest of bikinis, flirting blatantly with the pilots, some of them not bothering to check into their own rooms with other girls but going immediately to the pilot's room and pulling shut the drapes over the picture windows.

The hotel is managed by a young British couple who had emigrated to Australia to make their fortune, and ended up, as have so many, in the outer islands where it is believed money can be made more quickly and saved by enduring the deprivations of the wilderness. But this couple hates Australians and their country with the superb passion of those now economically and socially inferior to their braggart backwater cousins. The tropical climate and the year-round swimming are no longer attractions, and they can't wait to leave Rabaul and go home to London.

For those who stay any length of time, Rabaul has wisely left some war relics to amuse the tourists. The woman picked up the American and Australian very early on the day of their visit to the submarine base. Her first stop was the remains of the concrete bunker of the commander of the Japanese forces which is up the street from the police headquarters. The darkness inside was compressed by the very low ceiling. She carried a flashlight and played its beam into alcoves and sealed-off passageways. The musty smell was overpowering, and to get through the corridors, the three had to walk in a crouched position. Outside the bunker, scattered throughout backyards of private homes and behind the shops on the main street, are cement blocks from old gun emplacements.

The woman said she knew where most of the war relics were, though her sense of direction, once she was out of town, became confused, and she had to stop the car and ask two native children to show them the location of Japanese plane fuselages in an abandoned coconut plantation at the end of the airport runway. They were more than willing to go along, grinning wildly when she attempted to speak to them in pidgin English.

The children, having misdirected the woman down several muddy roads, finally spotted the fuselages being grotesquely lifted off the ground by the strength of young trees growing through them. Leaping from the car, the children splashed barefoot through the puddles, stirring into aggressive attack hordes of mosquitoes, and climbed up the fuselages to have their pictures taken by the tourists.

"These mosquitoes don't carry malaria," the woman said, slapping repeatedly at her bare legs and arms, leaving a trail of blood spots on her flesh. "It's not the season for malaria."

Farther up the coast road in the direction of Mount Uluwum is a cave several hundred feet off the bay road. It can be reached by a footpath trampled through a field of rugged plant stalks. Inside are eight rotting Japanese landing barges, huge chunks of metal plating rusting away. A total of 160 Japanese ships were sent to the bottom of Blanche Bay by American bombers, and most of the handful that made it to the beach are still there, deteriorating hulks, their bottoms covered with moist sand. Up the road from the cave is a huge crane, bent and listing toward the water. The Japanese had managed to get it to the beach before it was irreparably damaged by bombers.

Rabaul recently dedicated a Coast Watchers Monument in a clearing on a mountaintop ten miles outside of town. There is a wooden tower there with a splendid view of the harbor and the dormant volcanoes. At the base of the tower are a few large guns, a small underground bunker and a monument to the men who during the war lived in these hills and reported to the Allies on Japanese ship movements.

The woman walked down the tower stairs and said, "I'm reasonably happy here," her enthusiasm not quite believable but absolutely sincere. "At first it was difficult being away from the family, but then you get used to it, and it was so long ago. My home is here now. I don't mind living abroad."

She drove her customers back to the center of Rabaul. They stopped for a cold drink at one of the department stores, a long, one-story wooden hall without air conditioning, ventilated by panels dropped from the ceiling and moved mechanically by metal rods.

There was no great variety in the merchandise. It was practical rather than luxurious: underwear, socks, work pants, short-sleeved shirts, bathing suits, all simple without an attempt at stylish design. The food supply also had no variety. Most of it was frozen and brought in from Australia, and because of the high import duty, it was terribly expensive.

The closest thing to a roadside diner in Rabaul is a coffee shop in a new motel near the bayfront. It is immaculate and air-conditioned, catering to the white colony. Its menu has many items, almost all of them crossed off except coffee, ice cream and ham sandwiches. The music piped into the room is old World War II songs given mushy instrumental treatment.

One of the customers on a late afternoon was a talkative, plain woman, her hair pulled into an unattractive lump on the back of her head. She was fiddling with a cup of coffee, and it was cold before she brought it to her lips for the first sip. The teen-age waitress tried to ignore her without being rude, but the woman was persistent, practically raising herself off the counter stool to emphasize the urgency of her opinions.

"I'm in town visiting a friend. She's Jewish," she said, with the unconcealed scorn of an authentic anti-Semite.

Somebody asked her what was playing at the movie that evening. She interrupted without being directly asked, "You know there are two movies down the street. One is for the whites and the other for blacks. I wouldn't advise you to go to that one. They spit at you."

She received no response; nevertheless, she continued with suppressed hysteria in her voice. "I'm a Jehovah's Witness. I run a mission in the hills." Then, because she couldn't tolerate the silence her words created in the customers, she said, holding her back erect and tucking in her chin, "Would you believe I'm only thirty-six?" The assault of the tropical climate on her face and body had made her look fifty.

But she was not a singular character in Rabaul, rather a fairly representative one of the Bible Belt fundamentalists flocking to the islands to bring their pious religion and morality to the natives. To the white customers in the coffee shop, there was nothing particularly offensive about her anti-Semitism and her racism. Her only fault was she talked too much.

New Britain is a colonial territory with a native population that remains largely primitive and superstitious despite the ceaseless efforts of the Christian missions. There is one sect among the natives that offers nightly prayers for rain to bring money trees from the sky. Whites make up only a small percentage of the New Britain population, but they run the government and own the wealth-producing business, and they are trying to lift a primitive society into the second half of the twentieth century, a jarring experience for the natives and not without predictable responses.

There is a black separatist movement being organized by

young black students returning to the territory from schooling in Australia and England. One of their demands is control of the government of New Britain. In November, 1969, a protest rally of blacks was held in the native market, and for several days white Europeans stayed off the streets. But a show of force by the local constabulary dampened the revolutionary ardor of the natives. There is still talk, however, that New Britain, along with New Guinea, will become an independent nation, but if this does take place, it will be in the indefinite future.

Much of the improvement in the health and educational standards of the natives has, in fact, come not from the colonial administration but through the Christian missions. One of the largest is Roman Catholic and is a good hour's drive out of Rabaul along the coast road toward Mount Uluwum. It is spread over a grassy plateau up from the sea, and the main buildings are around a soccer field, the church at one end and the school rooms and dormitories along both sides of the other.

Christian missionaries traditionally followed the economic imperialists of their countries into the colonies. Christianity was often used as a religious excuse for the business operators, who took the land and minerals away from the natives, robbing them of self-government in the process. It also bred a moral superiority in its European practitioners because they believed, as they were told, that theirs was the true religion since only through a belief in Christ could one be saved. The natives not only didn't believe in but had never heard of Christ, and thus the moral dice were loaded against the natives.

Missionaries today tend to be middle-aged or older, the younger clerics preferring to teach in colleges or do social work in the urban areas of their native countries. Also the work in these missions has become quite complex and requires much greater specialized education. By the time a priest or a minister gets to the out-country, he can be well into his thirties, an age when men at home have usually made a mark in their parishes.

Though most whites give the missionaries credit for bringing much-needed education and health improvements to the natives, the practical results of these good works are difficult to document. Few missions keep records about mortality rates, life expectancies, job employments, and levels of education attained.

At the Catholic mission these records were practically nonexistent, but the enthusiasm among the priests for their work was tremendous. The head of the mission was a very likeable, literate priest from Ireland with a wealth of anecdotes about life in New Britain before the war. He had been interned in a Japanese prisoner-of-war camp. His two-room suite in one of the buildings off the soccer field, cooled by a floor fan, was a library of the highest-quality paperback books. They were piled in heaps around a well-used leather chair by a louvred door leading to the hill overlooking the bay. He was a stimulating conversationalist and a good host, having a generator-powered icebox filled with cold beer. Though he spoke well of his native students at the mission, it was with the strained affection of a father for children who are becoming rebellious.

Certain still of the principal goals of the Christian mission in black lands, he said, "We came out to give the natives something, a philosophy of life that would take them away from the introspection of the village."

But nobody had bothered to ask the natives if they wanted to be dragged from their primitive culture into a technological society of the twentieth century, the American said.

"It's never been done before, raising natives from the Stone Age to the present within a generation, but it's worth the try."

The beer lasted long enough for the tongues of the speakers to become heavy and the moral ambiguities posed by the work of the missionaries among the natives blurred.

The airport was crowded the next day for the noon flight to Port Moresby. The woman had volunteered to take the American to the airport, and she was at the hotel before he came down from his room, standing at the registration counter talking freely with the European women behind it, getting information about any recent check-ins who might need her services as a tour guide.

She had also agreed to take her priest friend and his entourage, including several black youths, to the airport. She was harried, her most appealing state, the one in which her essential friendliness came out. She had just finished collecting her flock from the houses they had been assigned to for the night; the priest and the whites in his group had been kept in a white European home while the blacks were placed in a hostel where race mixing is more easily accomplished among the young.

The priest's flight to Bougainville was supposed to depart first, but the plane had developed engine trouble, and white mechanics, protected from the sun by umbrellas held over their heads by natives, worked steadily into early afternoon to repair it. The woman kept busy in the terminal, first going to get hot coffee for her guests and then to the ticket counter to ask repeatedly the same questions about the delay. She acted almost as if she wanted her guests to leave, but when the priest's flight was called and the persons in his party collected their hand luggage and made their way to the terminal exit, a look of shock came over her face. The thing she feared most, being left alone again, was here with another departure. She would stay and they would leave.

"Ta-ta. Don't forget the Christmas card. . . ."

And when the American's flight was called, she walked him to the gate, where a customs officer checked passports and tickets. "Don't forget to write us, love," she said, offering up her cheek for a ceremonial kiss, one she had been receiving forever. But when his lips touched her flesh, she tightened perceptibly, her hands almost pulling his shoulders toward her body, resisting the impulse, before backing off quickly. "Good-bye. . . ." She stood at the fence with the natives until the plane left the runway.

It was a short flight to Port Moresby, only a few hours, and as soon as the plane left Rabaul the pilot informed the passengers they were in for a treat. He flew his plane low, parallel to the side of Mount Uluwum. And from the windows level with its cone, the passengers could clearly see smoke rising in puffs from the funnel. It was awesome in its suggested power.

# Port Moresby

The Japanese land forces were finally stopped after their spectacular victories in the Philippines, at Singapore, and in the islands of the South Pacific. The turning point came in the highlands of New Guinea 32 miles from Port Moresby on the Kokoda Trail, and the victory belonged to a handful of Australians who, though outmatched in numbers and arms by the Japanese, outfought them in the crucial moment of battle. At the time the Japanese reinforcements being poured through the Slot into the Solomon Islands made it still doubtful whether the Americans could hold their beachhead around Henderson Field on Guadalcanal.

By the summer of 1942 it was inevitable that New Guinea would be a major battlefield. The island of New Guinea was divided in half, the western section being a part of the Dutch East Indies. The less wild, more inhabited eastern half, further divided on the north into Northeast New Guinea and on the south into Papua, was administered by the Australians.

With the outbreak of the war in the Pacific, the Australians were in no condition to prevent the Japanese from raiding towns on the north coast of their continent, let alone to defend their Pacific territories. As part of the British Commonwealth, Australia had joined England in her war against the Axis, which had begun in 1939. Australia had a population of only a little more than 7,000,000, but she sent close to 9,000 men to fight with the British Royal Air Force. Most of Australia's combat planes were in Malaya when the Japanese attacked. Left for the home defense were an air force of twenty-nine medium-range bombers and fourteen flying boats, and an undersized militia of middle-aged men. The militia should have contained a quarter of a million men, but by the start of the Pacific war it only had half the number, most of whom were poorly trained.

When MacArthur arrived in Australia to set up his command post for the defense of the South Pacific, the Australians, already defeated in New Britain, were ready to write off Papua and its most important town, Port Moresby, and were preparing to fight the Japanese on the Australian continent. There were only 3,000 men to defend Port Moresby, and three times that number had been routed by the Japanese in Rabaul.

It was MacArthur's decision that the fight must be carried to the territories. Port Moresby with its docking facilities and adequate airstrips had to be saved. The general said the defense of Moresby needed at least 675 land-based aircraft and many more soldiers. Allied reinforcements began arriving there in April, 1942.

The Japanese carrier losses in the battle of Midway prevented an amphibious invasion of Port Moresby. The alternative was to reach the port by land, and on July 21 the Japanese put ashore troops on New Guinea, taking Lae on the north coast and Gona, northeast of Port Moresby on the other side of the Owen Stanley Range. The overland march through the mountains on the Kokoda Trail was begun in late August by two Japanese regimental combat teams. Assigned to defend the trail was the 39th Australian Infantry Battalion, less one company, and about three hundred native gun bearers.

The Japanese had covered most of the trail's length by early September with the help of 1,800 natives from New Britain impressed as gun bearers. The only opposition to this advance came from the sky when Allied planes were sent up from Moresby to harass the lines of Japanese troops and mule-drawn gun carriages struggling over mountain peaks rising to heights of 13,000 feet. The Japanese advance, considering the condition of the trail, was relentless and by September 17 had reached a red clay plateau 3,000 feet above the sea, where the ridges rising from the land around Port Moresby join the base of the Owen

Stanleys to make the terrain impassable except on native foot-paths.

Within 32 miles of Port Moresby, the Japanese halted their advance to wait for supplies and word on the outcome of the battle for Guadalcanal. It was a fatal delay.

By August the garrison at Port Moresby had grown to 28,000 men. Four airfields had been completed, two for the P-40 fighter planes, and two for medium-range bombers. While the build-up of military forces was underway throughout 1942, Port Moresby was subjected to one hundred air raids. It was then a frontier town of wooden and tin shacks scattered across two hills around the excellent harbor and very vulnerable to air attacks. But from this town and the bivouac areas on clearings in the hills, the Australian soldiers began their journey to rendezvous with the Japanese on the Kokoda Trail. They were taken from the town by truck to the flatlands around the Owen Stanleys where their forced march began at a place called MacDonald's Corner.

Today there is a simple memorial on a rubber plantation at the bend of the road at MacDonald's Corner. It is a wire sculpture of an Australian soldier holding a bayonet, and through the white lines of its frame the mountains loom in the background.

The road from here to the beginning of the trail is not paved, but the dirt has been worn smooth by car wheels and it is not a bumpy journey. The natives live in these highlands, although the soil and climate are not conducive to the growth of a variety of crops. For one thing, there is the rainfall, a tremendous problem throughout the whole island. During the rainy season there can be daily rainfalls up to 10 inches, and the annual fall may be 300 inches. The other factor is the terrain. The native huts are arranged in settlements on the ridges of these hills, and the farming is done on the slopes stripped of vegetation, the soil turned over into furrows. But the rains change these cultivated hills into chutes of red mud, and only plants and trees with deep, strong roots survive.

Natives are born, grow up, work, procreate and die all within a few hundred yards of these settlements, and their daily life is open to those passing on the road. Naked children swim and na-

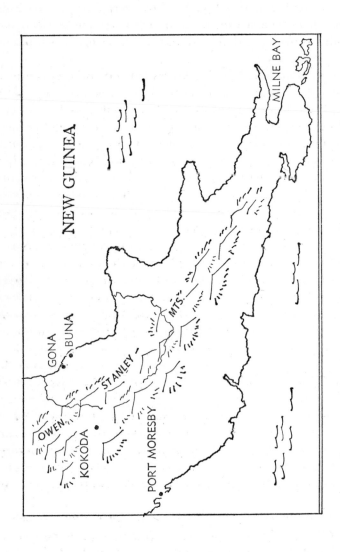

tive women wash clothes in the same pool. At roadside stands the males sell fresh fruits to the white colonialists out on Sunday drives to the highlands. Teen-age boys play European-style soccer in a field by a stream while under a tree another boy may carefully tune his guitar and begin hesitatingly to pluck an American pop song.

Schools maintained by the Australian territorial government are near these village settlements. One of them off the road to the Kokoda Trail is quite big with a number of barrack-type buildings around a well-kept square. The buildings are functional. One becomes a dining room when the desks and chairs are pushed back, and to keep it continuously clean, the boys daily scrub its stone floors. This particular school was recently made coeducational, and the girls, still somewhat shy, walk across the campus in groups, giggling when they catch the boys staring at them from the screened porch of the dining hall.

The only work outside the village farms for the natives is at the rubber plantations on the plains at the base of the mountains. Rubber is the main export of Papua. An estimated 300,000 tons of rubber were exported from New Guinea last year, most of it grown on the large plantations in Papua. There are some smaller plantations owned by individual Europeans, but the big productive ones are controlled by Australian companies. Each rubber tree must be tapped twenty-six weeks a year, and this requires a large labor force. The natives do the physical work, while the Europeans and Australians do the supervising. One of the largest plantations requires six hundred workers for its 6,000 acres of rubber trees. The workers live in settlements within walking distance of the plantations, and in the morning they all fall out on the road, machetes tied to the waist of their wrap-around cloth skirts, feet bare and skin worn pink on their soles.

There is something primeval about the mountains behind these villages. The sparse withered shrubs and stunted trees on the sides of the mountains, a purple color in the dull tropical sun, make them appear to possess a ponderous aura of death, as if life in the form of green vegetation had never existed on them.

The passable road suddenly ends and becomes a gnarled surface of large stones and deep ruts. It is here the trail begins, where the Australian soldiers, field equipment strapped to their backs, each man carrying a weapon, jumped from the back of the half-ton trucks and began the walk down the Z-shaped path through thick weeds. The descent can be treacherous even in the dry season, and after a rain, it becomes a slick ramp.

The path straightens at the bottom of the hill and continues on a direct line for two miles through a tropical forest, finally reaching a native village. This stretch of the trail is still well used. Natives regularly climb up it to get to a market near the plateau where fresh vegetables are daily sold. The man still rules the family, and if he is on the trail with his family, he walks in front, sometimes carrying the child, propelling himself by jamming a stick into the ground and pulling himself forward. The wife follows, often burdened with a net sack of produce on her back.

Four miles from this village on the floor of the valley, through more jungles and then around the side of the first tall mountain, is the exact location where the Australians engaged the Japanese in combat and drove them back. By mid-November, 1942, the Japanese had retreated the length of the Kokoda Trail. Port Moresby was now saved from land invasion, and thousands of Americans and tons of war matériel began to arrive regularly. By mid-November, too, the United States had 15,000 soldiers in New Guinea, the troops to begin the American phase of the New Guinea campaign, clearing out the Japanese from Lae and the mission stations on the north coast.

In March, 1943, the Japanese made their last major attempt to reinforce the garrison at Papua and sent 7,000 men by troop ship from Rabaul. The convoy was located by the Allies, and between March 2 and 5, in what became the battle of the Bismarck Sea, U.S. and Australian planes sank four destroyers and eight transports. Less than 1,000 Japanese soldiers made it ashore at Lae.

The Japanese were to try once more to take Port Moresby by land. In August, 1943, they sent a detachment of soldiers to Milne Bay on the southeast tip of Papua, hoping to outflank the

Allied troops stationed at Port Moresby. They were met east of
Milne Bay by a combined Australian-American force—most of
them, 8,000, were Australians—and driven back. The Japanese
were able to evacuate 1,300 soldiers.

At the height of the war there were an estimated 200,000 Australians and American soldiers crowded into Port Moresby with
not much more for them to do on leave than drink strong beer
at the Serviceman's Club, which still stands on the beach down
the hill from the main center of town.

"The Aussies and the Yanks got along reasonably well here,"
said Fred Turner, an Englishman who fought in the war and
has lived in Port Moresby for thirty-three years. "But they had
their usual fist fights."

Turner is a remarkable man. Retired from government service on Papua, he now runs his own travel agency, and though
he is in his late sixties, he still walks up and down this first hill
in the Kokoda Trail at least twice a week with the tourists.

It is impossible not to sweat on the climb up this hill. The
first few steps alone produce an outpouring of water on the forehead and chest and an expulsion of air from the lungs, leaving
them to pump in unbearably humid air that settles into the center of the body with a suffocating thud.

Ahead at eye level, progressing up the hill with a steady pace,
were the legs of Turner covered to the knees by wool socks. Only
the slightest line of perspiration was on his forehead, and there
were no wet spots on his shirt under his arms.

"Breathe deeply, lad. You'll make it."

If death had to come then on this hell of red dirt and stones,
would it please come quickly, the American said, his steps more
laborious as the soles of his shoes dug in for each painful thrust
upward.

The distance between the American and Turner began to
widen.

"We can rest here," he said on the last leveling of the trail before its final vertical thrust to the top.

Those which had been dots on the floor of the valley were
now a man, his wife and child going to market, moving swiftly
up the hill, past the American, almost overtaking Turner, their

breath registered evenly on their chests. The American's chest, however, was violently shuddering.

"They're used to this hill," Turner said kindly.

The native and his family were first to reach the crest of the hill because Turner had waited to help the American if it became necessary.

In the car, coming down the mountain road, the American held his sopping-wet shirt out the window and it dried almost instantly.

Halfway back from the Kokoda Trail, where the road unwinds for its descent on the last hill before the plain leading to Port Moresby, Turner stopped the car and led the American across a small ridge to a platform on an abutment of land over a gorge. Directly below was a ravine and the side of it glistened with a trickle of water.

"We're just in time," Turner said. From around a bend in the river came the sound of rushing water. "They've opened the dam up the valley. Watch what happens."

The level of the stream was tremendously raised by the water jetting into it from the open dam, and suddenly, what was a barely perceptible trickle was now a cascading waterfall, magnificent in its rumbling power. But it was an illusive, artificial creation, and as suddenly it was gone, the waterfall again a thin watery covering of a ravine wall.

"It's a pretty good show, isn't it, mate?" Turner said, covering his lips with the edge of a cool glass of beer. He was sitting at a roadhouse stuck back up the hill from the dam near where the power lines plunged into the tops of the trees. There was a pool below the veranda, but there was no water in it and the aqua-blue sides were cracked. The young natives in the roadhouse were intrigued by the pinball machine, and the manager, an elderly Australian woman, her gray hair wound in overly tight curls, spoke disparagingly of the indolence of the natives, dabbing the beer foam off her lips. Turner didn't concur; rather, he seemed bemused by the woman's bawdiness as she loudly greeted male customers, reminiscing with the older ones about the war years when from the veranda she could follow the line of trucks carrying her countrymen to the Kokoda Trail, bestowing favors on some who spent the night camped in the fields around the roadhouse, repeatedly slapping her thighs in the re-telling of her earthy stories.

Finishing the beer with a long gulp sustained by an automatic shutting off of the windpipe, Turner slammed the empty glass on the tabletop. "Those sure were the good days."

The Port Moresby they knew during the war is changed. It has been expanded in a disorderly pattern across the adjoining hills around the harbor, each of these having its own shopping center and residences, strung together by a road leading in from the airport, which has been enlarged to handle the big passenger jets. At any hour of the day there is more activity among the natives at the terminal than there is in downtown Port Moresby.

"They come here to meet their friends," Turner said of the native women and children who had taken every seat in the terminal building at the airport. "None of them are going any-where. This is a big treat for them to sit here and watch the ac-tivity."

There really isn't very much for a visitor to do in Port Moresby. There are some new gift shops in one block across from the docks on the harbor which sell native artifacts at almost double what they cost at a roadside stand in the interior. The main hotel in the center of town has two bars. One is air-conditioned and the other isn't. The first for white Europeans, a label stuck on any Caucasian staying in Port Moresby, is coldly correct: drab leather chairs, chrome tables and walls of glass; and the second, hot and rank-smelling from the sweating bodies crammed under whirling fans, is for the natives, who in their exuberance toss empty beer bottles on the sidewalk.

Around the corner from the hotel is a movie house, and at-tending it is an experience. A revival of the 1950's Metro-Gold-wyn-Mayer musical *Seven Brides for Seven Brothers* was being shown, and the projectionist had the film out of focus for almost its entire length. Jane Powell's jaw was going to one side of the picture while her eyes were traveling in the other direction. The few times it went into focus there continued in the print wavering black lines trailed by a school of wiggling white cells. The movie was supposed to begin at 8 P.M., according to the afternoon paper. A receptionist at the hotel warned there would be fifteen minutes of short subjects, so there was no need to rush through dinner. The management of the movie house had forgotten to say in the advertisement that they were showing a double feature and the musical didn't go on until 9:45 P.M.

The entertainment-starved audience didn't complain. The alternative was the radio and a bland selection of canned programs from Australia. There is no television on the island and it is not expected to arrive soon. The bars shut down at 10:30 P.M., conforming with the hours of closing in Australia. Nights can be long in Port Moresby.

While there is social stratification in the bars and movie houses between Europeans and natives, there is none on the beach, where black children splash in the surf with the whites and mothers look on without any apparent fears of the consequences of race mixing.

"This isn't much of a place for the young, anyway. Most of the Australians send their children back home to be educated, and then they pretty much want to stay away from here, coming back only for the holidays or funerals," Turner said. His three sons were gone, two into the Australian army and the third to Manila working for Quantas Airline. The life for him now in Port Moresby was a quiet one with his wife and old friends and their shared memories, remnants of their country's colonial period, living out their lives in a country that may be an independent nation before they die. They will probably be allowed to stay in their homes, harmless anachronisms of another era, for these are not the propertied colonialists, the ones who made a financial killing, often by cruelly exploiting the people and the resources of the country; rather, they came here before the war to do their duty in the service of government and Crown.

Of the Australian ground forces in New Guinea during the war there were 5,698 casualties, of whom 1,731 were killed and 3,533 wounded. Of the American troops, 687 were killed and 1,918 wounded. The American forces also suffered 5,358 cases of malaria. The Japanese had committed between 16,000 and 17,000 men to New Guinea. They successfully evacuated about

4,500 of them, but 12,000 died, almost as many from starvation and disease as from bullets.

Off the main road to the Kokoda Trail, about 12 miles outside of Port Moresby on a narrow dusty road, is the largest military cemetery in the territory. There are 3,002 Australians buried in it and each grave is marked by a white stone. The markers are spaced by lovely colorful bushes with gold and brown waxy leaves.

On the top of a rise at one end of the cemetery is a marble memorial to the more than seven hundred Australian soldiers missing in the New Guinea campaign. In the center of it is a sundial, and around the edges the names of places where Australian soldiers fought in the South Pacific. With the passing of the sun, the shadow of the arrow points to each name at least once a day.

Turner comes here often with his tourists, and while they are busy reading the names of the campaigns or taking pictures of the shrubs, he walks alone through rows of markers, stopping at some longer than others, his lips moving silently over the familiar names, then bracing his shoulders before moving on.

# Sydney

There is a city arranged across the hills outside the hotel window. Red slate roofs spread to the horizon where a white stone lighthouse stands out clearly against the dark clouds of early evening. This is the time of day when Sydney is most beautiful, a canvas of pastel-colored buildings on hills that slope into a natural harbor, and many Americans came here during the war in the Pacific to gain solace from people very much like themselves in a country in some ways very much like America. The Australians are genuinely fond of Americans. They still believe America was largely responsible, with a valuable assist from their friends down under, for winning the war in the Pacific.

It is to this city another generation of American servicemen are still coming to escape briefly from war. From the air, one of the first sights of Sydney is the main harbor guarded on each side by tall barren cliffs. For ships entering through these stone walls the water is swept a blue-black by the descending sun. Farther up the harbor the water becomes a mauve color from the shadows cast on it by blossoming trees in the parks along the water's edge. The fading sun also takes away the brightness from the restored and freshly painted pink, yellow, green and gray row houses in the Paddington section, and these residences become muted and solidified into a unified whole by their loss of distinctive coloring.

On a large hill five miles inland from the sea is the business center of the city. Here half-completed office buildings and apartments rise, and around these structures, balancing on skeletal necks, are construction cranes ready to begin again in the morning the transformation of the city's skyline.

The main port of Sydney is near the famous suspension bridge that spans the harbor. From the slips inside wooden sheds here, ferries shuttle across to the suburbs on the north shore. Middle-class workers rushing down the hill from the commercial buildings are lost in the steel glow of the drowning sun, their bodies outlined in refracted diamonds of light.

The hotel and the street outside are in Kings Cross on the next hill over in the direction of the sea, and it is a combination of London's Chelsea, San Francisco's North Beach, and New York's Greenwich Village: a section of Bohemia with all its cultural advantages—bookstores, little theaters, student cafés, plus the inevitable corruption by hustlers and pimps working from doorways next to strip joints and shady nightclubs.

The best restaurants are in Kings Cross, many of them cellar places serving fresh oysters in tart sauce, thick chunks of steak under sautéed mushrooms, and prawns garnished with garlic. But also in Kings Cross is the city's façade of cheap commercialism: overpriced tourist shops, gaudy clothing stores, and, despite strict censorship laws, movie houses and bookstores featuring the latest in vaguely salacious, if not pornographic, material.

In scenic beauty, Sydney is comparable to San Francisco, which it resembles in the Mediterranean architecture spaced over hills near the sea. But the life of any city is in its people, and below on the sidewalk and in the shops there is a vibrant sense of life being lived by a contented people. Young Australian sailors in white T-shirts and dark-blue pants, extravagantly bell-bottomed, swagger past a streetwalker who wears an expression of innocence painted on her face. The sailors ignore the silent pleadings of the woman; they continue up the street past a pancake shop done in the artificial colonial style of many roadhouses in New England; a new branch post office with a row of public telephones attached to the brick front; and a laundromat advertising in the front window in block letters fresh mint-scented dry cleaning in thirty-five minutes.

As the American stood in front of the window watching this human movement, a cleaning woman entered, pushing in front of her a carpet sweeper. She was an attractive middle-aged woman, her hair tinted red and her body softened by excess weight on her hips and thighs.

"I've seen plenty of this world. Don't think I haven't just because I work here," she said. "I've been to your United States. Traveled around it by bus for almost two months." She pushed the sweeper closer to the picture window where the American stood shielding his eyes to the sunlight, more glaring now in the late afternoon. "The United States is a grand place. But there's no better place now than Australia. I was sure glad to get home."

Across the street there was a smaller, less expensive hotel, only seven stories high, but each front room had its own balcony, and onto one walked a young American black, one of the hundreds of U.S. soldiers spending their six-day rest and rehabilitation leaves from Vietnam in this city. He wore gold pants and a sleeveless white undershirt. Around his neck was a large wooden cross hanging from a thick chain. He yawned, stretched, and the firm muscles in his arms shifted under his purple-black skin. The glass door to the balcony slid open and a white girl entered. She placed her right arm around his waist and cradled her head on his shoulder. To support this weight, he placed both hands against the balcony railing.

"Are you a soldier?" the cleaning woman asked. "There's so many around these days. But they're such nice boys."

The girl's fingers played at the gold cloth over his thighs, and they both laughed.

Up the street from the balcony where the man and woman stood were several late-night restaurants, and over their doors were signs with the flags of the United States and Australia joined in advertising for the trade of U.S. servicemen.

Americans in Sydney do look different from the natives. Their hair is neatly mowed into uniform crew cuts. They walk with backs held ramrod straight, as if they were just graduated from basic infantry training. They invariably carry a camera around their necks, stopping to take pictures of Australian girls in miniskirts or old men sleeping on park benches. They are wonderfully naïve and outgoing.

But not every Australian exhibits a friendly reaction to the new American invasion. Some soldiers complain of getting Mickey Finns with their drinks in cheap clubs and of being relieved of their wallets. Others charge some hotels exorbitantly raise rates when they approach. Most men, however, remain overwhelmed by the charm and willingness of the Australian girls.

It was soon dark, and a row of lights marked the end of the city and the beginning of the sea where it became a black carpet tacked over the night sky. The pubs were quickly filled with workingmen on their way home, their voices boisterous in natural affection for their drinking companions, the beer sloshing over the sides of the steins running in foamy rivulets along the bar.

In a park on the main square of Kings Cross an old man in a grimy tweed cap and frayed sports jacket set up his night's entertainment: a covey of tamed doves that perform for him on a wooden bar while he plays a tune on a bass violin.

An audience gathered around the old man. Parents handed children coins, and they walked timidly over and dropped the money in a hat overturned on the sidewalk. One bird fell off the bar and wandered in a daze on the chewing-gum-splattered cement before the old man picked it up and resumed the performance.

The girls take to the streets early in Kings Cross, filling the doorways before the last light of day has vanished in a scarlet sunset. They do not speak first. This would set them up for arrest as prostitutes, a profession illegal only on the books in Sydney. When business is slow, the girls leave the shelter of the doorways and gather in groups of three and four on the sidewalk, as if a human obstacle of many would get the attention of customers that an individual couldn't. Their conversations are limited by the inherent pragmatism of who they are and what they do. The cost for their trick, room expenses, whether it is all-night. Meaningful considerations for any streetwalker. And when the Sydney police crack down periodically, the girls hire cabs for the evening and solicit customers through a rolled-down window as they slowly pass by.

These are street scenes from modern Sydney, population 2,000,000, the largest city in Australia and the country's one claim to having a sophisticated metropolis comparable to London, Paris, Rome, Berlin, or New York. But Sydney's reputation is a recent development, a result of a growing acceptance that a city must have a culture to give it any distinction and an alternative life-style to what the Australians have long accepted: a rather comfortable, provincial cycle of hard work and long weekends of leisure with nothing fancy in taste; beer is preferable to champagne and television to the living theater.

But now most of the good theater companies make Sydney a stop on world tours. The Royal Shakespeare Company was here from England. *Fiddler on the Roof* and a revival of Arthur Miller's *Death of a Salesman* sold out. *Hair* played to standees for over fifty weeks. The fame of this American folk-rock musical, based on its first-act curtain with a stage of nude male and female bodies, did not reach every citizen of Sydney. Two men, not young but not old either, walked past the theater. One turned to the other and asked, "What's it about?" The friend said, "I think drugs."

A sign of the city's flourishing Bohemian culture is an arcade of coffee shops and jazz cafés off the main square in Kings Cross. Artists, hippies and intellectuals sit there by the hour to discuss war, peace, Fascism, and sexual freedom. This sidewalk cultural activity has about it a sense of newness and improvisation. The dress is still worn self-consciously as if the long hair and dirty jeans had been put on for the first time that morning.

One of the most arresting features of life not only in Sydney but across Australia is the struggle between Puritanism and paganism. The Puritan influence is pervasive. No liquor can be sold Sundays, except in hotels with special licenses. There are also strict censorship laws on books, movies and plays. It is still chic to smuggle in from the United States the latest pornographic novel. But the censorship laws are slowly being liberalized. Where James Jones' war novel *The Thin Red Line* was banned until recently, it can now be bought with all the words in it at one of several first-rate paperback bookstores in the city. Also the homosexual comedy *Boys in the Band,* with its strong language, was performed uncut in Sydney, though, when it was

taken on the road to Melbourne for seven weeks, some of the
dirtier words were yanked from the script.

The Puritanism is also here in less obvious, more Freudian
ways. There is an obsession for cleanliness in Sydney. Its streets
are spotless. There are stringent laws with heavy fines for litter-
ing, and they are enforced. Freud suggested that an overly obsessive affection for cleanliness was a psychological cover for deep
sexual repression.

Nonetheless, there is a seductive paganism about Australia
that breaks out in the love of the Australians for the beach. The
east coast of the country has some of the greatest beaches in the
world, and the Australians revere them, rushing to them on
weekends to burrow their bodies into the sand, positioning them
to get the best possible advantage from the sun's rays. For all
the country's repressive laws toward freedom in the arts, this repression doesn't carry over to bathing costumes. Australian
women and men wear the briefest bathing suits in the world,
outside a Scandinavian nudist colony. The girls' bikinis come in
bandage sizes, and men's suits are not much more than muscle-
men's posing straps. It's as if on the beach, practically naked to
the elements of sun and sea, the Australians are able to shuck
off repressions instilled in them by their society.

The devotion and care of the body—most everyone in Sydney
looks as if he were a model for health club advertisements—are
reflected in the country's passion for sport. No other subject is
better covered in the daily newspapers. On a Saturday afternoon
at the beach almost every transistor radio is tuned to the horse
races. The overseas competition of Australian tennis stars gets
more newspaper coverage than does the latest Middle East
crisis.

Sport is usually considered a masculine domain, and Australia
is often characterized as a man's country with mateship a ritual-
ized social institution. Nowhere else in the world, except possibly in some Arab countries, do men bond so closely. Intense
male friendship is the center of social life in this country and is
carried over to sports, work, and regular socializing at beach and
pub. There is practically a reactionary attitude to women, whose

place is thought to be in the home bearing children. When Australians gather privately for parties, the men most often end up in the living room with their mates discussing sports while the wives group in the kitchen.

Australians contend mateship comes from the historical development of their country. The first settlers were men, often from the prisons of England, and they were left alone on the huge Australian continent for months without women.

An Englishwoman, recently arrived in Australia, found mateship difficult to understand and accept. She and her husband were invited to an Australian home for New Year's Eve. This particular holiday is a very special one in England, she said, a night to be with family and close friends, and at midnight to exchange kisses with them. At this party, six of the husbands wandered off from the patio around 11 P.M. and were nowhere to be seen at midnight. They finally showed up at 1 A.M., and their wives didn't seem too concerned. They had only followed the rules of matesmanship and gone off to the local pub to discuss sports. The Englishwoman found this shocking.

Another characteristic of Australian men, and probably connected psychologically with mateship, is their apparent lack of any compulsive drive to get way ahead of their friends. The democratic egalitarianism in Australia's pioneer history, helpful in obtaining popular support for representative government and parliamentary institutions, may have had an adverse effect on social and economic ambition. Staying even, and not getting ahead, is much more desirable for the average Australian man. Talk to him and he says all he wants from life is a modest house, a nice-sized family—the number of children limited to two or three—and the weekend to be by himself, preferably on the beach. Rarely does he define his future in career advancements. Nobody seems out to get his neighbor because the goals for all are limited and obtainable in the good life that exists for most Australians.

There is a social contentment here observed in no other major country. Daily human intercourse is pleasurable. In his ability to live outside the material success ethos of the United States and still have a comparable standard of living, the Australian offers one of the more radical criticisms of the American way to success through obsessive hard work, hard drinking and an early heart attack.

But this social homogeneity on which Australian social stability rests was established in part by restrictive immigration laws. Australia's racial-exclusion policy is interpreted in the United States as being primarily directed against blacks, and there are very few of them in the country. The immigration laws, however, are really aimed at Asians.

There is a chronic labor shortage in Australia. The total population of the continent is just under 12,000,000, and the job opportunities, especially for men willing to go into the vast desert interior to the sheep ranches and mineral camps, increase daily. The official government policy is to encourage immigration of Europeans, and many refugees from Iron Curtain countries have found a haven here. Because of this postwar migration, only 80 percent of the Australians are now native-born.

This immigration liberalization did not apply to Asians, though. It is still extremely difficult for an Asian to obtain permission to settle, and hostility toward Asians is evident in even the most routine government functions. At Sydney's International Airport, for instance, a flight from Port Moresby brought in Australian students returning from holidays in New Guinea. At the passport window the only students treated rudely were two Asian boys. There was a mixup in their documents, and the immigration official ordered the boys to stand aside until all the other youngsters had been cleared by customs, then loudly berated them. Their humiliation was total.

But Australia may no longer be able to have this luxury of prejudice toward Asians. The Australian government seems to be catching on to the fact its country is closer to the markets of Asia than to those of Europe and the United States. Australia's biggest economic competitor now is Japan, not Britain or America. There are innumerable newspaper and magazine articles expressing the concern of Australian businessmen about the Japanese economic invasion of the South Pacific. The intent of many of these articles is to stir up memories of World War II and fears of Japanese military aggression.

Still, most Sydney newspapers project a charming provincialism. The coverage is parochial, a shark scare at the beaches getting bigger headlines than Vietnam. There is not much foreign news, and the reports on domestic politics are superficial. The headlines reflect an almost naughty-boy obsession with sex stories about lurid slayings, wife swappings and the latest methods of contraception.

Without much racial mixing, Australia has been able to develop a relatively secure middle class free of the tensions produced by radical politics and social strife. If one can be happy in a world beset with seemingly unsolvable problems and frequent wars, the Australians can be called happy with their marvelous beaches, good climate, booming economy and social stability.

But if Australia is a great place to visit, would it be worth living there? The things that make Australia a romantic, nostalgic continent for those Americans who keep talking about going back to their spiritual land, usually a mythological farm in the Midwest, eventually make it tedious. Man does need social and intellectual stimulation to grow and expand his ability to perceive the world on various levels of reality. Australia is flattening, one-dimensional. Too much social serenity can lead to social stagnation and a spiritual atrophy in which life becomes a ritual of the same limiting experiences: a beer with the boys, an evening with the television tube, a soccer match once a week, a child every few years. This can breed narrow-minded smugness.

A native Australian taxi driver was asked what, if anything, he thought was wrong with Australia. He took the question as an insult. "Nothing," he snapped. And then almost apologetically, "Maybe the traffic." Asked if he would like to travel overseas for a holiday, he said innocently, "Why? I have everything here."

Back in the hotel room, the cleaning woman said the same thing. "You've got a good country in the United States. But I like it here better."

And the American slowly drew the curtain across his window on Sydney.  ___

# Tarawa

In the vast sea, Tarawa is magnificently alone, a delicate curve of pink-tinted islets protected by a green awning of leaves from coconut trees. Over Tarawa the Pacific never seemed so awesomely large or lonely. The triangular-shaped atoll is made up of a series of islets surrounded by a 22-mile-long reef, and there had to be a Tarawa before there were the others.

As the plane circled the coral stone set in the placid dark-blue water, the British Air Force officer glanced down on the place of one of the bloodiest single battles in the war of the Pacific and said, "The Marines had to have a Tarawa at some time in the South Pacific to learn about amphibious landings." His judgment seemed cold and impersonal, made bloodless by the distance of time between the present and the morning of November 20, 1943, when Tarawa was assailed by thousands of Marines, stumbling under the weight of their packs, wading ashore waist-deep in water, racked by small-arms fire from the Japanese ashore, suffering such great casualties that newspaper editorials across the country demanded an investigation of the battle on an atoll few had ever heard of.

The young officer had just completed a two-year tour of duty there for the British government, planning and supervising construction of airstrips on the outer islands. To ease the loneliness and boredom of nights, he often read, by the light of a kerosene lamp, military histories of the war in the South Pacific.

For all the tactical blunders committed in the initial hours of the invasion and despite a loss of life so much greater than was

anticipated, Tarawa has to be considered a great victory for the
Marines, he said, and one that was achieved over almost fatal
misinformation about tides and the damage done to Japanese
beach installations from sea bombardments.

As were other islands in the Marshalls and Marianas, Tarawa,
a Crown colony of Great Britain since 1892, became a likely site
for an invasion when, in early 1943, the U.S. Joint Chiefs of
Staff agreed Japan would have to be bombed into submission.
The best road to victory was to move across the Central Pacific
capturing Japanese-held islands with good airstrips while Mac-
Arthur and his army cleaned out the Japanese forces from the
northern coast of New Guinea and moved on to the Philippines.
Because of the lack of troops, a majority of the trained military
personnel were still being sent to Europe, and plans to invade
southern China and establish air bases there from which to
strike Japan were abandoned.

In December, 1941, the Japanese had taken Tarawa and built
on it the best airfield in the Gilbert Islands. "A million men
cannot take Tarawa in a hundred years," its Japanese commander said. His boast had a foundation in fact. On the most
fortified of the Tarawa islands, Betio, where the airstrip was
built, the Japanese had put in the surf log barricades, barbed
wire, mines and concrete boat obstacles. A few feet in from the
beach was a five-foot barricade made mostly of coconut logs, and
behind this were machine gun emplacements and rows of
trenches. At strategic locations around the beach defenses were
fourteen coast guns, all of them surrounded by bombproof shelters for the men and underground ammunition dumps. Inside
the beach defense perimeter were more bombproof shelters and
twenty-five field guns.

The Americans knew the Japanese had about 5,000 men stationed there, an amazingly accurate count reached rather
uniquely. The sanitation problem for the Japanese had been
solved by building latrine stalls over the water. It was a natural
sewerage system, the tides flushing the waste away every twelve
hours. Through aerial photographs of these latrines, and by
counting the number of outhouses and working out a ratio of

buttocks to holes, the Americans came up with a count almost to the man.

Allocated for the invasion of Tarawa were 12,000 Marines, and they were brought to the battlefield by a convoy of sixteen transports, three battleships, five cruisers for fire support, five escort carriers for air support and twenty-one destroyers. In the days before the invasion there were thirteen air-strike missions with a total of 141 sorties against the beach defenses, and when the planes were finished, the ships moved in and laid down a barrage for two and a half hours at dawn of the invasion day. Aerial intelligence reported there was nothing alive on the atoll after the bombardment. But these pictures didn't show the Japanese waiting for the invaders in their underground bunkers. (Because of what it didn't photograph, air intelligence was largely discounted in later amphibious landings.) Though the bombardment did relatively little damage to the beach defenses, it did knock out the island's communication system, which proved to be very important when the battle was in doubt the first day.

Because no attention was paid to the tides, the Marines landed at a very low tide. Many of the amphtracs couldn't get over the barrier, so the Marines had to wade ashore weighted with too much equipment for this feat. Besides his battle dress of a mottled green cloth-covered steel helmet and green dungarees, each Marine had with him his weapon, several rounds of ammunition, three units of K rations, two canteens of water, a shaving kit, a toothbrush and a spoon. Many Marines fell through holes in the reef and were drowned under this weight.

Tarawa is shaped like a horseshoe lying on its side with the 291-acre Betio at the southwest end. At low tide a narrow sandbar rises from the sea, and natives, now numbering about 11,000 on the atoll, can walk from Betio to neighboring Bairiki, which contains most of the British administration offices. Betio can also be reached from Bairiki across a two-mile stretch of water on a slow, rickety native launch.

Betio barely rises from the sea and seems a vulnerable, thin line from a boat. Its only height is provided by the coconut trees bent permanently toward the sea by the winds. Its small harbor is on the northeast side of the lagoon, and since the invasion, new jetties have been built to permit larger ships to enter. Along the length of the jetty, naked children leap into the channel water, shouting and waving to their parents farther along the wall who squat in the water, bathing themselves and washing their clothes. At the end of this tree-lined jetty, which extends well

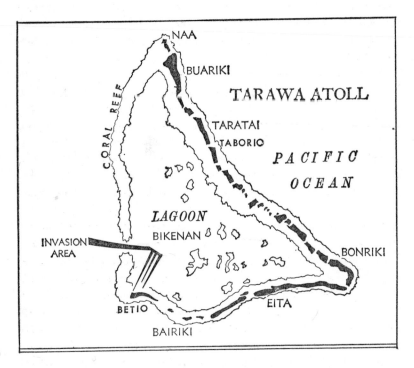

into the sea, is a plain white stone obelisk, a memorial to the men of the Second Marine Division killed in the invasion, and it is the first landmark seen on Betio from the water.

It was in this small area of Betio that the first day's fighting took place, and by noon, when the tide had risen and the amphtracs could float off the reef, 1,500 Marines had come ashore, only to be pinned down immediately on the beach. The officers in charge of the invasion doubted seriously if the beachhead could be held through the first night.

At the exact spot where the first wave of Marines landed there is a long stretch of beach with a line of palm trees pushing almost to the edge of the water, and at low tide, rusted frames of some of the stranded landing barges emerge eerily from the sea, reminders of how close the tide came to defeating the Marines.

By nightfall on November 20 there were 5,000 Marines ashore, and they controlled a beachhead 300 yards on each side of the pier. With their communications gone, and out of touch with neighboring bunkers, the Japanese were unable to put up a coherent, unified defense, and in the first day half of their troops were killed.

Around this battle site on Betio are many war relics. To the right of the harbor off the jetty and up the beach several hundred yards are bunkers banked in the sand and topped by stringy, tough weeds. Several bunkers still contain live ammunition, and a couple not too long ago lost their lives making love on what they thought was a harmless sand dune. Because the atoll doesn't have the money or the skilled labor to remove these dangerous shells, they have been stacked in bunkers covered with sand and designated off limits.

Inland from the invasion beach is a two-story cement bunker that was the Japanese command post. There are pieces of cement missing from the outside wall, and the space over the side door remains blackened from a scorching by U.S. flamethrowers. When the battle was lost, many Japanese fled here and it was shelled point-blank by a U.S. destroyer which moved almost up onshore to get it in range. When the ship failed to destroy it, the Marines drove a tank into the doorway and blasted directly into the bunker. After the battle an estimated three hundred charred bodies were found on the floor. Nobody survived.

Farther north on Betio, on the ocean side, are several large guns placed there by the Japanese who believed the Americans would invade from the sea rather than from the lagoon. These guns were alongside troop bunkers in accordance with the Japanese battle plan of putting their defense perimeter on the beach rather than inland, which would have been difficult since no part of Betio is more than 300 yards from the water. But once the Marines had established a beachhead and penetrated this defense line, moving beyond it so they were now behind the bunkers and coconut barricades, the Americans were able to isolate the Japanese into small helpless units and annihilate them.

The guns that were to stop the Marines still point to the sea, but they have become rusted, and a few, because of erosion from the tides, have been undermined and dip toward the surf. One of the bunkers on this side of the island has been put to use as the foundation of a civic club.

When Betio was secured, a batallion of Marines crossed to Bairiki and chased about two hundred Japanese around the horseshoe to the farthest end, where they fought to the death.

The battle for Tarawa was costly for both sides. In ninety-six hours Japan lost its entire military force on the island, except for the few soldiers who surrendered or were captured and a handful of Korean laborers. The Marine casualties were 990 men killed and 2,300 wounded.

There are no American cemeteries on Tarawa. The only one here is on Betio and contains the remains of eighteen Australians and New Zealanders who had been coast watchers. These men were captured by the Japanese and beheaded. The natives, who buried them in a plot of land almost on the beach in the shade of palm trees, decorated the cemetery with a line of amber-colored beer bottles half buried in the sand.

Although the bodies of the dead Marines were eventually taken back to the United States, natives digging in the soil of Betio occasionally uncover sets of dog tags around skeletons. The British dutifully notify the Pentagon of these discoveries. The British claim the Americans don't want to hear about the still-unidentified skeletons because they have closed out the casualty records on the war in the Pacific.

It is much easier to get to Tarawa in the paper-planning stage than it is by plane. Fiji Airways sends one flight a week which makes stops at minute grass airstrips on several islands in the Ellice chain that lies directly south of the Gilberts. It returns the next day, and if it is missed, the tourist is stranded on Tarawa for a week with little more to do than drink excessively to forget being cut off from civilization. There are boats, but they arrive from Australia every six weeks.

"The air service is a hundred percent better than it was two years ago," an Australian on Tarawa said, grinning. "There wasn't any then."

The trouble in getting to Tarawa can even begin in New York. Some of the islands in the Pacific administered by foreign countries, particularly Britain and Australia, require entrance visas, a fact the airline had forgotten to tell its customer until the day before his departure to Hawaii. "Can't you get to New York today and get the visas from the consulate?" the sympathetic ticket agent asked.

In New York the women at the British and Australian consulates were equally sympathetic, but said it was impossible to get visas from both countries within twenty-four hours. The customer's last hours in New York were spent in the waiting room of the Australian Consulate until his passport was returned to him with the necessary visas for New Britain and New Guinea. The British had assured him he could get his visa for the Solomon and Gilbert islands at their consulate in Honolulu.

The British Consulate in Honolulu is in the old section of the city in a two-room office in a bank building, and it is staffed by an absolutely charming middle-aged British lady, who when asked for visas to Tarawa and Guadalcanal replied with restraint, "Oh, do we own them?" The American handed her a map of the South Pacific, pointing out the islands and reading the labels on them, and assured her they were administered by the British. She seemed pleased by the acquisition of these islands for her already-shrunken empire and took his passport to the consul general. Within half an hour and at a cost of $3.50, he had his visas.

The jet plane ride to Tarawa from the Fijis took about seven hours, a journey of unrelieved tedium for the passenger when not looking out of the plane's windows. The first descent was to Funafuti, the administrative center of Ellice Islands, and it was unnerving. The plane came in low over the ocean, and suddenly, the airstrip, which is only a mowed grass field, appeared at the edge of the water. Even though the plane had only two engines, it was a jet and quite powerful, and before it stopped, it was almost in the water at the other end of the island, having shuddered and rumbled across an uneven surface. The terminal at Funafuti is a tin shack, and all the natives are there to see the plane, sitting cross-legged in rows under its roof. Across a square of burnt grass on the lagoon side of Funafuti is an eight-bedroom hotel, an elongated L-shaped cement block with an empty public room with one overhead fan whirling away. Once the plane touched down, a native bartender ran from the customs shack and took his place behind the cleared bar, setting on it cold bottles of Australian beer for the transients.

The plane then continued to Tarawa, clearing the rocks at the end of the runway at Funafuti by inches. The fact that Tarawa is a British possession is immediately established at its primitive airport. Flying above the customs shed is a small Union Jack. The plane's arrival is the social and commercial event of the week, bringing in the mail and crates of fresh vegetables and fruits for inhabitants accustomed to a diet of frozen meats and canned foods imported by ship from Australia. Everyone turns out for the plane: European men in shorts and long knee socks and barechested natives in sarongs.

The customs work was done by a native officer in white shorts and pith helmet. He was friendly and carefully read every visa in the American's passport, which took some time since he travels widely.

"Where is Tarawa visa?" he asked in halting English.

"Right there," the American said. He did a double take. The visa issued at Honolulu was for the New Hebrides, a colony jointly administered by the French and British, several thousand miles southwest of Tarawa.

"You can't enter without visa."

"But I'm only going to stay for the night and get the plane back tomorrow."

He conferred with a white man and returned smiling. "You can stay."

"Where?"

"In town."

Once the plane was unloaded and the cargo inspected scrupulously by often-bewildered native customs officers—they act as if they don't quite know what the British want them to find in the packages—everyone piled into two nearby vehicles, a dilapidated bus with no glass in the windows and a dusty, dented Land Rover, and took off for a jolting ride to the Hotel Otintai, seven miles east on Bikenibeu, which is connected by an uneven causeway, the water having chewed out sides of it, to Bairiki and the British colonial offices.

The road to the hotel is rutted and often shrinks to a barely passable strip of land separating the pounding ocean surf and the tranquil blue water of the 17-mile-long lagoon inside the horseshoe. When the road widens again, it goes through villages whose inhabitants live not much differently from their ancestors. After a modern war, Tarawa seems to have been gently nudged back into history.

The natives live in one-room thatched huts, many without walls, resting a few feet off the ground on wooden stilts. They sleep off palm mats on the floor, and they go to bed at dusk because there is no electricity. They cook over outside fires, and their utensils are washed in the sea. Most of their food comes from the sea, and at dawn the men push off from the beach in bark boats to fish the untroubled lagoon. Some of the native boys being educated at British or missionary schools play soccer in clearings near the huts.

The hotel has ten bedrooms, each a cement cell containing twin beds with mattresses which feel as if they were filled with stones and a shower with no hot water. The tap water in the bathroom basin is undrinkable; the water to be consumed comes in the form of rain and is caught in huge metal drums outside the hotel and bottled for the guests' use. The best feature of the hotel is that it's built on the lagoon side of the atoll, and its dining room is an open veranda extending to the water. The bedrooms also have doors opening on the lagoon, and at night palm trees and the brilliant stars in the clear blackness of the sky are beautifully outlined. Only in the daylight is the litter of empty beer cans on the beach noticed.

The hotel is the center of European social life on Tarawa. The bar to one side of the veranda is the collecting place for the young British men who, early in their careers, are assigned there for two years of government work. With them are a few army officers, two or three businessmen, the wives of civil servants, and if a man is flaunting convention—something being done more often—his native girlfriend. The topic of conversation is rarely about leaving Tarawa, these colonialists having accepted their sentences with stoic grace.

The meals at the hotel, considering the limited menu and the fact that everything is either frozen or canned, are quite good. The native chef is able to do remarkable things with water, bits of meat and some vegetables to make a first-rate soup. The steak, from Australia, when it is thawed, tends to be stringy, but the chicken, especially when broiled in a butter sauce, is good. And when the meal is not quite right, there is always good Australian bottled beer to wash it down quickly.

The hotel is run by the Wholesale Society, a government subsidiary, and is managed by a young Australian who has lived on Tarawa four years. He is now married to a beautiful native girl addicted to Hollywood movies, and the few nights a week when ancient films are shown on a screen outdoors he and his wife get on a motorcycle, she holding the canvas folding chairs —there are no seats in front of the screen—and they roar into the darkness to see Joan Collins in *Esther and the King*.

The girl is from a leading native family. Her father is one of the chiefs and is often seen wheeling and dealing down by the docks among the natives who are waiting for the launch to Betio. The girl is in better harmony with the fluctuations of natural island life than is her husband, although he says he finds Tarawa very relaxing. He is constantly running, even when there is no place to go, seeing everyone gets his meal hot and on time in the hotel dining room, then bolting down the long corridor to check on the conditions of the guest rooms after the native maids have finished cleaning them.

There are few recreational opportunities for the colonialists. They include a couple of tennis courts—the game can only be played comfortably in late afternoon—a very small library, a local radio station broadcasting a few hours each day, and a social hall where Europeans hold their dances.

The advantage of being a European on Tarawa is that the best housing is available to you. These are wooden frame buildings, some of them with two floors, and, unlike most native huts, they have ground-level stone floors. The few natives able to obtain this type of housing are those working for the British administration.

Most of the natives on the Gilbert Islands are Micronesians, while those on the Ellice Islands are Polynesians. There is a great visual disparity between the native and European cultures in the colony. One is modern, efficient and hurried, the other is ancient, slow-moving and tradition-bound. The Europeans have brought to Tarawa better health and education standards, but their presence has created a cultural dislocation among the natives who are being asked to adapt to ways alien to their backgrounds. The older ones still follow traditions established by their ancestors, but there are noticeable changes in the younger natives. Though education is not compulsory, many of the young Gilbertese have gone to schools run by the missions or the government, and they now wear Western dress instead of the sarong. The boat between Bairiki and Betio on a Saturday night is filled with noisy, flirtatious boys and girls clutching well-thumbed jackets of American rock 'n' roll records and smoking filtered cigarettes down to the filter.

This colony has also been overtaken by the modern problems of overpopulation and labor surpluses.

Tarawa is the base from which the British administer this Crown colony comprising the thirty-seven atolls in the Gilbert and Ellice islands. A mimeographed bulletin posted by the British outside the administration headquarters on Betio explains why. The population of the colony has grown at an annual rate of 3 percent, the fastest of any British colony in the Pacific, and the population density is greatest on Tarawa, 2.5 persons per acre. Since most of the natives are nominal converts to Christianity—mostly Roman Catholics or evangelical Protestants— the British haven't been too specific about birth control, but they have suggested the natives restrict their families to two or three children instead of the present average of five to seven.

Overpopulation has created an alarming labor surplus, and the British want to relocate 3,000 natives in other islands where there are better prospects of work. In addition, many of the young Gilbertese men are being trained at a local maritime academy to work as crewmen on the world's merchant ships.

The economy of the Gilberts has benefited since the war from a booming phosphate industry on Ocean Island, 240 miles southwest of Tarawa. But the British estimate the deposits will be exhausted within seven years, creating an annual shortage of $2,000,000 in the budget for the islands. If no local industry is developed to take up the loss, the money will have to come from already debt-plagued England. The only commercial crop now exported from Tarawa is copra, but hardly in the quantities necessary to make any difference in the economy of the atoll.

Tarawa is also adversely situated geographically. Isolated from the major trading islands of the South Pacific, it is also far from the regular air and shipping lanes. Because there aren't enough ships scheduled to make stops in Tarawa to bring in the necessary goods, the British have set up a list of priorities. In order of current importance, they are medical supplies, mail, food, and building materials.

Though Tarawa has better resisted being civilized by Europeans than most other islands, its children are bothered by cultural confusions. A native boy, who had been educated at a mission school and can fluently speak English, talked about a trip to Sydney, Australia, where he found life too hectic. "Time is very important to people there. They rush, rush, rush." He then described his own life on Tarawa, making it sound very idyllic, with much leisure time to fish the lazy water of the lagoon. He was not controlled by a passionate ambition to be other than who he was or to be in any other place but Tarawa. But asked what he would bring back to his native atoll from Australia if he had the money, he did not say electricity, adequate medical supplies, a hospital or a satisfactory sanitation system. He said, "Television!"

The cultural shock of the Western influence can be gauged in the increase of juvenile delinquency, especially in petty thefts. "Shame is still a great vice for the natives," the Australian hotel manager said. "To steal is to be shamed. But even the fear of being shamed hasn't prevented the kids from stealing." Another problem is alcoholism. The native men, who used to consume

a drink made from fermented coconut milk with enough kick
to get a man through the night, now drink beer and whiskey
and don't know how to handle it.

There is still no great social mixing between the natives and
the Europeans. A British government official said. "The Europeans just don't know the native language, and if some of the
men do, their wives don't." This is only a partial explanation of
the continued social segregation. There are Europeans who still
adopt the superior attitude of the typical colonialist toward all
natives. Even so, many of the young single white European men
take native girls as their mistresses, sleeping with them in huts
on the lagoon away from the European compound. This is permissible as long as display of affection between lovers is not
made public.

But there is still an uncorrupted majesty in the simple rituals
of the natives. One evening at dusk, a funeral procession moved
slowly along the main dirt road in Bairiki. There was no priest
or minister in the line of mourners. At the head of the procession was a young father, barechested in a bright-red sarong,
carrying a tiny wooden box containing the body of his son. Behind him several yards away came the women of the village,
whispering and nudging each other in animated conversation.
Some were even giggling. But there was no emotional response
from the father. He walked carefully, balancing the box on his
right shoulder, holding it steadfast with his right hand while
his left arm lay flat against his side. Inside the cemetery many
of the small tombstones had settled into the sand and were
barely visible above the weeds. At a few, candles were burning
in red glass holders. The father entered the cemetery, walking
alone and erect, to the edge of a freshly dug hole. Nobody was
there to conduct an official religious burial, but it was still a
painfully moving religious expression of a father for his dead
son.

The ways of the Tarawa natives are attractive to a foreigner,
and when it is time to go, he may prolong his leaving by the
repetition of the things that have filled his daily life on the atoll.
The British air officer did that on his day of departure, asking
his native driver to stop at the post office, even though he had

checked his mailbox immediately after the plane had arrived the day before. He also stopped at the native food store and shook hands good-bye with the clerk for the second time in one day. And then he was on the plane, and below it for just a few minutes was the panorama of the surf breaking in rolls on the coral, the leaves of the palm trees driven by the wind, the little straw airport and, standing in front of the flagpole, the native customs officer in his white uniform.

# Saipan

The tour bus with fifteen elderly Japanese turned off the main road and lifted a trail of white dust until it stopped at the edge of a cliff overlooking the sea. In two days in mid-July, 1944, thousands of Japanese soldiers, along with women and children loyal to Japan, walked to the edge of this cliff and threw themselves to their death rather than surrender to the Americans in the conclusion of the battle for Saipan.

The Japanese got off the bus carrying with them a large bottle of sake, a favorite white rice wine in Japan, and walked with measured steps to one of the two wooden stick memorials on the cliff's edge. The leader of the group stepped forward, knelt and poured some of the wine around the base of the stick. The group then formed a semicircle around it, bowed their heads with hands held together in the position of the worshiper, and then moved to the second wooden marker and repeated the ritual. When they finished the ceremony they snapped to rigid attention and, throwing their arms straight above their heads, yelled "banzai" three times, their voices echoing down to where the waves crashed on rocks half submerged in the turbulent sea.

There are two plain stone monuments back up the hill from the cliff, put there by students of the University of Tokyo. At the base of the smaller stone is a plaque with the cryptic inscription in both Japanese and English: "Devote Yourself to the Creation of a Pacific Global Era." To some Americans the inscription resurrects memories of the strident Japanese economic and military expansionist policies of the 1930's that led to America's entrance into World War II.

One of the Japanese men stepped away from his group and walked to an American standing beside the monument, and with a pleasant, unforced smile said, "No more war," repeating the phrase once more before returning to his countrymen to participate in the ceremony of the pouring of sake to appease the souls of the Japanese who died on Saipan. This time the shouts of "banzai," a call of honor to the dead, were not repeated. The Japanese posed for a group photograph and climbed quietly back into the bus.

From Banzai Cliff, one of the more popular tourist attractions on Saipan, the bus went back over the graveled field to the main highway, paved and smooth, and proceeded north on it before again turning onto another dirt road, this one circling up the side of a mountain to a heavily tree-covered rock formation at the top. It is called Suicide Cliff, and from here more Japanese soldiers leaped to their death, down past the green sides of the mountain to the gray rocks below.

The group remained subdued, despite the Japanese tendency to be more animated when on exhibition in other lands. After the same sake ritual was completed on Suicide Cliff, some quickly returned to the bus while a few men knelt in the corner of the abutment, the sake bottle in the center of them, and posed for photographs.

The men in the group were well into their fifties and sixties, and, though none had relatives who had died on Saipan, they had come to honor the dead. They were men haunted by the memories of their defeat here which presaged the inevitable defeat of Japan and the occupation of the homeland by foreigners for the first time in the country's history.

The driver of the bus, owned by Micronesia Tours, could speak fluent English and Japanese, and he said his passengers talked throughout the journey about the battlefield sites of the mass suicides, condoning them as an extreme but honorable method of answering to their ancestors for the defeat of their army on Saipan.

"The attitude of these old men," the driver said, "was that if they had been stationed on Saipan and faced with capture, they would have rather died as heroes by committing suicide than surrender to the enemy." These Japanese, however, were of two minds about the war. "Though still very much influenced by the war," the driver said, "they thought the military leaders were mad for having started it when the odds said they would lose it."

After their visit to Suicide Cliff, the Japanese began to relax. The bus took them to a beach where they had a picnic of raw fish prepared by Micronesia Tours. Knives and forks had been placed in the picnic baskets. But these were old traditionalist Japanese, and they insisted on using chopsticks. A young imaginative Californian, Bruce Kuhn, who is director of the tours and was following the bus in a private car, remembered a Saipanese man who owned many pairs of chopsticks, and he sent his aide back to the village for them. The gesture was greatly appreciated by the Japanese.

After the Japanese left the cliff, white birds drifted serenely in the sky over the flat green field below, a short, deserted airfield strip from the war knifing through it. Beyond it the frantic surf beat on the rocks. The guide said there is a legend on Saipan that there weren't any white birds on the island before the war. They arrived in flocks after it and contained the souls of the Americans and the Japanese killed there.

Many soldiers on both sides died in a battle that for bloodletting was comparable to Tarawa and Peleliu. It began on June 15, 1944, when seven hundred landing crafts carrying 8,000 Americans came ashore in the first twenty minutes of the invasion, and it ended more than three weeks later when almost the entire Japanese garrison of 30,000 men was either killed or had committed suicide. The American casualties were 3,426 Marines and soldiers killed and 13,099 wounded.

MacArthur, assigned to clear out the Japanese from New Guinea, was against the invasion of the Marianas, contending his army could move up through the Philippines to Hong Kong and capture the air base there for the air attack on Japan. Airfields were a prime target because of the development of the long-range B-29 bomber capable of traveling 1,500 nautical miles without refueling and carrying 10,000 pounds of bombs.

In March, after it was decided MacArthur would take Hollandia in New Guinea and Mindanao in the Philippines by November, Admiral Nimitz's amphibious fleet was given the task of capturing the Marianas, the most important being Tinian, Guam and Saipan, which in the spring of 1944 had the most suitable air base for the long-range bombers.

The Marianas were part of Micronesia which Japan had been awarded control of by the League of Nations after World War I. The Japanese transformed a number of these islands into substantial military bases even while remaining a member of the League of Nations and therefore pledged to the general concepts of mutual national disarmament and peaceful means of finding answers to international political problems.

Saipan was the site of the Japanese government in the Marianas and at the start of the war in the Pacific was one of its best fortified bases. Thirteen miles long, with a maximum width of two and a half miles, Saipan is unlike the other islands on which the Americans had conducted amphibious landings. The Marianas are volcanic islands, not coral atolls, and they have mountains suitable for a defense away from the beaches. But, because materials were late in arriving, the Japanese again relied on a beach defense, something that had not worked for them in Tarawa.

For the American invasion of Saipan, there was a fleet of 535 ships and auxiliaries carrying 127,571 men, over two-thirds of them Marines. The Americans came ashore on a four-mile-wide stretch of beach after their amphtracs crossed without the difficulty they had in Tarawa.

Although the preinvasion assault from planes and ships had worked better than it had on Tarawa, it was still faulty. Little of the gunfire was aimed behind the beach defenses where many of the Japanese artillery guns were located, and not much attention was paid to the Japanese machine gun and mortar nests on the flanks of the beachhead. This small-arms fire on the flanks harassed the amphtracs as they pulled to the shore to empty their human cargo. Some of the Navy guide boats caught in crosscurrents veered off course, and a number of amphtracs bunched up on the beach, making them vulnerable to the Japanese artillery. The amphtracs were supposed to carry the men

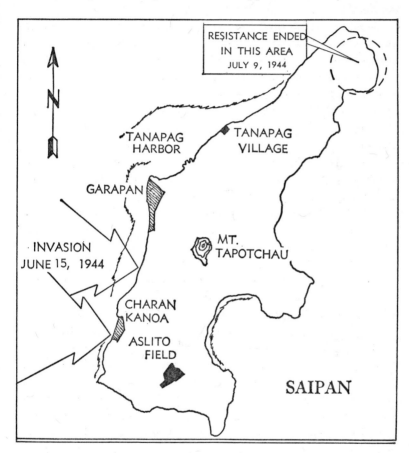

inland, but the debris on the beach of trees, supplies, and fresh shell holes made this impossible, and the men rushed off the beach on foot. Even with the extremely heavy casualties during the initial part of the landing, 20,000 Americans came ashore before the day was out.

The Japanese used almost entirely artillery to try to stop the Americans. They waited twenty-four hours before committing their infantry, and then they sent a thousand men and 37 tanks down the main coastal road. This force was met by the Marines and was driven back by a barrage of fire from machine guns, mortars, rifles and bazookas. In this futile charge, the Japanese lost 24 tanks.

Two days after the invasion, the U.S. Army's 27th Infantry Division was sent into the battle. By the next night, attacking in parallel offensive lines, the soldiers and Marines had cut the island in half and captured the important Aslito airfield. The combined forces then turned north, moving on the Japanese mountain defenses. The going was cruelly slow, measured daily by a few thousand feet. In this advance, the latent interservice rivalry erupted. When the Army's 106th Infantry Regiment of the 27th Division was accused of starting late on its advance north, subjecting the Marines to attack on their flanks, Marine General Holland Smith relieved Army General Ralph Smith of his command on June 24. Later investigations showed the Army officers in the division were not adequately combat trained, and many were overaged.

But the Army proved its valor on July 6 when the Japanese, mustering what was left of their ground forces, launched a banzai attack. About 5,000 Japanese charged the Americans with anything they could carry, from clubs to bayonets attached to the end of rusty rifles. It was a suicidal maneuver, and up to 4,000 Japanese lost their lives.

The American advance continued up the island into what became known as the Valley of Death, a thickly weeded field with no real protective covering at the base of the mountain at Marpi Point. From the sides of the mountain, the Japanese rained round after round of shells and bullets on the advancing Americans, not aiming at individuals but indiscriminately firing at a moving mass. Still, the Americans came on, engaging the Japanese in hand-to-hand combat, driving them back into the caves on the side of the mountain, and then sealing them off until the screams from within were silenced by the wall of stone.

When the Americans reached Banzai Cliff, they looked down and saw thousands of bodies floating in the water. There were so many corpses that a small naval craft was unable to steer through them.

The island was declared secure on July 9, and this was made possible by the efforts of the U.S. Navy in a decisive naval battle that took place on June 19 and 20, and that was known as the Battle of the Philippine Sea.

Preparing for a sea rescue of Saipan by carrier-based air attacks on the American landing force, the Japanese launched an air strike against the vessels of the U.S. Fifth Fleet, which was participating in the invasion. During the battle, which was known also as the Turkey Shoot, the Americans lost under 30 planes and only 20 pilots, but the Japanese carrier air force was decimated, losing 476 planes and 445 pilots. The Fifth Fleet went in pursuit of the Japanese and sunk two carriers and two tankers and severely damaged four carriers, one battleship, one cruiser and one tanker.

Saipan was one of the crucial battles of the war in the Pacific. With the fall of Saipan, the Japanese inner-island defense perimeter protecting their mainland had been cracked and the Americans had captured valuable air bases from which strikes could be made against the major cities of Japan. The first of the almost-daily bombing missions by B-29's from the Marianas began on November 24, 1944.

The capture of Saipan also brought about the fall of Prime Minister Tojo, the architect of Japan's disastrous military adventure in the Far East. He was forced to resign and his departure strengthened a peace faction within the Japanese Cabinet.

At the invasion beach site today a number of tanks are still sunk in the waters of the lagoon, their decomposing, rust-colored turrets sticking above the surface at all tides. Two of these tanks are in the water directly in front of the Royal Taga, the island's only first-class hotel. Young Japanese skin divers have made it their headquarters on expeditions to Saipan, and when not in the water, they are bronzing themselves on towels spread over the prickly, stiff grass by the hotel's pool.

The hotel has the feeling of being much larger than it is, more massive in bulk because of the thickness of its walls which must withstand the pounding of waves pushed across the coral reef to the undefended shore during a typhoon. The rooms are quite comfortable, and most have small balconies facing the sea, radios and air conditioning.

At the Valley of Death, the site of the heaviest American casualties, a road sign reading HISTORIC MARPI is stuck in a field of beautifully somber wood roses growing around human bones. Another sign warns DO NOT REMOVE ANY HUMAN REMAINS. Many skeletons of Japanese soldiers are still scattered through the thick growth of bushes and trees, bleached white by the sun yet still resisting ultimate decay. Piles of bones have also been left in the entrance to the caves in the side of the mountain, an orderly housekeeping job done by the Americans after the war. The local government wants to keep this part of the island an historical park, and it is treated as if it were the Acropolis, with tourists forbidden to pick up pieces of the rubble for souvenirs.

Saipan is the capital of Micronesia, a U.S.-administered trust territory of 2,100 small islands spread over the Pacific in an area roughly the size of the United States. Only one hundred of these islands are inhabited, with a total population of 100,000 natives. There are 11,000 people living on Saipan, of whom 200 are Americans, most of them working for the trust territory government. The United States was given the administration of Micronesia by the United Nations.

As was all Micronesia, Saipan was closed to tourists until the mid-1950's. The United States restricted travel for strategic military reasons. Saipan had a large Central Intelligence Agency complex where Nationalist Chinese agents were supposedly trained to be infiltrated into Red China. Some of these CIA buildings are now used as a post office and library by the local civilian government.

Saipan is easily accessible from Guam, which is 135 miles south. There are daily flights, some on jets which take only twenty minutes to reach Saipan. But there is very little to do on the island for a tourist if he doesn't like to fish and sun. There are two movie houses, one of them with seats not secured to the floor, and a number of native bars, the more daring having

earthy floor shows. There is also a television channel in operation during the evening hours six nights a week. The islanders
also hope someday to get their oasis of community salvation, the
bowling alley.

But there are the girls from Truk, their promiscuity legendary among the Americans on Saipan. The girls gather at
dusk on a pier used by native fishermen and then go off into the
sand, walking several yards up the beach before sitting down,
their loose-fitting cloth skirts billowing around their crossed
knees, waiting until dark and the arrival of the men. Then they
pair off with their dates, both sexes dropping their clothes
as they race into the water for a moonlight swim before going
off into the bushes bordering the sand to make love. This is
what the girls from Truk will freely do with men they are taken
with, so the rumor goes, and every night the American visiting
the island goes to the pier and waits for his girl from Truk, but
she was there the night before, or so he is led to believe by the
old fisherman pulling his bark boat over the pebbles in the
shallow water, the keel making a piercing, scratching sound.

Even without the uninhibited Truk girls, Saipan is much
more naturally primitive than is Guam, and the natives want to
keep it that way, fearing that the Americans might reactivate
the military airfield next to the commercial one at Asilto if they
are eventually forced to leave Okinawa, their largest island
military base in the Pacific and the one nearest the Asian mainland. The Saipanese enjoy their uncluttered sandy beaches and
acres of semitropical wilderness.

The island cannot escape nature, though, and Saipan was
almost completely devastated by a typhoon two years ago, when
wind and tides flattened practically every building on the coast.
The United States has since spent more than $2,000,000 to build
permanent stone buildings to replace the old Quonset huts used
to house government offices. Most of the residential dwellings
appear today to have been put together with any material left
on the ground by the storm: wings of houses being of tin and
wood while the foundations remain stone.

Because the island is open to the fury of ocean windstorms,
the Saipanese use five huge concrete bomb shelters, constructed

by the Japanese before the war, as havens in typhoons. They are huge, empty rooms, the dampness sealed in. Names of those who fled into them during the typhoon are scratched into the concrete. Each bunker holds three hundred people, and those who can't get into them during a storm flee to caves left by the Japanese in the sides of the mountain.

Saipan was agriculturally self-sufficient before the war, but its economy was ruined and has never been revived by the United States. Most of the food has to be imported, and the prices are exorbitant. Carrots and cabbage sell for 48 cents a pound. About the only fresh fruit on the island is watermelon.

Many Saipanese still have warm regard for the Japanese. The agricultural economy was started by the Japanese, who were also responsible for the first school system. This affection for the Japanese—one of the considerations given before the Americans invaded Saipan was the loyalty of the natives for the Japanese—may play a role in determining the future political status of Saipan.

There was a referendum in the fall of 1969 in Saipan, Tinian and Rota, the northern Marianas Islands, and the vote was heavily for joining Guam in an Independent Territory of the Marianas. Guam already has an independent-territory status and is not a part of Micronesia. But the Guamanians voted down the proposal, presumably because of hard feelings from the war—when Guam was occupied by the Japanese and overrun by Saipanese workers.

There is also the possibility that if Micronesia is given the freedom in a referendum to choose her political or territorial affiliation, she may elect to be returned to Japan. It is doubtful the United States would let the election get that far out of hand. The choice for the Micronesian voters will probably be affiliation with the United States as a commonwealth or independent territory or complete independence as a new nation.

Whatever happens politically to Saipan, the tourists will still be drawn here because of the battlefield. Along the main road, from the airport in the south to Marpi Point in the north, are many relics of both war and nature: a fishing boat resting on a bank where it was tossed by a wave during the typhoon; rusting tanks, their sides splintered by shells; stumps of coconut trees with their tops shorn by the wind; crumbling pillboxes and sunken barges.

There is also man-made debris. The site of the initial American landing where engineers later built a sturdy pier is now the native garbage dump, and heaps of trash stand sentinel the length of the road to the pier.

Probably the best-kept war relic is the Japanese command post at Marpi Point, a maze of heavy artillery and machine guns arrayed around paths at the entrance to a cave, and the guns still point not toward the sea but around to the Valley of Death where the white birds fly.

# Tinian

The coral airstrip is empty, the shells of dead crabs scattered over its rough surface and thick bushes in dense clumps at its edge, but from here, in the late afternoon of August 5, 1945, the age of atomic warfare was commenced. The first tactical atomic bomb, whose complete destructive force was still unknown to its inventors, was loaded on the *Enola Gay,* a B-29 Superfortress to be piloted the next day by Colonel Paul W. Tibbets, Jr., to the Japanese city of Hiroshima. The crew of the *Enola Gay,* living in tin huts off the flight strip, knew they had been trained for a very secret mission, but only Tibbets was told what the plane would carry when it took off from Tinian the next day. The bomb was dropped at 8:15 A.M. on August 6, 1945, killing in one brilliant explosion at least 80,000 people and destroying all buildings, except those made of reinforced concrete, within a two-and-a-half-mile radius.

The pit from which the first atom bomb was mechanically lifted into the belly of the Superfortress has been filled with loose dirt, and from it grows a coconut palm tree and a tall plant bearing a pale, soft-yellow flower that gives off a suffocatingly sweet smell. There is also a white stone marker, about three feet tall, with a metal plaque noting why the location is commemorated.

Across the wide loading area is another bomb pit filled in with the same type of flowering shrub and palm tree. It was here three days later that the second atom bomb was loaded on another B-29, this one named *Bock's Car,* piloted by Major

Charles W. Sweeny and flown to Nagasaki, where in another blinding white flash accompanied by an awesome explosion at least 35,000 people were instantly killed and a sizable suburb of the port city demolished.

The next day the Emperor of Japan decided independently of his badly divided cabinet to accept the Allied terms of unconditional surrender and to end the war. More than half a million Japanese soldiers had already died in a war which the emperor really had no heart to pursue.

In the last months of the war, a continuous line of American bombers left from the four airstrips on the northern end of Tinian, winging over rocky cliffs that resemble the rugged coastline of Maine. This part of the island is now completely deserted, left to snails and frogs to crawl among the broken coconut shells on the airstrips, some not making it across, crushed by falling shells.

The silence is almost total, the sound of the surf blocked out by the impervious covering of trees and bushes. The Quonset huts near the loading pits where the pilots and crews flying the *Enola Gay* and *Bock's Car* lived and were briefed before their flights of destiny have been removed by a scrap metal outfit which stripped the island of most of the salvageable war metal in the early 1950's. Their exact locations have been hidden by scraggly thin bushes with whiplike branches growing in abundance in uncultivated fields.

The feeling of desolation on this end of Tinian is absolute; only an acute imagination can bring back the sights and sounds of the B-29's lifting off the runway, the ground crews rushing across the crushed coral with backs bent to withstand the winds stirred to storm force by the departing planes. The awareness of its being an historical wasteland is heightened by a modern dual-lane highway—empty at every time of day except for an occasional farm truck—which connects the northern and southern ends of Tinian. It was built to carry the atomic bombs the length of the island from a pier on the southern end and was made dual-lane to prevent any head-on collision of cars. Today the road eerily goes nowhere, passing between points of inconsequence, its center island filled with head-high bushes.

Much of the land in the northern part of the island is now owned by a wealthy American who runs the Micronesian Development Company, which is cultivating this once-unproductive land so the Tinianese can raise their own food supply and sell the surplus to neighboring islands in the Marianas.

The only way to get to Tinian from Saipan now is by open launch. There was passenger plane service but it has been temporarily discontinued. Instead of three minutes by air in a one-engine sports plane, the trip by water between the two islands, separated at their closest points by a channel three miles wide, can take up to three hours. The slowest boat trip is on the twice-weekly mail boat. The fastest is on an 18-foot, dual-powered outboard motorboat piloted by Herman T. Palacios, a native of Saipan who served with the U.S. Army in Korea during the early 1960's.

Palacios' round stomach gives him the appearance of an outsized Buddha, one who is flabby from easy living and too much drink. But on closer inspection, even though the stomach is convex, it's a protuberance of solid muscle, not fat.

Palacios is the kind of boatsman about whom legends are made. Saving money by working on the docks, supporting his pretty, equally plump wife and many children with a portion of his weekly salary, Palacios went south to Guam to buy his outboard motorboat and then proceeded to sail it back the 135 miles over open seas alone with only a hand-held compass to guide him. This exploit is still recalled with respect by the Saipanese.

As a boatsman, Palacios manipulates the sea rather than allowing it to overpower him. The trip across the channel in a small boat is frightening because the water here is very rough, alternating huge waves and deep troughs. When the boat descends into one with a sudden rush, the sky is lost behind a crest of mountainous waves, and for a moment the boat, shuddering as its engine is out of the water, seems about to be engulfed by them. But Palacios knows intuitively how to ride the waves in the channel—when to cut the motor to prevent the hull from slamming into the trough and when to rev it up to guide the boat over the crest smoothly. It is a masterful performance, although only routine to him, and one he executes while looking frequently away from the sea to talk to his American passenger.

Once out of the channel, the sea becomes relatively calm on the leeward side of Tinian. From the water the landing beaches, guarded on both sides by large rocks and topped on the bluffs with clusters of weeds, are postage-stamp size. Now the passenger could admire the flight of a solitary flying fish as it cleanly broke the water's surface and traveled in a perfect trajectory parallel to the sea before reentering it with a sudden swish.

At the southern end of the island, 23 miles away from Saipan, is the only usable docking facility. Its metal bulkhead, put up by the Americans after they captured Tinian in 1943, is rusting away, and much of the cement behind it is eroded, so the steel reinforcement bars are exposed and bent. At the seaside of this L-shaped harbor the U.S. cruiser *Indianapolis* unloaded its cargo of two atomic bombs. It was an ill-fated voyage for the ship. On the way home, in the last days of the war, the cruiser was sunk by a Japanese submarine and went down with an appalling loss of life. Most of the sailors survived the sinking, but many of them died while in the water from drowning, exposure and shark attacks.

Although there are still a few empty crates and rusted oil drums on the dock, most of the daily activity comes from the village boys playing in the water. The only sizable ship arrives on Saturday with food supplies from Saipan. Ironically, the sign on the dock reads, WELCOME TO TINIAN. GATEWAY TO ECONOMIC DEVELOPMENT.

Palacios spun the wheel, smoothly turning the boat into the harbor's water, cutting the engine's power at the last minute as it slid, like a ballplayer stealing second base, into the steps of the dock where strong young boys caught the rope and secured it to a piling. For their work, the boys were tossed fresh watermelons by Palacios, who had picked them that morning in Saipan.

Palacios is a familiar person on Tinian, and the island residents pause in their daily chores to give him a wave as he passes.

When he stops at a village canteen to buy cold soft drinks, the
owner gives them to him without asking for payment.

The island's population consists of about eight hundred
Chamorros natives. Most of the men are farmers, and in their
fields there are half-destroyed Japanese bunkers around which
grow fresh vegetables. Buildings left on Tinian, even some of
the remains of those half-destroyed by the war, are put to use.
The mayor lives in a freshly painted white Quonset hut. The
town hall was built over the ruins of a Japanese blockhouse used
in the battle for Tinian as their command headquarters. The
island's young police lieutenant lives in another damaged
bunker, the outer walls still torn and jagged.

The village of Tinian Town is really a collection of private
homes spaced among public buildings, none of them in any coherent pattern, on a main street. The official center of the town
would seem to be where the Catholic mission church and town
hall face each other on the road halfway up a slight hill from
the harbor, but the real life of the island is focused around a
cockpit next to a combination bar-community center on a street
near the dock.

"You should meet the mayor," Palacios said to the American,
who had rented his boat and navigating services for $40. How-
ever, since it was Sunday afternoon, he didn't drive the car,
which he had rented from a native, to where the mayor lived,
but to the cockpit. The men of the village were there in force,
jammed around the arena, clutching money in their hands. The
floor of the ring is brown dirt, and there is a wooden circular
barrier in the center high enough to prevent the birds from escaping and low enough for the customers to see the fight. Just
after noon, barechested men, sweating in the heat, bring the
birds they have trained to the arena. The fight begins with the
pitiful screeching of the cocks engaged in a contest in which one
will probably lose its head. The native men crowd closer to the
ring, shouting encouragement to the birds racing around in ter-
rified bewilderment before striking each other with a brutal
violence. A young spastic boy, moving with the jerkiness of a
cerebral palsy victim, went among the men collecting bets and

bringing cold beers from the bar. The mayor was there in the middle of the men, a glazed look on his face.

Gambling is legal on Tinian, and cockfighting the most popular way of making bets. Any reports of expanding gambling on the islands are happily received by the natives; their favorite rumor, and a persistent one, is that an American syndicate wants to build a luxury gambling hotel there. Law and order are no problem, the Tinianese say, because gambling, a source of crime on other islands, is legal on Tinian. For a rather easy life, the fourteen-man police force is well paid. Each man gets $1.14 an hour. In fact public service is fairly lucrative on Tinian. The mayor's salary was just raised to $200 a month, and in the next election he suddenly has opposition for the job nobody had previously wanted.

The cockfights don't end at once; rather, the men begin to drift off before the last battered bird, its head half off, is snatched from the ring and the sand, moist from blood, is raked over. The winners go to the bar and set up their friends with a round of drinks. Palacios doesn't drink, though the spastic boy hands him a beer. He presses a few American coins in the boy's palm, which the boy is trying to restrain from shaking uncontrollably by holding his right wrist with the talonlike fingers of his left hand.

Driving down the empty four-lane superhighway, Palacios snapped off the lid on a can of soda and said he didn't drink hard liquor on the job, though he and his wife had been known to close the bar of the Hotel Taga in Saipan. At the northern end, Palacios drove his car onto the *Enola Gay* airstrip, parked it and walked alone down the strip until he was in the middle of a ribbon of mustard-colored stone, the unencumbered wind flapping his shirttails and long dark-brown hair.

"It was here that it all started." He yelled because his back was to the American and the wind carried his words to the side of the runway. The American moved behind Palacios, and for the moment the enormity of the event which had begun on this runway overwhelmed both of them in the self-imposed silence. The American said something that was not a word but a sound of profound dismay.

There was no further exchange between Palacios and the American until they were back on the boat, and Palacios said, "Not too many tourists get over here. But they should. It would give them something to think about!"

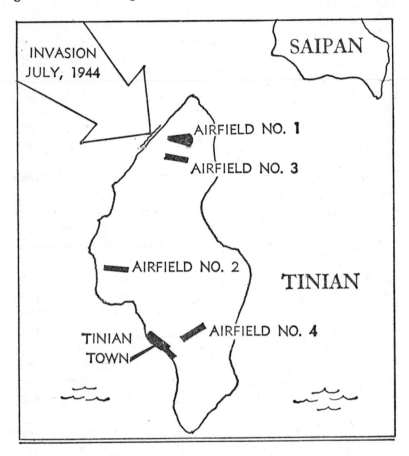

As the boat moved past the landing sites, Palacios took his hands off the wheel and plunged his knife into a fresh melon, slicing it with a blade still carrying the stench of fish. The melon juice ran across the scale-crusted bottom of the boat. Then, later, when the boat entered the channel, he again left the wheel, rummaged through a drawer under the panel, pulled out a gun, and with his right leg against the edge of the right side, braced his arm and fired at a sea gull. The bird, arching above the boat, was arrested in flight and fell dead weight into the water. Palacios slapped his stomach and grinned.

The northern coast of Tinian vanished behind a trough of a gigantic wave.

There was a very good reason why the Americans wanted to take Tinian. In the summer of 1944, it had two 4,700-foot runways and three more airstrips under construction, all of them on the north. The only suitable place for an amphibious landing is at the southern end, and this is where the Japanese expected the invasion to take place.

To capture the airstrips of Tinian, the U.S. Marines executed probably their most successful amphibious landing of the war. From the start the Americans had planned to land on the northern beaches, not much wider than 160 yards, cutting up from the beach through hard coral bluffs rising to 150 feet.

On June 20 the Americans began their preinvasion bombardment from air and artillery positions on Saipan. In the next two weeks, 7,571 rounds of artillery fire were directed on the island, and Tinian Town was reduced to rubble by air strikes.

The Americans also experimented for the first time with napalm. On July 22, two days before the invasion, two P-47's flew in low over Tinian, dropping fire bombs made of napalm gel and gasoline packed in aircraft fuel tanks. Observing their devastation from the air, the flyers reported the bombs were good for burning off the cane fields and exposing Japanese underground positions in the thickets. The next day, thirty more napalm bombs were dropped in the fields around White Beaches 1 and 2.

The first Marine amphtracs touched down on the beaches of Tinian about 8 P.M., and within minutes twenty-four of them had landed Marines and pulled back to offshore transports. Within forty minutes, the entire assault battalion of the 24th Marines was ashore on White Beach 1.

The landing went off without a hitch. By nightfall more than 15,000 Marines were on Tinian, with only 15 killed and 200 wounded. The beachhead on the night of the invasion was 2,900 yards wide and a mile deep.

The Japanese counterattacked the next day in a five-hour sustained drive against the American beachhead. It was repulsed, and four hundred Japanese soldiers were killed.

The American advance south toward Tinian Town proceeded swiftly along a terrain flat and suitable for tank charges. Ushi Point, the island's main airfield, fell on July 26 and was made operational by the Americans July 29, a little more than a year before it was used by the *Enola Gay*. Tinian Town was taken on July 30, and the next day the island was declared secured. The Marines lost only 389 men; their wounded numbered less than 2,000. The entire Japanese garrison was lost. The Americans counted 5,000 Japanese bodies and took 252 prisoners. The rest of the garrison, about 4,000 men, since there was no escape possible, presumably committed suicide off the cliffs on the southern end of the island.

After Tinian there was only one other Marianas island of importance to capture: Guam, where the Americans had been routed by the Japanese in the first days of the war in the Pacific.

# Guam

The NO SMOKING signs over the seats came on with the noticeable slowing down of the plane's forward motion. Outside, lights glittered on the horizon. There was the clicking sound of seat belts being fastened.

"It's like this every night," the hostess said, rushing up the center aisle holding at arm's length a bag containing the supper of an airsick bride. It was a Monday night flight from Tokyo to Guam, and every seat in both tourist and first class was filled, almost entirely with Japanese newlyweds.

The airsick bride had her head back against the headrest, her face the complexion of the white doily. The attentive groom pressed a wet towel to her forehead, taking the wave out of the curl there, flattening strands of hair on her alabaster skin.

"You'd get sick, too, if you had to eat what he fed her," the hostess said knowingly. "He poured enough champagne in her to sink a ship, and on top of supper, too."

Of the 30,000 tourists to visit Guam last year, three-fourths were Japanese, many of them young honeymooners filling the nightly flights to Guam, and the airlines have made it quite inexpensive for the Japanese to fly to Guam. The fare is only $130 round trip from Tokyo.

Because of the Japanese, Guam, an independent territory of the United States, is thriving as each jet passenger plane brings reinforcements in what has become the new Japanese invasion of Guam. The planes also bring in Japanese businessmen with money to invest in everything from resort beach hotels to wholesale food businesses. And their vigorous economic activity on an American-owned island is an irritant to Americans who had been trying to make a living on Guam long before its economy began flourishing as a warm-climate resort for expense-account Japanese.

One of the unhappy Americans is Al Waller, the owner of the Sleepy Lagoon, a modest motel-restaurant on a choice location: a grassy bluff with a sandy path down to a protected cove beach. Running away from a bad marriage—most of the established Americans on the South Pacific islands seem to be running away from something—Waller showed up in Guam in 1949, and after working at odd jobs, he saved enough money to invest in his hotel on the outskirts of Agana, the capital of Guam. Waller's motel business benefited from Japanese young love until Japanese adults discovered money could be made in the honeymoon business. Waller contends the Japanese travel agencies began practicing unfair competition by booking guests at his motel without any intention of delivering them from the airport. Their scheme was to fill up his hotel on paper and then direct the young Japanese to the hotels they own on Guam, leaving Sleepy Lagoon deserted, though every room was reserved.

Waller's business began to falter, its decline helped by a typhoon in the early 1960's which carved out chunks of the bluff, dumping half of his motel units into the water. He now has only twenty-six rooms, less than half his original number, and no capital to rebuild.

What money he makes to support his Guamanian wife and their children, one a college-aged boy, comes from a bar and restaurant business, and most of that from civilian American pilots with a sense of loyalty for his trying to make a go of it. But even his bar empties early, the young American servicemen sitting there until it is obvious no young Guamanian girls are going to show up. When they go, he makes one last swipe at the big wooden bar, closing the door by midnight, by which time the plane from Tokyo has already landed and dispersed the newlyweds among the newer, more elaborately furnished motels on flat beaches nearer Agana.

Waller said some Japanese businessmen offered to buy him out, but he refused and plans to fight the Japanese. He is constantly reminded of them, however, even when they aren't at his motel. Sleepy Lagoon is built over what was an underground Japanese mortar position, and just off the entrance to the restaurant is a path through a dark tunnel to an opening on the water. A mortar gun is in the ground half-covered by overhanging sod on the bunker's roof. Waller leaves the military excavation and gun there as tourist attractions, but the few young Japanese who come to Sleepy Lagoon are not very interested in World War II. They take a meal of American steak, sip some European wine, and retire early.

If much of Guam's original postwar prosperity came from the heavy spending of the United States on Navy and Air Force bases on the island, almost all the new investment money has come from Japan.

For many young Japanese, Guam is the first U.S. territory they will have visited. As a popular slogan says in the masthead of the morning newspaper, "Guam is where America's day begins." Because of the International Date Line, Guam is always a day ahead of the American mainland.

The young Japanese come to Guam well indoctrinated in American movie Westerns. "To these kids," a Guamanian said, "this island is the last real American frontier. To them the Americans living here are modern-day cowboys. The first thing they buy on this island are cowboy hats, and we sell plenty of them."

The young Japanese are, like youths around the world, attracted to any place they can sunbathe, and Guam has many wonderful beaches offering a brilliant sun, its intensity diminished by almost always cooling offshore breezes and pastel-blue water separated from the rougher open sea by coral reefs. The new resort hotels front on the better beaches and more are being built yearly.

The Japanese businessmen know the United States has shown very little interest in expanding the private economy of the island, leaving to them the opportunities for investment in the lucrative tourist business. To emphasize how much Guam is being transformed into a Japanese community, a television crew was in Agana shooting a commercial for a Tokyo television station. A young Japanese actor with the sharp features of a Caucasian was sitting on a fishing boat, a straw cowboy hat on the back of his head and a cigar in his mouth. He was on the steps to the boat's cabin, staring at a pretty Japanese girl standing on a jetty. The theme of the commercial was that Guam was becoming a fisherman's paradise for the Japanese. The point of the commercial was not lost on several American fishermen on a boat in the next slip. Over gulps from beer cans they made appropriately derogatory remarks about the Japanese economic invasion of Guam with the testy chauvinism of the Americans on Guam today.

Guam's permanent population is still very much American. Of the 100,000 people living here, 45,000 are Americans, most of them military personnel and their dependents. As residents of an independent territory of the United States, the native Guamanians have many of the rights of U.S. citizens, among them service in the U.S. military. Guamanian males are eligible for the draft, and many do serve. Stories about the death or injury of young Guamanians in Vietnam are not infrequent on the front pages of the island's newspapers. Although one of the few rights denied Guamanians is the vote in U.S. Presidential elections, they do elect their own island governor now. Until recently he was appointed by Washington.

Though Guam is much nearer Asia than the mainland of the United States—it is only three hours by air to Tokyo and Hong Kong and less to Manila—it looks American, especially to anyone returning from a lengthy stay in the Orient. The main roads feature a typical American conglomeration of unattractive shopping centers, many of them trashy discount houses, hamburger stands, gas stations and taverns.

Since the Spanish-American War of 1898, Guam has been a possession of the United States. First to discover it was Magellan, who sailed the Pacific for ninety-eight days without sighting land until he reached Rota, a Marianas island directly north of Guam. He landed on the southern coast of Guam and was greeted by unfriendly Chamorros Indians who chased him off.

Because of their inhospitableness, Magellan called Guam the
Isle of Thieves. The United States took possession of Guam
for the same reason it did many other islands in the Pacific: to
provide a coaling station for its Pacific Navy. The other Mari-

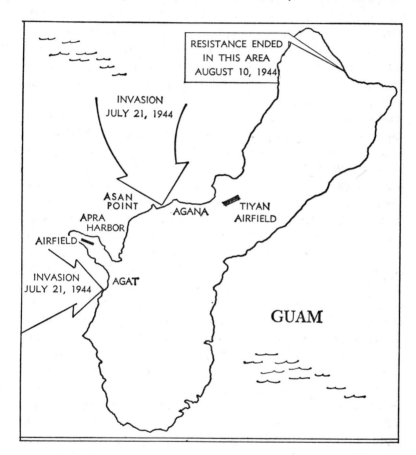

anas were purchased by Germany for $4,500,000 and were lost
by them to Japan after World War I.

   After a few hours of fighting, Guam was lost by the Americans to the Japanese on December 10, 1941. The Americans
had thought so little of Guam's military potential that on the
day of its invasion there were only 450 U.S. Marines and sailors
on it, armed with thirteen machine guns and 170 Springfield

rifles. The Japanese put ashore 5,000 men, and after a brief skirmish near city hall, the small American force capitulated before the Japanese had spread out beyond the city limits of Agana.

The Japanese occupation at first was not too harsh on the Chamorros, though native men were forced to work on Japanese military installations and Japanese was made the language of instruction in the schools. But when it was apparent the Americans would invade Guam, measures under the occupation became stringent. The Japanese navy was relieved of administering the island, and army units took over control of its military and civilian governments. The Japanese closed schools and churches, The number of Chamorro men pressed into forced labor battalions increased greatly. Food was rationed, and most of the civilian population by early 1944 was rounded up and placed into concentration camps.

When the Americans arrived to retake the island, the Japanese, even though they knew the invasion was imminent, were ill-prepared to put up a strong defense. The Battle of the Philippine Sea had left them with a decimated air force, which allowed Americans to bomb Guam almost at will, and for thirteen days before committing its troops to the beaches, the Americans rained bombs and naval shells on the island's fortifications. The Japanese had less of everything on Guam compared with their garrison on Saipan—fewer men, tanks and artillery guns. The Japanese defense plans were also the same as they had been for Tarawa and Saipan: meet the Americans on the beaches and drive them into the sea. This might have been effective if the military strengths were equal, but now the American amphibious troops were well supported by air and naval forces, and at Guam on July 21, 1944, the Americans landed some 20,000 Marines and soldiers within a twenty-four-hour period on a stretch of flat beach below the town of Agana. Then, as they had on Saipan, the Marines and soldiers split into pincer formations to outflank the Japanese troops. The strongest Japanese counterattack was assembled on July 25 outside Agana. After hours of hand-to-hand combat, the Americans left 3,500 dead Japanese on the field. The night before this decisive battle, the Japanese launched one of their more bizarre charges. The island had been the liquor storehouse for the Japanese in the Central Pacific, and before this charge, the Japanese troops broke into the supply and drank themselves into fighting shape. Many Japanese strapped explosives around their bodies, planning to throw themselves against the advancing American tanks. But this formation became a shambles of stumbling, drunken men, and the Marines picked off these human bombs, detonating them before they reached the tanks. Still the Japanese pushed forward in drunken waves, many of them carrying sticks, pitchforks, baseball bats and empty bottles. When it was over there were 400 dead Japanese.

By August 10, when the entire island was under American control, the Japanese had lost their complete garrison of 18,500 men while the Americans suffered 7,081 casualties, of whom 2,124 were killed.

For a number of Japanese soldiers, the war didn't immediately end with the official surrender. They fled into the caves in the north of the island to wait out the American occupation until Japanese reinforcements came. Some of these men starved to death; others went to the high cliffs over the sea and committed suicide. For two, the war didn't end until 1962. They were found wandering in a daze on a village road in the north, and when they were taken by the natives to American officials, the Japanese said they thought the war was still going.

By then most of the debris of battle had been cleared from Guam. Up from the beach, in the low hills around it, there is a field of rusting tanks. Where the Americans landed, there stands an elementary school and beside it, farther down the beach, a memorial of a used shell stuck on top of a stone marker. Soon the Japanese will have their own memorial. They have been given permission by the Americans to scour the jungles in the north for skeletons of their soldiers. The bones will be collected and buried under a proposed memorial park in a remote site on the northern, uninhabited part of the island where a few tourists or even permanent American residents visit. It will not just be another commemoration to war dead, according to the Japanese planners; the stone memorial will symbolize world peace and brotherhood. But these are idealized conditions of the future. Guam today is still much a part of the American military commitment in the Far East.

If anything, Guam's importance to the United States has tremendously increased since World War II. The major U.S. military base in the Pacific now is Okinawa, but that island will revert to Japanese control in 1972. The United States hopes to keep a military base on Okinawa, but it is doubtful the Japanese will allow it to remain in its present size or let the Americans have nuclear weapons there. If they are removed, Guam would be the most likely receiver of them. It already possesses airfields large enough to handle bombers making air strikes against Vietnam.

Some of the more seriously wounded from Vietnam are brought to Guam for convalescent leave, and they stay at a naval base hospital on a cove south of Agana. It is a settlement of depressingly routine wooden two-story barracks, many of them now closed, an indication of the decreasing number of soldiers fighting the ground war in Vietnam. The wounded in striped pajamas and blue robes sun themselves on the grass between the barracks. Those completely ambulatory wade in the cove water inside a seawall built out from the beach in a circle.

For these servicemen, Guam is not an easy place in which to move about easily. The stores of Agana are spaced widely apart on the main road, making them impossible to get to without a car, and there is no real public transportation, except for a bus that goes hourly through town to the U.S. military bases. Cars are essential because taxi fares are outrageous, and there are an estimated 33,000 private vehicles. Promptly at 4 P.M. on weekdays, the road leading out from the commercial section of Agana becomes clogged.

Agana is not a good leave town. Most of the American civilians on Guam are government workers whose lives are secured by Civil Service, pensions, seniority and low-cost hospitalization, breeding in them the natural conservatism of the true bureaucrat, who is the staunchest defender of the military-government establishment. Through it the bureaucrat is afforded economic protection in what is essentially a modified Socialist state. The basic needs of the bureaucrat here are taken care of by the government. Curiously, his public morality is a reflection of his slavish devotion to the idealized American past of small town, Midwest life, with its mythology about rugged individualism, something completely absent from his life on Guam unless he is one of its few store owners. Public decency in Guam, as it presumably was in Indiana at the turn of the century, is measured by the extent of the curtailment of public places of pleasure. There are taverns in Agana, some even with go-go girls, though by the standards of San Francisco they are overly dressed. These are few in number. There are very few eligible girls for the servicemen to date, most of them being rushed after puberty to schools back in Hawaii or on the American mainland. The few still here can be met in the lobbies of local movie houses or in the few restaurants with combos and dancing. The best places for servicemen interested in girls but not in permanent relationships are the hotels catering to airline personnel. By midnight the bars at these places fill up with pretty hostesses willing to experiment with their leisure time while waiting for their flights out.

The inherent conservatism of society on Guam is also reflected in the island's religious fundamentalism. The only major bookstore in Agana is a religious one carrying tracts by obscure Protestant theologians. The island's road signs also indicate a definite moral preference. TO HEAVEN. TURN RIGHT. GO STRAIGHT, reads one on the outskirts of Agana.

Despite a religious fundamentalism that is often not conducive to racial and religious toleration, Guam seems to show signs of little racial prejudice except for letters to the editors from American Southerners complaining of race mixing between Guamanian girls and American servicemen.

"Guam is a mixture of many races. Polynesian, Micronesian, Melanesian, Caucasian," an old-time Guamanian said. "Everyone gets along here. There's no such thing as race prejudice on the island. That's what makes it such a nice place to live."

Many American servicemen who have married dark-skinned Guamanian girls do settle on Guam after their military duty is over rather than return to America and face social ostracism. "My mother was more concerned that her daughters married Protestants than whether they married Guamanian boys or American mainlanders," said one young Guamanian woman whose two sisters had married American servicemen. For the mother to find candidates for sons-in-law among Guamanian boys with the right religious background would be very difficult. Guam is 90 percent Catholic.

While there is hardly any hostility between young Guamanians and the Japanese visitors, there is a residue of bitterness among the middle-aged who lived through the Japanese occupation. "The Japanese were pretty mean according to the old folks on the island," the young girl said.

The Guam Tourist Commission recently advertised in the local paper for Guamanian families who would be willing to invite into their homes visiting Japanese students. Only one native family responded favorably, but there were a number of acceptances from mainland American families living temporarily on Guam.

# Peleliu

The justification for 1,950 Americans dying on Peleliu, the southernmost of the Palau Islands, is an unused airstrip almost completely lost now to weeds growing profusely through cracks in the cement. Several hundred yards in from the beach where the Marines landed on September 15, 1944, it is in a stickily humid trough formed by the ridge behind it and the high jungle growth around it. There is no chance the airstrip could be used again in war since it is too short for long-range bombers and would need expensive resurfacing for jet fighters. It is even of doubtful value as a tourist attraction. The few who come to the Palau Islands usually get no farther than Koror, 30 miles to the north.

Peleliu is 7 miles long and 2 miles wide, and its basic topographical tedium is relieved by the spiny ridge of rock that runs its length. At low tide the beaches on the eastern side are wide expanses of mushy white sand bordered by a coastline of tough coral reefs. The fighting for the airstrip, begun by the First Marine Division and later pursued by the 81st Infantry Division, lasted one month, and it has been called by military historians the fiercest single-division battle of the war. The American casualties included 7,000 wounded, while the Japanese lost 11,000 men on the coral barriers and the fractured rocks of Bloody Nose Ridge. The controversy is still unresolved as to whether the cost in lives was worth the taking of the island.

Peleliu became a military objective in 1944 because of its location along the route of the island-hopping American forces.

The strategic debate was whether to proceed to Japan through the Philippines or to bypass them and go on to Formosa. Mac-Arthur argued the Americans had to liberate the Philippines to honor the commitment made to 16,000,000 Filipinos when their country fell, and for the invasion of the central Philippines, Mac-Arthur insisted Peleliu and its airfield first had to be captured. Nimitz, however, wanted to bypass the Philippines, take Formosa, and break the Japanese line of communication and supply between their homeland and their forces spread out in Asia and the Central Pacific. When it was decided the Americans would take the Philippines, landing there in the fall of 1944, Nimitz concurred that Peleliu was necessary as a staging area for the invasion of Leyte.

For the defense of Peleliu, the Japanese drastically changed their battle tactics. No longer did they plan to commit most of their troops to the beaches. Instead they established positions in 30-foot-high coral ridges, honeycombing them with fortifications in the hope of repelling the invaders in a counterattack.

On the morning of D-Day, Peleliu was burning from fires started by twenty-four hours of naval and air bombardments, including the dropping of canisters of napalm on the high ground. Walter Afflitto, a Marine platoon sergeant with combat duty in Guadalcanal and New Britain, was in the first line of amphibious tractors pushing off from the transports. He saw Peleliu burning and told his men they would probably be off the island by nightfall. But when the tractors were about 60 yards from the beach, the Japanese opened with machine gun fire. Afflitto's tractor was temporarily stalled on an underwater coral reef, and the driver shouted over the whine of bullets that he couldn't get the boat off. But Afflitto forcefully told the man to keep trying, his responsibility being the forty-eight men of his platoon huddled on the bottom of the tractor protected by the metal plating.

With a wrenching motion, the tractor scraped over the reef and was steered to within ten yards of the beach. Rather than having the driver stop there and drop the ramp, presenting a concentrated target of men to the Japanese, Afflitto ordered the Marines to jump over the sides, and they waded through the waist-deep water until they could crawl up the coral beach. It was then the Japanese hit the Marines with mortar fire.

Afflitto saw a ridge of coral about 7 feet high some 20 yards in from the water, and he told his men to get behind it, but in

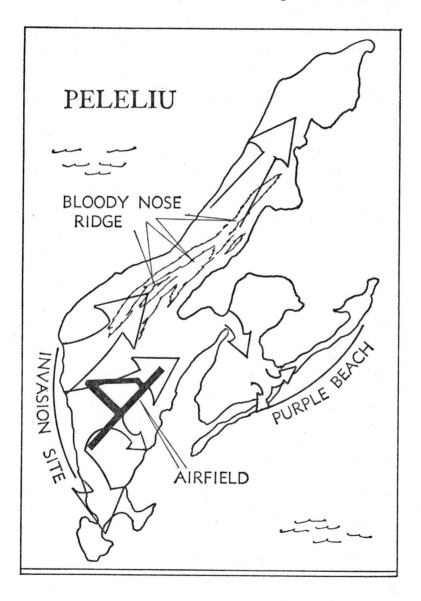

the stumbling charge over the coral a half-dozen men were killed, among them the corpsman and the Marine carrying the platoon's largest weapon, a Browning Automatic rifle.

"We couldn't see the enemy. There was nothing to fire at. The Japanese had dug themselves into the coral ridges. I picked up the Browning rifle and waited until I saw a few Japs running around helter-skelter in front of me about seventy-five yards in from the beach. They were probably trying to change defensive positions. I fired at them and saw a couple go down."

Afflitto's platoon had come ashore at 8 A.M. and by noon had reached their first day's objective, the side of the airfield nearest the beach. It was an unprotected clump of weeds, and the Japanese fire on the position was murderous. His men were being slaughtered. "I told them to take as much coverage as they could, even if it were nothing more than a vine or a tree branch." A Marine next to him had his left shoulder shot away, and in front of him a close friend took a bullet directly into his navel. "He had a hole in him the size of a melon. With the corpsman dead, I was giving first aid, and I remembered I wasn't supposed to give a man with a stomach wound any water. But I knew my buddy was dying, so I held him in my arms and gave him water from my canteen and two sulfur pills. He told me he was dying and asked when I got back to look up his family. He was coherent up to his last breath, and then he just died, went limp in my arms."

In the wait for further orders, all but eighteen men of Afflitto's platoon were killed or wounded.

Afflitto moved back from the weeds and with a friend took cover in a hole in the coral. The two men were inside resting when they heard a rumbling noise. Afflitto peeked over the edge and saw a small Japanese tank, with two armed men strapped to the sides, moving down on them. "We threw aside our weapons and took as much coverage as we could in the hole. We pretended we were dead and held our breaths while the tank came right up to the hole, and the driver turned the gun barrel down into it so it was no more than three feet away from our heads. I have never been so scared in my life. I didn't have time to think or even say a prayer, I was so scared. Then the driver suddenly backed the tank away. He probably thought we were dead and didn't want to waste a shell. Also, the hole was of such an irregular shape that he couldn't have run us over without getting the tank stuck."

There were six other Japanese tanks near the airfield, and the Marines asked for air support to get them. American carrier planes swept in low over the beach, strafing the tanks and accidentally killing some of the Marines, Afflitto said. But several of the Japanese tanks were crippled, and one of Afflitto's friends, a man from Brooklyn, leaped on top of one, opened the turret and threw grenades inside. He slammed the lid but took the force of the grenade blast in the stomach, seriously wounding himself.

The few men left in Afflitto's platoon stayed on the beach side of the airstrip overnight. The next day they were ordered to move across it, and in the dash over the open concrete, Afflitto was shot in the shoulder. Because the bullet smacked into a metal plate he was carrying under a shoulder strap, he suffered only a superficial flesh wound.

During the first week the platoon stayed in the vicinity of the airfield, going out daily on patrol. There was very little action, and that limited to sporadic rifle fire and light artillery barrages.

In the second week Afflitto's platoon was directed to take the ridge, and the men began to climb up the stony footpaths through trees and bushes shredded by the gunfire. On the side of the ridge the Japanese had constructed pillboxes in caves, and each had to be taken in close-quarter fighting with rifles and grenades. As the platoon neared the top, American ships offshore laid down a support barrage that dropped on the wrong side of the ridge, and the Americans were caught in a crossfire between the enemy and their own men.

In the trek up the ridge, the commanding officer, a young first lieutenant, was killed and Afflitto took command. "I was not very military. I tried to lead the men by being a prankster, making jokes."

When they reached the top of the ridge, Afflitto found he had lost six more men from his original platoon.

Down below, in a valley, twenty Japanese were wandering as

if lost. "We began tossing grenades on them and all but two or three were killed."

For his leadership on the ridge, Afflitto was awarded the Silver Star for "heroism and intrepidity in action against enemy forces, and with disregard for his own safety aided the wounded and assumed command of his platoon when the platoon leader was killed."

Afflitto said, "The Japanese were very tenacious fighters, but they became directionless when they lost their leaders. It was the exact opposite of the Marine. He was an individual fighter, taught to assume command if his officer was killed."

After the battle of Bloody Nose Ridge on November 24 and 25, the island was considered secured except for mop-up operations. Even though they lost almost every man on it, the Japanese rated the battle of Peleliu a victory because they had tied down 42,000 Americans and a sizable naval task force.

A scrap metal company has cleared much of the war debris from Peleliu, and it has regained the serenity expected of an untroubled Pacific island. Rusted barges and guns are gone from the landing beach, but the terror experienced there came not so much from the visible enemy and his weapons as from the Japanese who had burrowed themselves into pits in the coral reef, waiting until the Marines were almost upon them before poking up their rifles and firing.

A single lane of tracks worn into the grass of an elevated bank leads from the beach to the airfield. Shaded by trees, the road has stretches of white sand, mucky at low tide, flanking it. This road levels out beyond the sand swamp at the airfield, and it passes the side of Bloody Nose Ridge with the caves still above the field. At the entrance to one there is a pile of human bones capped with a dented Japanese helmet.

For years after the war, the side of Bloody Nose Ridge was covered with an impenetrable growth of trees and bushes, but a few natives have cut a path over fallen logs and around massive boulders to the top where there is a stone memorial to the U.S. infantry, reading, LEST WE FORGET THOSE WHO DIED.

It is still an exhausting climb. The humidity is trapped within the jungle growth, and the air is an unbreathable mass of stillness. In places torrential rains have reduced the path to an ankle-deep ravine, and in parts it is so steep one has to grab hold of low-lying branches and pull oneself up to move on. So few tourists make the climb that there are still mortar casings and empty rifle shells from the war left undisturbed at the side of the path. The monument at the top of the ridge is gradually decaying. Stones from its base have been removed, some of the letters from the legend have fallen off, and it is now practically concealed by a leafy covering.

Between the airstrip and the village on the southern bend of the coast is a natural cove of green water. After the war the Americans sailed surplus landing barges here and sunk them in a shallow watery grave. They are still there, emerging ghostlike at low tide, their sides decomposing into oxidized orange flakes, their bottoms a mat of sand.

Peleliu remains a very remote battlefield to reach. The only access is by water, and the fastest route is down from Koror outside the coral barrier where the sea is made rough by waves cresting before they beat down on the reefs. An open launch, the most popular means of transportation to Peleliu, is easily tossed about and slammed down into the troughs, drenching the passengers.

But inside the coral reef the ride in a waterway through deserted mushroom-shaped islands, wearing tight caps of rope vines and green fan leaves, is stunningly beautiful. These are called Rock Islands, and the work of erosion and sea urchins cutting away their water level has given them their distinctive, squat-necked shapes. A few of the Rock Islands have beaches, narrow protrusions of sand and palm trees on which boats can be grounded while passengers, using masks and snorkels, float over the coral reefs, dipping under the water's surface to investigate the tremendous variety of fish and rock formations on the crystal-clear bottom. Some of these islands have huge natural caves which were used by the Japanese as storage bases, and a few are still filled with piles of corroded tin containers and rotting wooden boxes. One of the larger ones was used as an ammunition dump, and the front wall over the entrance and the inner sides are still black from the explosion and fire that occurred when the Americans blew it up.

For tourists who really like to go native, one of the Rock Islands near Koror has wooden huts on the edge of a wide beach that can be rented for weekends. This island is without water and electricity, and guests must bring everything with them from fuel to food.

The voyage through these primeval Rock Islands is almost sensual. Their beauty has been unchanged by war, and the sight of them in the morning, rising serenely from a purple mist on the calm water, is a source of joyous satisfaction.

At Peleliu the one serviceable dock is near the village on the northern end of the island where the Japanese built a narrow concrete pier. The water is constantly smooth because it is funneled through a natural channel between two islands. Off to one side is a Japanese barge half-covered by the drifting beach sand.

The one paved road on the island was built by the Americans after they captured Peleliu. It has been kept in excellent condition, possibly because there is so little vehicular traffic passing on it. Several small trucks cart supplies up from the dock to the village, and a few beat-up passenger cars, their paint pitted with white marks left by the salt air, can also be found.

Most of the island's two hundred permanent native residents live in the village, which is dominated by a community center, open with no side walls, under whose pointed thatched roof rows of backless wooden benches lie in front of a raised platform where the business of the village is conducted. A school across the street is in rather dilapidated condition, its color faded by the hot sun, the storm shutters half off, and one wing unfinished. Near the school is a small store with very few items on the shelves other than American soft drinks and chewing gum. Most of the native men make their living from the sea, the main source of food for Peleliu. A few crops are grown, but many more have to be imported by boat from Koror.

Ringing the uncut lawns and squares in the center of the town are houses put together from surplus war matériels, the most popular being tin from Quonset huts flattened into ribbed wall panels. Also converted into a private home is a stone blockhouse, built by the Japanese and left intact by the battle, except for some gunshot holes in the front.

There is another airfield in the Palaus, on Babelthuap, the largest island in the chain and located next to Koror. From the air it is an unnerving sight, a strip of coral and concrete bowed deeply in the middle and plunked down on a leveled-off hilltop. The plane lands on the strip as if it were hooked to the tracks of a roller coaster, dipping and rising quickly before slamming to a halt at what passes for the terminal, a group of parked trucks and native women under umbrellas around a table for customs officials. There is no shelter from the sun for those waiting for the plane. About a half mile away is a bombed-out two-story Japanese bunker where the luggage is stacked for the departing guests.

Since no bridge connects Babelthuap and Koror, the only way other than plane to get across the small channel with its vicious current is a cable ferry. On alternate days the cable breaks and an ancient ferry, carrying only two cars each trip, is put into service. The regular ferry can haul up to seven cars a trip. If the old one is in use, the two-minute water trip can be preceded by a two-hour wait at the end of the dirt road from the airport where a line of traffic piles up. And the road from the ferry to the town of Koror, a distance of only three miles, presents an almost unsittable voyage over potholes and mound-high ridges that diminish the expected life of a new car to six months.

Koror has one major hotel, a distinction it has achieved not because of any great service it offers but because it has the only decent restaurant—it is air-conditioned and the soup is safe from a can—and a bar in the lobby. The hotel is an insubstantial one-story tin structure with tissue-paper-thin walls separating the rooms along one long corridor. When a person speaks in a room at one end, he can be heard from a room at the other even with the door closed. Only two rooms have private baths, and if you happen to be sleeping next to the communal bathroom, the flushing of the toilet sounds like Niagara Falls. The rooms are furnished sparsely: a bed, a dresser and a bug light in the closet which can't be turned out unless you break the bulb. Most of the rooms have sinks with water that runs whenever workers are not accidentally destroying the pipes that connect the town with the water reservoir.

The bars in Koror close officially at midnight, but the hotel shuts down all its operations at 10 P.M. when the staff locks up and goes home. This proves to be a problem if a guest happens to be out for the evening and has left his key in the hotel office. He must then climb on a chair, break the screen in the transom, crawl halfway through the opening, swing his upper trunk low and in the same motion, with one hand, swipe the key off a rack on the wall beside the locked door.

Koror officially comes awake at 6:30 A.M. with a common reveille, a long, wailing siren sounded from the town hall. Shopping in town can be done in a half hour. There are several stores modeled on the American supermarket. Most of the shelves are taken up with native wood carvings. The food supply is short on variety. Almost everything is frozen and shipped in from Hawaii. Fresh vegetables and fruits are exorbitantly priced. Fresh milk and eggs are scarce. Canned foods are cheaper and easier to come by.

Having been awakened at dawn, the visitor finds there is very little to do on Koror. The tourist attractions are few. There is a museum behind the town hall with a room of wood carvings and displays of native boats. Outside, there is a Japanese tank beside the school's volleyball net. Connected to the town hall is the local jail where the inmates make story boards, the most exportable item from Koror but one that has difficulty getting by customs. The stories are quite racy with most of the male figures adorned with enormous erect phalluses and the women with exposed genitals. In the tales of Koror, sex has replaced superstition as the best way of warding off evil spirits and natural catastrophes.

There are no good bathing beaches near the town. It is imperative to meet someone with a boat who can sail a guest to one of the outer beaches. The best one is around the cove from the town and was used in the Hollywood movie *Hell in the Pacific*. A wooden shelter was built on it by company carpenters and a litter of camera bulbs and paper wrappings was left. But skin diving off the beach is still superb.

The Palau chain is the westernmost part of the Caroline Islands and is in the territory known as Micronesia, over which the United States acquired jurisdiction after the war in the Pacific. All totaled, there are more than 2,000 islands in Micronesia, with some 100,000 natives living on the 100 that are habitable, including Saipan in the Marianas, the capital of the American Trust Territory of Micronesia. The Micronesians are a mixture of Polynesian, Mongoloid and Negroid races.

Most of these islands would be considered primitive by Americans, lacking as they do electricity and rudimentary sanitation facilities. But much of the attractiveness of Micronesia is its isolation from conventional consumer civilization. Days can go by without anyone knowing about current affairs. Few of the islands have newspapers, and only some have radio stations, with greatly curtailed broadcasting schedules. It is at first distracting, then rather pleasant, to realize one can exist without knowing what is happening in the outside world.

For the United States these islands have both a military and a tourist value, and a not-too-subtle tug-of-war is going on between her and Japan for their control, an issue to be resolved in a United Nations-sponsored plebiscite. Both countries obviously want the territory. The United States sees its military importance, especially if she rolls back her front-line defense from Okinawa and Vietnam. Japan, which is barred from having an army under the constitution imposed upon her by the victorious Americans, sees Micronesia as a gigantic business investment. The older Micronesians, born and raised under a benevolent, progressive Japanese administration in the years after World War I, would like to go back with Japan, while the younger ones, educated at American schools and tuned into the social mores of American teen-agers, want to become part of the United States.

The Japanese government can't publicly speak out on this issue since the territory was lost because of a war Japan started. Besides, it would be almost indecent to seem too greedy at a time when negotiations are being completed for the return of Okinawa.

Recently the Americans offered Micronesia a commonwealth status similar to that of Puerto Rico's, but this was rejected in favor of a self-governing "free association" status with the United States, which in turn was vetoed by the Department of the Interior, which is technically in charge of the administration of Micronesia.

If American liberals want a new cause, they can investigate Micronesia, which has been given shabby treatment by the United States ever since she received the trust territory under United Nations authorization. The Americans living there have exposed the Micronesians to the presumed good life of fancy electrical appliances and electronic gadgets, yet the islanders have not been given the economic means to buy washing machines, transistor radios and cars, even if they had the electricity and the roads for them. After the war the United States made no attempt to revive the agrarian economy which was developed under Japanese rule and has done little to improve the daily life of the natives. A few more schools have been built and some of the local health services improved, but the United States is not willing to spend very much on Micronesia. The annual budget for this operation is $50,000,000, of which a large percentage goes for the salaries and transportation of trust territory workers.

The most promising way of improving the economy of Micronesia is through tourism. About 25,000 Americans traveled through Micronesia last year, and an increase of another 5,000 is expected this year. The recently organized Micronesia Tours, Inc., with its headquarters in Saipan, will take a tourist to almost every inhabitable island in Micronesia, most of them now serviced by Micronesia Airways. However, traveling this airline is in itself an experience. A weekend trip to Koror from Guam can last much longer since planes have a recurring habit of not returning on the expected day.

Where Koror's share of the current budget goes is not readily discernible. The main road is an abomination. Though there are a few new classrooms and a new community cafeteria is being built across the street from the hotel, the dormitories for boarding high school students remain a scandal, with toilets backing up and overflowing constantly. The Americans contend

they are providing adequate facilities but that the native youngsters don't know how to use them.

The report prepared by Micronesia's locally elected officials
in which free-association status was requested stated that a commonwealth solution would fall "well below the minimum
standards of self-government acceptable to the Congress of Micronesia, the people of Micronesia and the United Nations."
Charging that Washington sees in Micronesia only her "security
interests," the report continued, "under our present quasi-colo-
nial system, the identity, individuality and dignity of the people
of Micronesia are being suppressed.

"American power and influence are currently so dominant
that Micronesia and its people are being 'Americanized' at an
ever-increasing rate. This is having a tremendous effect upon all
aspects of Micronesian life and society, and it will be impossible
to control this influence until the people of Micronesia can establish their own government."

Some local native chiefs, however, have learned to live with
the Americans, adopting business ways learned at the feet of
their masters. Getting a car off the dock after it has been shipped
in from the mainland may cost a few extra dollars in port taxes
imposed on the spot. Any number of these hidden taxes are uncovered by Americans as soon as they receive shipments from
the States. When one native working for an American-owned
tourist agency refused to pay the money to get a new bus off the
docks, it stood there until he paid up.

The uncertainty of Micronesia's future has created some tensions within the American community in Koror, numbering just
under two hundred people, most of whom work for the trust
territory government and now call this Palau island home.

A certain Hemingway-type personality is attracted to places
like Micronesia because here, in direct confrontation with nature, he can operate with fewer restraints. One such in Koror is
Peter Wilson, a robust, gregarious man in his early forties who,
as the director of the marine biological laboratory, is currently
in charge of a project very important to the future of Koror and
all the islands in the Palau chain. The coral reef protecting them
from the devastation of severe storms is being slowly destroyed

by an invasion of starfish which are stripping off the hard covering of the reefs and subjecting them to the adverse effects of tidal erosion. Not only will the islands be exposed to the full force of the typhoon waves if the reefs go, but the fish will be driven from the still waters within the lagoon created by the reefs, and with them will vanish the source of fresh food.

Wilson and a team of divers, several of them from the Peace Corps mission, swim down to the reef each day and kill starfish with hypodermic needles shot from guns. In one month Wilson and his men killed more than seven thousand starfish.

A native of Hawaii, Wilson married a fashion model from his home state and brought her here ten years ago. They now have three boys, and they live in a comfortable house on a hill with a splendid view of the harbor. Their life is very pleasant. The work is not too difficult, and the discomforts from the shortages of food and things to do are compensated for by the joys of raising children in the outdoors. When he is not in his office, Wilson is often on his boat off the islands, fishing with his family, stopping to water-ski or to skin dive. Most of their social life is constructed around entertaining at home, and Wilson's living room, ventilated by breezes off the hill, is equipped with an excellent stereo system and has one wall containing an extensive library of paperback books, most of them well thumbed from being passed around the American community.

Not just his job but his imposing, vigorous physique has given Wilson a stature in the American community, and often on public issues he automatically becomes its spokesman. Wilson has been on Koror long enough to know he wants to make it his home. He doesn't plan to leave the trust territory unless the government reassigns him to another Pacific island. But, like most of the older Americans on Koror, he is disturbed by the Japanese encroachments and believes the United States is not sufficiently aware of the threat.

And Wilson is almost always annoyed with the activities of the Peace Corps volunteers who are great advocates of bringing participatory democracy to the natives. These young idealists are dedicated to the liberal principles of democratic self-government and hope to convert the natives to them without any philosophical or even practical groundwork.

The only newspaper on Koror is a weekly mimeographed newsletter put out by the local antipoverty agency, run by young Americans with a native staff. The paper is stridently anti-American, proving again that some of the most anti-Americans in the world are Americans. In one issue the paper eagerly reprinted the testimony of a Peace Corps volunteer before a U.N. investigating team visiting Koror.

The corpsman said, "Your coming every three years is not helping anything around here. You have to have an observer every day on that hill [the residence of the high commissioner] to keep those people doing what they are supposed to be doing.

"Every year that you come around roads get built, schools are repaired—everything looks fine and dandy but after you leave we return to the same old conditions."

Wilson takes offense at this because, like many Americans living abroad in underdeveloped countries, he doesn't have the disdain toward the natives that would make him a really good colonialist in the mold of the old British imperialists. While he doesn't socialize with many natives—the American community bands at a clubhouse where community meals are served several nights a week followed by the showing of old movies—he works with them at the laboratory and supports programs of economic self-improvement. However, the Peace Corpsman thinks the Wilsons on Koror are patronizing anachronisms from the era of American imperialism in the Pacific.

# The Philippines: Victory

## LEYTE

*On this occasion of the return of General MacArthur to Philippine soil with our airmen, our soldiers and our sailors, we renew our pledge. We and our Philippine brothers in arms—with the help of Almighty God—will drive out the invader; we will destroy his power to wage war again, and we will restore a world of dignity and freedom —a world of confidence and honesty and peace.*

—FRANKLIN D. ROOSEVELT

A set of footprints in a square of cement marks the official location where the Americans landed on Leyte to fulfill the pledge of General MacArthur to return victorious to the Philippines. Because tourist business is scarce on Leyte, an island more than 300 miles south of and a two-hour flight from Manila, villages on the eastern coast still argue over the exact site where the American landing barges first came ashore on the morning of October 20, 1944, when seven hundred ships and 174,000 U.S. soldiers and sailors participated in the invasion of the Philippines. The troops struck almost simultaneously at four places on an 18-mile section of the Leyte coast, including its capital at Tacloban and a village which has since been renamed MacArthur. To settle the argument, the beach where MacArthur himself waded ashore at Palo, a few miles outside of Tacloban, has been designated Red Beach, the place where the Americans returned. About noon on the day of the invasion, MacArthur, his pants still wet from sloshing through knee-deep water, stood in front of a radio microphone set up on the sand and said to his Filipino audience, "People of the Philippines, I have returned. By the grace of Almighty God our forces stand again on Philippine soil. . . . Rally to me. Let the indomitable spirit of Bataan and Corregidor lead on. . . . For your homes and hearths, strike! In the name of your sacred dead, strike! Let no heart be faint. Let every arm be steeled. The guidance of divine God points the way. Follow in His name to the Holy Grail of righteous victory!"

Two years before his death, MacArthur paid his last visit to the Philippines and came to Leyte to put his footprints in cement across the street from a soft drink stand named Red Beach. A multimillion-dollar memorial has been proposed for Red Beach, but with the Filipino treasury always skirting bankruptcy, nobody expects it to be erected soon. On the site now is a tall stone obelisk flanked by two smaller tablets honoring the Americans and Filipinos killed in the battle of Leyte. The sidewalk around the obelisk is fenced off by a chain and some scraggly shrubs. Nearby, hulks of landing barges are partly submerged in the beach sand.

Every October 20 the Filipinos reenact on Red Beach the invasion of Leyte. It is a realistic show with soldiers splashing through the surf from landing crafts and dodging detonations exploded in the shallow water and on the beach. The 25th anniversary of the invasion, celebrated in 1969, turned out to be an extravaganza. Parachutists from the Filipino army were used for the first time, and the American military participated by lending a mine sweeper.

Back up from the beach through a grove of coconut trees is a swamp of rice paddies, and over this ground American paratroopers were dropped in 1944, placing them behind the thin line of Japanese pillboxes on the beach. There was little initial Japanese resistance to the invasion; that came later in the mountains of Leyte where more than twenty thousand Japanese lost their lives.

The road from Red Beach, passing through the rice fields, graveled and rutted, is in almost the same condition as when it was built by the Army engineers. It is now lined with native straw shacks, almost every one of them with naked children playing in front, and it has been renamed MacArthur Boulevard.

Several miles in from the beach is the Cathedral of Palo. The original cathedral, used at the time of the invasion as a hospital for wounded Americans, was torn down after the war, and all that is left is a gilded altar carved from Filipino hardwood. Like most of the churches in tropical climates, this one has open doors and windows and birds swooping freely over the altar at the worshipers kneeling at the railing.

Since the war, Leyte's tranquil rural life has been restored, and most of its 1,200,000 peasants live from earnings made on small farms. The future for the province is not promising. It will probably remain plagued by extreme poverty, with the natives living in one- and two-room shacks, their food consisting of what they can get from the fields, trees and sea around them.

"While not many peasants are starving," a Leyte health official said, "malnutrition is a major problem on the island." The number one killer disease, however, is tuberculosis.

On most other islands of the Philippines, the larger, wealth-producing farms are owned by absentee landlords with the peasants living on them as tenants. On Leyte, most of the peasants own their own land, even if it is only an acre or less. "We have no problems about land reform in Leyte," an official said. "We have no rural capitalists here. We are an outpost of civilization, and the men here are not as greedy as they are in Luzon."

The crops that are not locally consumed are exported, a difficult process. They have to use a middleman who controls the prices paid the farmers and sometimes gets a 100-percent profit on the marketing. The peasants are often indebted to the middleman because he usually owns the local stores and a peasant will get goods on credit only if he promises to sell his crops through the middleman. Private farm cooperatives, some of them administered by the church, have been attempted, and all of them failed. However, the provincial government is planning to start a marketing cooperative for copra, rice, corn and sugar. Fish is also exported, but only to other provinces in the Philippines.

Farming is not financially rewarding. The average agricultural income is 500 pesos a year, about 125 American dollars.

Tourism, as it is to other Pacific islands, is a possibility for bettering the economy. "I don't know why American tourists wouldn't want to come to Leyte," a provincial government official said wistfully. "It is the scene of the greatest American military victory in the Philippines."

Tacloban is not a typical tourist town. It has no first-class hotel or decent restaurant. Native crafts there are not systematically marketed, though at the harbor there are several shops selling grass-woven floor mats and wall decorations. Still there are things to see in Tacloban. There is a lumpish building near the harbor which was the provisional capital of the Philippines from October, 1944, to February, 1945. It now has attached to its front wall a gold relief of the scene of MacArthur coming ashore. There is usually a civil servant inside the building, even on weekends, to show visitors the rooms where MacArthur directed the fight for Leyte and the chamber where the provincial legislature now holds its governing sessions. There is also the University of Leyte, a collection of functional buildings grouped around an athletic field. But housed inside one is a fine collection of artifacts from Leyte's ancient civilization: broken pottery, arrowheads and crude maps of the water routes off the island. There are also very nice beaches south of Tacloban, and on one secluded stretch the president of the Philippines has a cottage to which he can go for long weekends. There is nothing on either side of the house but fine black sand and palm trees majestically reaching toward the sea, bending to it but never touching the surface, the curve of their trunks arched gracefully by the wind.

The climate, though extremely warm in the dry season and unbearably humid when the rains come, is much nicer than in Manila, and the natives are the most genuinely friendly of the Filipino people. Nonetheless, there is, almost predictably, anti-American sentiment on Leyte, particularly among the young government workers. The older Leyte natives remember that in the days before the invasion the Americans dropped leaflets warning them to evacuate the beaches. One old man said fondly,

"We saw the American planes come and we heard the bombing of the beaches. We knew the Americans would soon liberate us because a few days before the landing an American submarine dropped off some sailors on the beach and they passed out chewing gum." Another old peasant said, "The Americans are still liked on Leyte. They behaved well here after the invasion."

But the war has been over for many years, and the men born after it know America from what they read in the newspapers: how U.S. business controls most of the real wealth in the Philippines, and how U.S. servicemen stationed at Clark Field and Subic Bay get drunk and rape Filipino women.

A young official in the Leyte provincial government said he once believed with blind faith everything good said about the United States. "But then I read a book by a white American in which he described the lynching of an American Negro. I cried. Since then I've been able to make a difference between the stated ideals of America and her actual performance not only at home but all over the world."

The Philippines gets financial aid from the United States from both private and public sources, but very little of this money now comes to Leyte, and the little that does rarely trickles down to the peasants. One private American group continues to send primary school books. "But these books are useless to us. They are written by Americans for Americans, and the life shown in their pictures is the life lived in the United States, not the one lived here by poverty-stricken natives," the government worker said. "Americans want us to see them the way they do. But the children don't understand the part of America they see in these books. It is so alien to their own standard of life."

He said this while having lunch with an American guest at the governor's residence in Tacloban. There were three courses to the meal. A peasant woman carried to the table platters heaped with fresh fish, rice, and pieces of chicken and vegetables floating in a thick sauce. While he spoke, an American tape cassette played American music, the background for the movie *The Graduate.* Outside the dining room on the open veranda the peasants continued to line up to seek redress for a life over which they have little control. Along the curb were parked several long black Mercedes, and beside them stood armed guards waiting for the government officials to emerge from the residence.

The Americans almost didn't come to Leyte in the fall of 1944. The original plans called for the invasion to take place on

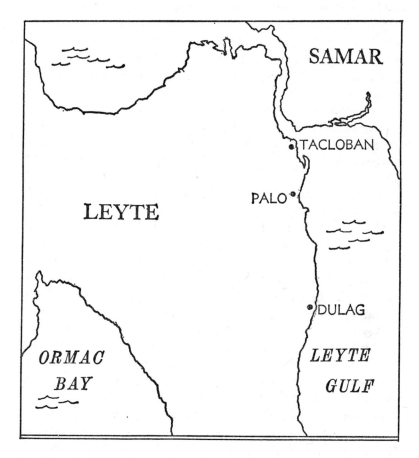

the island of Mindanao. But when, in his forays along the coast with his carriers, Admiral Halsey discovered a lessening of Japanese resistance from Leyte, he advised the landing at Mindanao be canceled.

In the first five days of the invasion, 145,000 Americans came ashore with another 55,000 to arrive later. Within three days, a large beachhead had been established. The airfields at Dulag and Tacloban were taken the day after the invasion, as was the town of Tacloban. But the beachhead was not really secure. At the end of the second week, the Japanese managed to land 20,000 soldiers to join their original garrison in fighting in the mountains and swampy plains, and this ground fight, prolonged by the rainy weather, continued through early 1945.

As if they knew the Americans couldn't be stopped once they came ashore, the Japanese decided to go after the fleet bringing them to the beaches. Four days after the invasion of Leyte, 64 Japanese ships sailed into Leyte Gulf to engage 216 American ships in one of the great naval battles in history. It contained everything from gunfire between facing ships to submarine attacks and air strafing. It also had the first kamikaze attack of the war.

In the late sixteenth century, when Japan was about to be invaded from the sea by the Chinese, it didn't have the military force to resist. But, as the legend goes, a Heavenly Wind in the form of a typhoon was sent by the gods to do what the Japanese couldn't, and the wind drove the enemy back to their own coast. "Kamikaze" means "Heavenly Wind," and it was a last desperate act for the Japanese to send their best pilots to dive their planes into the American ships.

The Japanese strategy was first to attack the U.S. Third and Seventh fleets on three fronts over a 500-mile stretch and then to get past the ships to drive the American soldiers from the beaches. One group would draw the carriers of Admiral Halsey north, another force would strike through San Bernardino Strait, and the third group would attack through Surigao Strait.

The first U.S. ship to be hit was the carrier *Princeton,* and before it was sunk by the Americans, rather than have it captured by the Japanese, 450 sailors were rescued. Then, in the riskiest maneuver of the battle, Halsey headed north with his Third Fleet of sixty-five ships to seek out the Japanese carriers, leaving the American ships in San Bernardino Strait largely unprotected. Fortunately for the Americans, the Japanese had practically no land-based planes.

The first full-scale engagement was at Surigao Strait, and through torpedo attacks by the destroyers, this part of the Japanese fleet was demolished. It was a night battle and the last in which air power would play no part. It also marked the last use of the battle line formation, in which ships send continuous salvos against each other, sometimes at point-blank range. Air power would make this naval formation obsolete.

The main force of Japanese ships sailed through San Bernardino Strait into Leyte Gulf on October 25. Though the Japanese inflicted severe damage, the attack was prevented from becoming a disaster by the application of the superior American air strength and the relentless mobility of the American destroyers of the Seventh Fleet which moved in and out of a smoke screen to confuse the Japanese. Halsey was urgently requested to return, and he did so after his ships finished off several crippled Japanese vessels, without sinking any of their carriers. Meanwhile, though, the surviving Japanese ships had slipped through the undefended straits and escaped.

Still the Japanese losses were devastating: four carriers, three battleships, six heavy cruisers, three light cruisers and eight destroyers. The only losses for the Americans were one light carrier, two escort carriers and three destroyers. After the Battle of Leyte Gulf, Japan's fleet was finished. Her carriers were sunk; and, without them, the six remaining battleships were of no value.

By Saint Patrick's Day of 1945 the mop-up of the Japanese on Leyte was reasonably complete. In the opening battle on land and sea in their return to the Philippines, the Americans suffered 15,584 casualties, of whom 3,508 were killed.

At the Tacloban airport, the American tourist waited for the early-evening flight to Manila. A Filipino boy, not much more than five or six, was shining shoes in the small restaurant which served sandwiches and soft drinks next to the main terminal building. He spoke English and said he didn't go to school because his mother had just died and his father was unemployed and all the children had to do something to make money. It was a sad story, and after the American tipped well, the boy picked up his shoeshine box, walked outside, and spat disgustedly on the ground.

# THE LIBERATION OF MANILA

War lives for men as a collective remembrance. This is how Jack Higgins remembers the liberation of Manila:

"We landed at Batangas, Luzon, in May, 1945, and our mission was to truck matériel from the port there to the depots at Manila, seventy-five miles to the north. The port of Manila was unusable, some four hundred vessels of various types had been sunk in the bay and their masts stuck up out of the water like trees from a swamp. The highway, a two-lane macadam road, was pockmarked with shell holes, and the seventy-five-mile trip often took a truck convoy four or five hours.

"Manila itself was a mess! Every government building was destroyed, partly by Allied bombardment and partly by Japanese demolition to deny us the use of the buildings. General MacArthur set up his office in the front section of the badly damaged city hall, and he could be seen entering it every morning, wearing his familiar cap, sunglasses and open-collared shirt.

"The Jones Bridge over the Psaig River had been dropped into the water by bombs, and the Army engineers had built a Bailey bridge alongside of it. A long line of trolley cars had been burned at their depot in the center of the city and their tracks had been torn up.

"There was no gasoline for civilian use and the principal means of transportation was by *caratelas,* the two-wheeled buggies drawn by ponies. The few Filipinos who had owned cars before the war had buried them in mounds of dirt and hidden them from the Japanese. The power plant in the city had been destroyed and the streets after dark were an eerie sight.

"Still, it used to give us a warm feeling when riding around the city to have the natives run after us giving the victory sign and calling, 'Victory, Joe. . . .'"

In liberating the city from February 3 to March 3, 1945, the Americans engaged the Japanese in hand-to-hand combat and close-range artillery gun duels, and block after block of the city was leveled. In the ruins of liberation was born some of the bitterness that has since contaminated relations between Americans and Filipinos. After the war the Filipinos asked both countries responsible for the destruction of Manila to pay reparations. Japan agreed but the United States balked, arguing that she had already sent men and material not only to reconquer the island but to assist the country's postwar rehabilitation. The Filipinos resented America's not paying for what they thought was her share of the destruction.

The American administration of the Philippines ended after World War II, but the Philippines has remained very much an unofficial American colony. Her economy continues to be dominated by American business, a condition perpetuated by her constitution. To get American financial aid, excluding reparations for the destruction of Manila, the Philippines agreed to have written into her constitution a provision giving American companies parity rights in exploiting the country's natural resources. To many Filipinos, the persistent poverty of their country can be explained by the United States' continual drain on the profits from the few wealth-producing industries and resources in the Philippines.

The disparity of wealth in the have-not nations of Asia is very apparent in the Philippines. The average weekly income of many Filipino males is barely a few American dollars, and their naked, ill-fed and uneducated children roam through the slum streets of downtown Manila. But a newspaper can report that a girl from one of the few families controlling most of the country's wealth was paying $12,000 for a wedding dress. The grossly unequal distribution of wealth, shaping Filipino society into a pyramid with most of the Filipinos mired in its base, is a legacy of the American rule which left the country psychologically and economically maimed. Many Filipinos remain wards of America's clumsy attempt at European-styled imperialism, and it should be a lesson for those today who want to have Americans again stationed throughout Asia.

Time has eased from the minds of many Filipinos the memories of friendly, sincere GI's handing out cigarettes and candies during their liberation march up from Leyte to Luzon. The younger Filipinos, having been born after the war, never possessed these images of kindly young Americans. They see now only the tourist and the businessman coming not as friends to their country but as potential exploiters. These Filipinos see the affluent Americans in their hotels and shopping centers, their brothels and nightclubs, and they know more than most that it is an American era and what their place is in it.

The following interludes are with two young Filipino males who are uniquely typical of those born in the post-liberation years in the Philippines and whose lives are so tenaciously connected to Americans.

## INTERLUDE ONE

The plane banked effortlessly, went into a circle as if attached to the smooth rim of a gently spinning vortex, and then leveled over the concentration of night lights below. It was an early-evening flight from Leyte to Manila and the round-faced Filipino stewardess, her steps restricted by a tight, plain skirt, walked down the aisle asking passengers to buckle themselves into their seats before the landing. She was especially solicitous to a young male Filipino sitting at a window seat near the middle of the plane.

In a country decimated by government corruption, overpopulation and poverty, the young man was among the chosen of the Philippines, and it was understandable why the hostess had selected him for her attention. Until recently, his father, a respected businessman from one of the country's ruling families, had been a cabinet officer in the government of President Marcos, and though almost every Filipino government official is eventually accused of civic wrongdoing, his father had retained the respect of even the most cynical of his countrymen.

The youth attended the University of Leyte, a southern island province governed by another of his relatives, and he often flew home from school on weekends to visit his family and friends in Manila and to go to the better restaurants and clubs—the enclaves of the wealthy Filipinos that encircle the rotting core of the city. Because of his connections with the national airline, he had traveled on several occasions to Europe and the United States.

He carried himself with the sophisticated casualness of one secure in his place in society, yet he was not indifferent to the conditions of his country and the rampant poverty among his people. He was knowledgeable about trade deficits, balance of payments, diseases of the natives, and inadequate schools. And his dress, a starched white shirt worn outside his solid-colored dark pants, was traditional with all classes of Filipino men: It could not separate him from the people of whom he spoke with the abstractions of those who think of men collectively when trying to determine what is good for them individually. He was very much like the young men attracted to government service in Washington in the first days of the administration of John F. Kennedy. Politically liberal, he, like many of the disciples of the Kennedys, was also a nationalist, believing his country's culture had something to offer other countries. He sounded very much like those New Frontiersmen who piously believed American idealism could be exported.

This young man doesn't feel indebted to America for liberating his country, and he would now support any government policy that would lessen American domination. Although he wants to enter government service after he finishes his studies, a goal easily obtainable since his family holds positions of power in both the national and provincial governments, his plans are vague. In his middle twenties, he is older than most of his classmates, who earlier that day on the campus moved out of his way as he walked with an American, publicly treating him with the respectful detachment of those who know their place.

The plane made no further circles of the Manila International Airport and slowly descended through the humid night air until it touched down on the ribbon of concrete. When it stopped at the ramp near the terminal, the passengers, most of them peasants from Leyte, waited, without being told to, in their seats until the young man and his foreign friend made their way to the back of the plane. Then they got up and fell in line behind, carrying with them packages wrapped in soiled brown paper and fresh vegetables in baskets of cord. Before the door of the plane was opened, the young man put on dark glasses, a disguise that failed to confuse the hostess or the airline official outside, who nodded courteously to him, welcoming him with words made silent by the idling engines of the plane.

While most of the passengers stood on the sidewalk outside the terminal waiting for cheap transportation to Manila via dingy painted buses, the young man went to a taxi and gave the driver the address of a house in an exclusive residential development across the boulevard from the Intercontinental Hotel in the Makati section of Manila. The entrance to the development, at the end of a long drive from the boulevard, is barred by a gate raised and lowered on command of an armed guard, and then only after the driver is identified or, as in this instance, the passenger in the taxi is known. The houses are mostly low stone structures lying behind voluptuous dark-green bushes. The only visible light at the young man's address was extended from the ceiling of the carport. After the taxi door was slammed and feet were heard shuffling up the driveway, the door to the kitchen opened a crack, revealing a man holding a pistol. When he identified the new arrival as the son of his employer, he warmly greeted him and put the pistol away in a holster tied to his hip.

The rooms inside were sealed from the world by heavy shutters. As the guard disappeared into another part of the house, his steps lost in the clinking sound of the air conditioner, the young man went to his room and flipped on the television set in a console built into one wall. His back was turned when a picture of a dead Vietnamese peasant emerged through the wavering white lines on the face of the set. He went into his private bathroom and changed from his simple white shirt and dark pants into a smartly tailored suit that snugly fitted his lean chest. He tied a wide knot in his tie before once more putting on his dark glasses, then returned through the kitchen to the carport, slipped across the smooth leather seats of the Mercedes to the driver's side, and steered the car down the dark driveway.

Driving across the boulevard to the shopping center in front of the Intercontinental Hotel, he arrived at one of the city's better restaurants. It specializes in native dishes and is very popular with wealthy Filipinos when they entertain American business acquaintances. The restaurant is in a one-building complex that contained another restaurant featuring a floor show and an arcade of small, expensive boutiques. Its design was vaguely Spanish: white stone walls, heavy, dark wooden tables and chairs, and vaulted doorways. The clientele was decidedly young. It was a Saturday night and the young of the wealthy, driving their own cars, often ate here before proceeding to the fashionable night spots. Most of them chattered in English, and their taste in food was more American than Filipino: milk shakes, Cokes, thick steaks and hamburgers. The one concession some made to their Filipino heritage was the wearing of barongs, the starched white shirts worn without ties and outside the pants, the intricacy of the lace designs on their fronts providing the formality of neckties and jackets in the West.

The young man knew many of the customers, particularly the girls, and he greeted them without standing as they passed, his recognition being a barely perceptible nod and a wink that became a slow-moving, heavy shadow on the lens of his dark glasses. In their dress and hair length, the girls effected the modish international look of the rich that changes as quickly as one can turn pages in a fashion magazine. In the background, overdressed call girls, their faces held in somnolent smiles by cementlike white makeup, listened impassively to the small talk of their equally bored escorts, who often were the thuggish, moon-faced army and police officers who are the bodyguards of the country's status quo.

The table conversation was about the young man's future: an attractive job in the government, frequent trips abroad, and marriage with good connections, if he desired it. Shining through all was a youthful idealism to reform the national government. There is a good life for this young man in the Philippines. He was living life well and was able to move freely among both peasants in their hovels and the upper class in their homes and exclusive restaurants.

After the meal the young man took the wheel of his Mercedes and dropped his foreign friend off at the entrance to the hotel.

The young man then proceeded alone to a supper club before going back to his family's home, past the road barrier, the armed guards and the vicious dogs prowling the grounds—the inconveniences wealthy Filipinos accept to give them a sense of security in a country threatened perennially by rumors of revolution.

# INTERLUDE TWO

There are other young Filipinos who are barely able to make a living, and one of them was waiting in front of the hotel. He was a few years older, but still under thirty, married, with a child. Standing in a parking lot in front of a line of polished American cars, he was one of the several English-speaking drivers who worked for a tourist agency.

The Philippines is not the most popular country in Asia for American tourists. There is a grapevine for international travelers, usually the airport waiting rooms and the lounges in the front cabins of the superjets, and the reports circulating through it about the Philippines are generally unfavorable. The crime rate is intolerable; murder of police officials in rural towns north of Manila is commonplace. The Huks, Communist-led guerrillas, are still active in the provinces. An airline representative said his American-owned company was not having jets remain overnight in Manila because several hostesses had been raped on the streets. The city is fearfully run-down, filled with dirty-faced children begging shamelessly for American dollars.

Yet, like most Filipinos, rich and poor, the young driver found his livelihood inexorably tied to the United States. His economic survival depended on the American tourist, and his subservience to foreigners had conditioned him to wear an emotionless expression consisting of an open smile encircling white teeth. He impartially displayed it to matrons from Ohio with blue rinse in their hair and brash, cynical journalists from the East Coast.

His English, if not spectacular, was serviceable. Though it had a limited number of usable nouns and adjectives, the vowels kept dropping from the verbs, giving them a lisping sound at their endings. But his smile prevented Americans from becoming too annoyed. Politeness toward Americans abroad is difficult to find, and when it is displayed, its bearer is quickly adopted.

There are not enough tourists to justify the number of drivers standing idly in the parking lot, but the men must wait there for the few who do come. The drivers arrive at the hotel early in the morning, often before the darkness is drained from the sky, and they leave late in the evening when they have safely brought the last foreigner back from a naughty club or driven him to the night flight from Manila.

This young man was born and raised in one of the slums that twist through the heart of the city, corrupting its streets with foul-smelling garbage and the murderous instincts that are bred in the despair of the poor. He believed his chance of escaping the poverty of his parents and their parents was to advance in the government-sponsored tourist business. It was a matter of pride that he advance himself. His wife was a schoolteacher, and her weekly salary was higher than his. He considered his wife more intelligent because she had gone to college, but he could increase his stature if he brought home more money.

His salary is meager; the major source of income is tips; and those drivers who speak passable English naturally make the most since they are in greater demand. Being a tourist driver is a seven-day-a-week job that leaves him very little time for his family; on a few occasions, however, he has phoned in sick and taken his wife and child to a public beach. He has almost no hope of ever making enough to move his family to a spacious middle-class home in the flat lands outside the city, but he recently moved them from a wooden shanty to an apartment. Although it has only two rooms, running water and electricity were available, and these represented a tremendous step up.

Even so, he could not escape the sights of his past, for all roads in Manila eventually go through slums where old women carry their clothes and dirty dishes to the gutter to wash them in water from a fire hydrant and where children dart from behind parked cars to beseech foreigners for a few coins.

Throughout the tour of the city, he remained protective of the welfare of his passenger and refused to stop his car at Tondo, the most notorious of the Manila slums. But this young man couldn't disguise his feelings about Tondo. His reaction was stronger than embarrassment for his country and the way many of her citizens are forced to live; it was a disgust common among those who have raised themselves, if only slightly, above the conditions in which they were born. It almost bordered on snobbery, but it was tempered by his genuine concern for the poor Filipinos.

There were instances when the young man's loyalty to his countrymen and his passengers were tested, and the most severe test was in front of the presidential palace, usually a quiet tourist attraction. On that day, however, it presented a scene of turmoil, with students nailing revolutionary posters to unpainted sticks and youths running recklessly among the passing cars. One boy in his early teens came up to the young man's car and pressed his face against the closed window on the passenger's side of the front seat, a motion which distorted his features into a grotesque shape. Through puffy lips he shouted to the American to go home.

The young driver's foot hovered over the gas pedal, waiting to slam it down if the youth showed signs of committing an act of violence. He said he was sorry for the words of the youth, not condemning the cause or the actions of the students as much as apologizing for the conditions of his country that made rudeness against guests a frequent occurrence. But the boy's belligerency was reduced to the mute formations of his lips into an "o" and his fingers into a clenched fist, a gesture whose threat of harm was reduced by his youthfully thin fingers.

As the young man moved his car away from the boy, he said, "I should not have brought you here," and said it in a subdued voice with a genuine sorrow in eyes usually rounded by hopeful anticipation of the best. "They don't really mean anything. They're too young to understand what they are told to say by the troublemakers. But they can be dangerous if led too far."

Through the rear window of the car, the youths were seen hoisting their hand-drawn placards over their heads and beginning a slow circular march in view of the armed palace guards standing behind the gates. The guards attempted to give the appearance of disinterestedness without ever permitting their glance to range away from the demonstrators.

The car went around the corner and down a boulevard of cheap movie houses, their fronts barricaded by grilled gates in the morning, and dingy counter restaurants where pieces of dark meat rested on grease-encrusted flat stoves. They were watched over by old persons trying to establish a connection with life by placing themselves in the middle of a city's daily activity.

The morning editions of the English-language newspapers were out, and boys who had neatly folded each paper moved down the line of cars stopped by a traffic light. They pushed a copy through the open windows, intimidating passengers into buying one. Other children spread their papers over the sidewalk on mats in the shade of the shopping arcades.

The young man drove his car down a street walled on both sides by unimposing, multifloored buildings. "This is a school where there was rioting," he said, referring to an event of the recent past which had already lost its preciseness by having since been repeated at other schools. In this particular demonstration, however, several students had been killed by the police. A man from the slums, still young, though aging is more rapid among the poor, he sympathized with several of the demands of the students. He knew corruption permeated Filipino society from the greedy rich with bank accounts in Switzerland, the universal protection against revolution, to the poor whores working with male accomplices to get unsuspecting tourists into dark alleys. He was almost schizoid in his reaction to the repeated promises of a good life in the Philippines. He knew the life of the mass of his countrymen was bad, yet he lived in dreams of the future based on his ambition of being his own tour director, dealing with affluent Americans who would pay him the money to get his family farther away from the slums, someplace halfway to the wealthy residential homes. His expectations had been raised by his contacts with Americans and his viewing, in Hollywood films, of the way Americans supposedly lived. His survival as a man depended on his being able to fantasize about a life removed from the mayhem and corruption around him. Driving daily down the crowded, filth-littered streets that abound behind the few lovely boulevards of Manila, he could cling to the American promise of a better way of life for those who worked honestly by their hands, and he believed in this more than he did in the rhetoric of the professional radicals and the zealous students.

He was witness to daily tableaux of affluence. Standing in the hotel driveway while black limousines discharged prosperous Filipino businessmen, he saw the rich go into the arcade shops to buy, at inflated prices, shirts, dresses, jewelry and wood carvings, both sacred and profane. On the shelves of even the exclusive gift shops are statues of saints next to those of a man in a barrel, who, when the barrel is lifted, springs an erect phallus. He saw customers take the hotel elevator to plush restaurants where an abundance of meat and shellfish are served in rooms of red velvet wallpaper while Filipinos in stiff tuxedoes move slowly among the tables plucking out familiar melodies on their violins. He saw the hotel guests stroll to the pool and adjust fashionably lean bodies on lounge chairs, their sweat making dark stains on the cement.

He was not a part of this rarefied life. He only had his movie houses. He took his wife to those that were in the shopping centers near the wealthy residential areas, and there, in the darkened hall on a wide screen, he renewed the dream that made him as equally representative of the new young Filipinos as were the students rampaging in front of the presidential palace.

But even the image of the American was being diminished in the new Filipino films. One of the more popular ones recently was about a Filipino guerrilla band fighting the Japanese during World War II. The real villain in it was not the Japanese conqueror but an American sailor stranded on Luzon after the American defeat. He bullies and murders his way into command of the band and, once its leader, proceeds to rape the dedicated, pure Filipino heroine in front of her father, later repeating the act on the grave of her father whom he has murdered. The American ends up a frothing lunatic who has to be shot down like a mad dog. The Filipino audience burst into spontaneous applause when the American was killed.

One of the difficulties of living with this untainted dream of the American good life is that it had removed the young man from the actuality of the government that represented him. Steve McQueen was more important to the essence of his life than was his elected senator. And he could drive past without acknowledging the massive presence of the government buildings on the less-populated side of the Psaig River. These buildings are on flat fields cleared unnaturally by the shells and fires of the battle for Manila at the end of the war. Many of the government offices have already been moved to Quezon City, the new capital of the Philippines, and the lethargic steps of the pretty female workers, immaculate in short white dresses as they move on the sidewalks fringed by sun-scorched grass, indicate the diminishment of activity within the government buildings, evidence of a further drain on the vitality of life in Manila.

The one place of reasonable social activity in this area is the Hilton Hotel, a walking distance from the government buildings, where the first-floor bar is the meeting place of foreign businessmen. But even the hotel is vulnerable. It is located near where student demonstrations take place, and to vent their anti-Americanism, the young periodically throw rocks through its windows, knowing it is safer to attack an American corporation abroad than to attempt a personal confrontation with the U.S. Marines guarding the American Embassy on the shores of Manila Bay.

The young man was asked to take his American passenger once more along the street ringing Tondo, and he grudgingly did so. It had to be seen and recorded permanently in memory: the naked, listless children and violent armed men, garbage banked around the utility poles that bring light only to the fringes of Tondo, and, above all, the overpowering stench. It is there, in Tondo, not in the lobby of the Intercontinental Hotel, where the rage will build until someday it could conceivably break through the barriers of indifference erected by the church and corrupt governments. There where a genuine revolution would start, and all that would be left of the young man's dream of attaining peacefully the better life would be a river of blood from the bodies of countrymen and former allies.

The one factor uniting these two young Filipinos, the rich, anointed child of a frightened oligarchy and the poor childlike aspirant to the practically nonexistent Filipino middle class, was the history in this century of the special relationship between the United States and the Philippines. This common history makes these two young Filipinos brothers to the future.

# Iwo Jima

In his command headquarters on Iwo Jima, in a cave on the ash-gray slopes of Mount Suribachi, General Tadamichi Kurbayashi knew the war was lost. All that was left for his men to do was fight and die courageously for their country. Aware that theirs was a lost cause, he sat down at his portable desk and wrote to his wife and children in Tokyo: "No one here expects to return alive. Do not plan for my return."

The Americans would come to Iwo Jima—one of the Bonin Islands about 750 miles south of Tokyo, halfway on a straight line between the Marianas and Japan—because of its two airfields, from which the Japanese were sending up fighter planes to harry American B-29's on their daily bombing runs to the Japanese mainland. In addition, the Americans needed the airstrips to provide a place where disabled bombers could make emergency landings and as a base for fighters to accompany the B-29's on their runs to the major cities of Japan.

All the Japanese could do now was slow down, not stop, the American advance. With the fall of Saipan, the Japanese inner defense perimeter had been breached. Their troops and ships couldn't drive the Americans from Leyte, and the Americans were in Luzon. On February 15, 1945, the southern tip of Bataan, where the infamous Death March had begun a little less than three years earlier, was taken, and the next day infantry parachutists were dropped on Corregidor to engage in an appallingly fierce battle which left 4,500 Japanese dead.

In his letters that February, Kurbayashi showed himself to

be an intelligent, dedicated, professional soldier doing his duty. He devised a battle strategy for the defense of Iwo Jima which he hoped would take such a toll on American lives that the enemy might give up its plans to invade the Japanese mainland. He spoke glowingly of the plan to his subordinates and in his letters to his wife. It was similar to the defense plans used on Peleliu, of which the general was unaware. Instead of trying to stop the invasions at the beaches with fanatical banzai charges, his men would wait for the Americans in a system of seemingly impregnable underground fortifications which could survive constant sea and air attacks. The plan appeared sound during late January and early February when, for weeks before the invasion, Iwo Jima was struck almost daily by U.S. land-based aircraft from the Marianas. Some 6,800 tons of bombs were dropped on an island only 4½ miles long and 2½ miles wide, and still the defenses held.

In his letters, Kurbayashi was obsessed with the physical safety of his wife, son and two daughters. He urged them to evacuate Tokyo for the country, and when they refused, he carefully instructed them in how to bank their wooden home with sandbags, protection against the fire bombs the Americans were dropping on the capital. He predicted the Americans would expand the radius of their bombing attacks to take in residential areas of the city, and he was correct. He also frequently admonished his son for his bad spelling, fretting that he wasn't being properly educated.

Yet in every letter there was the same fatalistic mood. He was a professional soldier, and having lived by the military code, he knew he had to die by it. Death by suicide was the ultimate payment the soldier made for the shame and dishonor of defeat. "Do not plan for my return," he said over and over again.

He wrote his letters at night, after the 21,000 men in his garrison had gone about the tedious business of seeing that defenses, already long completed, were kept in working condition, testing shore batteries, releasing bursts of machine gun fire into the empty sea and, when this was done, going through a half hour of vigorous calisthenics before eating their ration of rice and sake and writing nightly what might be their last letter home.

There were now only Japanese soldiers on Iwo Jima. The more than one thousand Japanese civilian farmers who had been there until the previous year, raising sugar and pineapples, extracting sulphur from the volcanic ash and operating a rudimentary sugar mill, had been evacuated in late 1944.

After ten weeks of almost daily bombardment, the Americans arrived on February 19, 1945. Edward Bradshaw, then a nine-

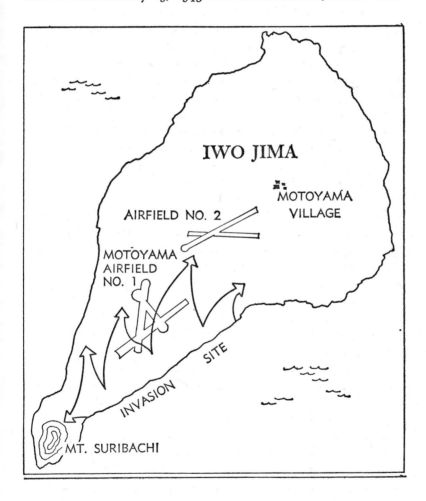

teen-year-old first-class seaman in the U.S. Navy, remembers that morning: "I was a coxswain on a landing craft, and I was in the fourth wave bringing in a mortar attachment with a senior officer. The boats on either side of us got hit by mortar fire from the beach and all I could see was everything flying, and a machinist on our boat shouted above the noise that we were in the range of the Jap mortar fire. I steered the boat too close to the shore and the back end of it was hit by a mortar. We managed, however, to make several more runs between the ship and the beach, a distance of one hundred yards. We kept the craft afloat by pumping out the water by hand pump.

"What I remember of the beachhead that day was the black volcanic ash, and one young Marine lieutenant standing up to draw the enemy fire from his men. Miraculously, he wasn't hit, but the guys in the foxholes around him were getting killed right and left."

The Marines almost didn't make it ashore. The men had expected firm footing on the beach after a smooth ride in. Unlike the Pacific atolls, Iwo Jima, a volcanic island, was not surrounded by a coral reef. Instead, the beaches were covered with soft volcanic ash rising at places to create walls 15 feet high. The landing barges couldn't gain any traction on the ash and kept banging into it futilely, their ramps unable to be lowered. Bobbing like toy targets in a shooting gallery, the barges were easy prey for the Japanese firing from their intricate network of gun emplacements in the caves. These gun positions were so cleverly camouflaged that the Marines had to come ashore to see them before they could radio their positions to the ships offshore.

Thirty thousand Marines landed on Iwo Jima the first day, but not before 519 were killed (47 more were to die from wounds suffered in the first assaults on the beaches). Newspaper correspondents who arrived with the first combat troops reported there was greater violence than usual to the bodies of the dead. Many of the corpses were not intact, with arms and legs found up to 50 feet away from the torsos.

Bradshaw: "On one of our runs after dark that first night we had to wait at the side of the ship to load up, and doing nothing there, the boat finally sank. Another landing craft came over to us and we were pulled out of the water. We weren't in it for more than a few minutes when this craft was hit by fire and we were back in the water again. This time we stayed there for several hours, hanging onto the floating wreckage. Then we were picked up the second time, and I spent the first night off Iwo Jima in the engine room of the ship trying to keep warm."

The fight for Iwo Jima became a continuous series of personal encounters between Americans and Japanese in the caves and tunnels on the side of Mount Suribachi. Casualties on both sides increased frighteningly. The Americans had expected to secure Iwo Jima in seventy-two hours. Instead, the battle wore on and progress was measured in the inches it took to climb the high ground around a volcanic crater of Mount Suribachi at the southern end of the island. (The northern part of the island is a plateau with inaccessible rocky beaches.)

Once again, Edward Bradshaw: "A few days later we heard over radio communications on our landing craft that the Marines had reached the top of Mount Suribachi and were raising the American flag. I grabbed the binoculars from a guy standing next to me and I watched the whole ceremony."

There were really two flag raisings on top of the volcanic crater on February 23. The first was done by a Marine sergeant from Florida who had raised a very small battle ensign, about eight feet long. Then, about 10:30 that morning, five Marines and a Navy corpsman hoisted a much larger one aloft on a pole, and the photograph of these six men pushing the flag upright against the stiff wind sweeping across the crater top, taken by Joe Rosenthal of the Associated Press, became probably the single most famous photograph of World War II.

Of the six men who participated in the event, three of the Marines were killed within two weeks on Iwo; the fourth Marine, an American Indian, was found frozen to death on his reservation ten years later. Of the two survivors, the Navy corpsman lives today in Wisconsin, and Rene A. Gagnon works for a travel agency in Manchester, New Hampshire.

"The Marines had been pinned down around the base of Mount Suribachi for four days," Gagnon said. "On the morning of the fifth day, a Marine detachment began to climb up the side. Halfway up, the reconnaissance patrol lost contact with the men at the base, and I was sent up by myself to bring the patrol a radio. The footing wasn't bad. The side was hard lava rock and there was only occasional Japanese sniper fire.

"We then proceeded to the top. We knew a small flag had been raised, but our patrol leader had given us a big one and said when we got to the top to fly it. The raising was not staged by Rosenthal as it's been charged. We did it on our own."

Beginning in late February, the Marines began to push north, herding the Japanese into a small corner of the rugged part of the island, pushing them back from Mount Suribachi. By mid-March, knowing the rest of the island was about to be overrun by the Marines who were crawling to within sight of the entrance to his cave, Kurbayashi knelt on the ground and plunged a ceremonial sword into his stomach.

The Japanese had died as they had fought, fanatically and with utmost loyalty to their emperor. Of the garrison, only 216 men were taken prisoner; the rest died in the caves and on the sides of Mount Suribachi. The toll of American lives was equally horrible. In the three Marine divisions committed to the battle for Iwo Jima, there were 21,000 casualties, of whom at least 4,500 were fatalities.

After winning it in one of the bloodiest battles of the war, the United States formally returned Iwo Jima to Japan in late 1968. Reclaimed by wild vegetation and rising slowly each year —26 feet since the war—from the sea, a geological phenomenon being watched closely by scientists, the island's only function is as a weather and navigational station, and two small detachments of Americans and Japanese live near each other at one end of Iwo Jima.

The U.S. contingent consists of thirty-five Coast Guardsmen who send around-the-clock navigational information to ships sailing between the Marianas and Japan. A tour of duty for these men is one year. There are no accommodations for families, and they live as men without women, getting one seven-day pass during their tour.

The Japanese keep a fifty-man detachment from their Maritime Self-Defense Force. Although they now have no military units, the Japanese do possess internal security troops, and the group of navy men on Iwo Jima maintains a radio communications center for ships and aircraft.

Because of their isolation, the Americans and Japanese have to more than coexist to make life comfortable. The men have organized an international baseball league, playing a regular schedule between the units. They swap movies, which is an advantage for the Japanese: The Americans get a new movie each night. They exchange books. The American base library has several thousand volumes. And, most importantly, they exchange language classes.

Each American has his own air-conditioned room in the one-story concrete bunker, and almost everyone has a stereo set. But the Americans don't have an unlimited supply of liquor and are allowed only beer, while the Japanese can have anything. This promotes cooperation and instant friendship on a very meaningful level.

"The relations between the Americans and Japanese on Iwo Jima today are more than formally polite," a Coast Guard officer said. "They actually are quite good. The men seem to enjoy each other's company."

Their numbers were recently increased when a Japanese construction firm sent out a few men to help resurface the airstrip which had become pockmarked by erupting sulphur vents.

Under the terms of the treaty returning Iwo Jima to Japan, the Americans were awarded a daily supply of fresh water, up to 2,000 gallons of rainwater collected in huge vats, and unlimited use of the airstrip, the single most valuable piece of real estate on the island. The 7,000-foot-long runway provides the only regular contact with the outside world. For the Americans there is the weekly Coast Guard flight on Friday, bringing in supplies and mail. It is difficult for an American civilian to get on this flight, which stays on Iwo only an hour before returning to Tokyo. The military has to grant permission, and then the authorization is subject to change. A civilian was bumped from one Friday flight because the plane was carrying explosives to be used by the Coast Guardsmen on an excavation project.

The Japanese flights are less regular, but are equally anticipated.

The treaty also gives the Americans right of access to their
two memorials on the island. One, near the Japanese camp, was
carved in the side of a rock after the war by an ex-Marine. It is
a large Marine Corps emblem topped by a U.S. flag, and around
this a list of names of those who died on Iwo. The other memorial is on top of Suribachi, and it was the only one there until
late 1969, when the Japanese erected one next to it.

The American memorial is a bronze plaque with the flag
raising depicted on it. It is set in a white stone. The Japanese
memorial is a simple black marble stone. Next to these two
monuments, the flags of both countries are now flown.

Mount Suribachi was permanently disfigured by the Americans after it was captured. A volcanic island, Iwo has only one active crater, Suribachi, and the Americans, afraid it might erupt,
showering lava down on them, sent engineers into the crater to
blow out one side so that the comb would tilt toward the sea.
If Suribachi erupts now, the lava will presumably run harmlessly away.

There are a few war relics still on Iwo Jima. Several rusted
Japanese battery guns are directed toward the sea where 60,000
Marines prepared to come ashore, and live ammunition remains
hidden in the brush. The Coast Guard reports that fires are
frequently started in the dry vegetation by ammunition ignited
by the hot sun.

While the bodies of the American dead were almost immediately taken off Iwo, many skeletons of Japanese soldiers still
can be found in the sealed-off caves in the sides of the ravines
and in the sea bluffs. A Japanese government Graves Registration Commission continues to come to the island to search for
bones of their fighting men.

Every battle has its survivors, and for them there are anniver-
saries to celebrate. The twentieth anniversary of the battle of
Iwo Jima was celebrated in Tokyo in 1965, and Gagnon, his
wife, and their son attended.

"When we got off the plane at Tokyo, I wondered how the
Japanese waiting for us there felt. Among the delegation at the

airport were some of the Japanese who got off Iwo alive. I was worried some nationalist nut might take a shot at us. But as soon as the plane door opened, everyone started to applaud and cheer. It surprised us, but we learned the Japanese are like the Germans. They admire warriors. It doesn't make any difference what side they're on, so long as they won.

"The first Japanese survivor I met was the chief engineer responsible for building the island's fortifications. I asked him through an interpreter if he thought they could have won the battle. He said no when he looked out that morning, saw the island surrounded by Americans, and realized the Japanese couldn't get any reinforcements.

"These survivors, about thirty of them, have their own club, and they made me an honorary member. They even gave me one of their pins."

The veterans from both sides were flown on an American military plane to Iwo. At that time it was still under American control, and the U.S. Air Force maintained some nuclear weapons there. The visitors spent four hours on Iwo and were given a luncheon by the American military brass before they once again climbed Mount Suribachi to stand silently at the memorial.

The 25th anniversary, in February, 1970, was organized by Charles Early, a lawyer from Sarasota, Florida, and Yoshitaka Horie, of Tokyo. Early had been a private in the 28th Marine Regiment, and Horie an executive officer who had been transferred from the island just before the battle began.

Early made a generous gesture, greatly appreciated by the Japanese and reported widely in their press and on television. He invited widows of Japanese soldiers killed on Iwo to visit with his delegation of fifty-four Marine veterans in their Tokyo hotel. "It was the first time in Japan the wives had met their former enemies and it was very moving," Horie said.

Asked to comment about his feelings on the war, Hori remembered a remark attributed to MacArthur when he was head of the American occupation of Japan. The general had supposedly said that the Japanese acted like twelve-year-old children.

"After the war we studied the American democracy. We looked at its economy, education and politics, and we liked what we saw. Now we have a prosperous economy, and the Japanese have become smarter and smarter. Maybe now we are fifteen or sixteen years old."

Was the slaughter at Iwo worth it? Military historians think it was. Before the war ended, 2,251 American Superfortresses made emergency landings on the island, and the line of bombers continued uninterrupted over Iwo Jima, bringing to the Japanese mainland destruction and fiery death from the sky with load after load of incendiary bombs.

But Iwo itself? Is it still the same to one who fought there? "Coming to it once more, this time by air, and not seeing it the first time from a boat, I was amazed how small it has become," Gagnon said.

# Formosa

Throughout late 1944 and early 1945, Formosa was slated to be the next site for a major American amphibious invasion. In preparation for it, the island was blasted almost daily by American bombers. Like Rabaul earlier in the war, Formosa now stood as the greatest, most threatening Japanese military fortress outside the mainland, and it was the home for what was left of the Japanese land-based air force.

Formosa would not be easy to capture, and it was estimated that a number of American divisions would be needed to do the job. The timetable called for the assault to take place in mid-1945. But in the early months of the final year of the war, the Americans, realizing it would take too many men to invade Formosa, chose another Pacific Island, Okinawa, for the next amphibious landing.

Along with Rabaul and Yap, Formosa was thus bypassed, to wither like the others on the strategic vine. But Formosa, now better known as Taiwan, is still very much an American concern and an outpost, in the rhetoric of the cold war, of liberty as ranged against the tyranny of the Chinese Communists. Occupied by Chiang Kai-shek and his Nationalist forces after they had been pushed off the mainland, Formosa received $1.4 billion from the United States between 1951-65, as well as tons of encouraging words from American politicians, who, ignoring the jails filled with political prisoners in Taiwan, saw a moral distinction between the totalitarian aspects of the civil governments there and on the mainland.

Formosa has prospered from American support, with an industrial growth rate of about 15 percent, second to Japan in Asia, and a foreign trade of a billion dollars a year. The per capita income is $189, one of the highest in the Orient. While they would like to take total credit for these economic advances, the Nationalist leaders periodically acknowledge that some of this progress is due to both private and public American investment.

The relative prosperity of Formosa is obvious in Taipei, the island's capital. The shops are filled with consumer goods and crowded with customers until the nightly 10 P.M. closing. As word of the bargains in jewelry, silks and watches spreads among international tourists, more and more of them are making Formosa a day or two stop on a trip between Hong Kong and Tokyo. Consumer goods are not the only reason foreigners enjoy Taipei. An aging white-haired businessman from New Zealand, sitting at the bar in one of the better hotels, said, while stroking the arm of a pretty Chinese whore many years his junior, "This is sure a man's town."

U.S. servicemen stationed here or arriving on leaves from Vietnam have discovered a plethora of bars and brothels with lower prices than prevail in Tokyo and Hong Kong. At the best Taipei hotels, the clerk, while the guest is checking into his room, will ask whether he would prefer a woman for the night or for the length of his stay. If he accepts the nightly rate—a minimum of 20 American dollars for the whole night—the girl will arrive at the room and let herself in with a master key supplied by the enterprising head clerk at the main desk who gets a cut of her profits. There are other hotel personnel in the flesh trade. Each floor has a night clerk with a black book containing the names of enough girls to satisfy even the most sexually jaded tourist. Prostitution is no longer left to the general practitioner; there are specialists for almost every sexual taste.

Whores, old Nationalist soldiers and Americans: These are the leading characters in the street scenes of daily life in Taipei. The American soldiers are everywhere, in civilian clothes, cameras slung over their shoulders, most of them holding hands

*U. S. Army Photograph*

The Americans landed 20,-000 men in twenty-four hours in retaking Guam. *Above:* troops of the 77th Army Division bivouac on White Beach. *Left:* a Japanese mortar on the grounds of Sleepy Lagoon. Today the island is a popular resort with the Japanese.

*Above:* restored row houses seem to stand guard before the suspension bridg
that spans the Sydney, Australia, harbor. *Below:* Sydney's famed Bondi Beacl
where the bikinis are among the briefest and the sands the cleanest in th
world.

The assault on Peleliu, lasting one month, has been called the fiercest single-division battle of the war. *Above:* American planes drop bombs on Bloody Nose Ridge. *Below:* tanks and infantry move in on Japanese fortifications in coral ridges.

*Right:* Americans stand atop Bloody Nose Ridge at monument to the nearly 2,000 Americans who died on Peleliu. *Below:* the rusting remains of war: a Japanese tank in a Koror schoolyard and American landing barges. *Bottom:* the Peleliu invasion site as it now appears.

Leyte, scene of MacArthur's triumphal return to the Philippines. *Above:* American troops unload supplies in Leyte Gulf, October, 1944. *Below:* Red Beach at Palo where MacArthur waded ashore and later exhorted the Filipinos to rally to him and let "the indomitable spirit of Bataan and Corregidor lead on."

In twenty-five years the horrors of life in Manila have changed from the destruction of war to the waste of poverty and despair. *Above left:* American troops move through Intramuros section in wake of bombings which left Japanese fortifications along the Pasig River *(lower right)* in shambles. Lower left and upper right photos are of Manila's huge slum, Tondo.

Four days of bloody hand-to-hand fighting occurred between the time the Marines landed on the volcanic ash of Iwo Jima *(right)* with Mount Suribachi looming in the background, and the moment the men, including Pfc. Rene A. Gagnon *(second from right)*, raised the American flag on the top of Suribachi *(above)*.

The Coast Guard weather station on Iwo Jima today where 35 Americans live, sharing the island with a 50-man Japanese Maritime Self-Defense Force detachment.

*U. S. Army Photograph*

*Defense Department Photo*

*Defense Department Photo*

The final great land battle of the War in the Pacific began on Easter Sunday, 1945, and ended three months later with 100,000 Japanese and 36,000 U.S. troops dead and Okinawa under American control. Photos on these pages show U.S. soldiers and Marines in action clearing out the island as they marched toward Naha and Shuri Castle.

*Above:* Invasion Beach on Okinawa where the Americans, meeting little resistance, secured a beachhead 15,000 yards long and 5,000 yards deep with amazing ease. *Below:* downtown Naha today, completely rebuilt after the war.

*U. S. Army Photograph*

The devastation of Hiroshima was nearly total after the detonation of the first atomic bomb over the city on August 6, 1945. This photo was taken 550 feet from the explosion's hypocenter.

*U. S. Army Photograph*

Aftermath of the holocaust: A temple archway stands amid the ruins of Nagasaki, target of a second atomic blast on August 9, 1945. *Above right:* Hiroshima's Industrial Exhibition Hall, the only building permitted to remain standing today in the same condition as it appeared after the bombing. *Below:* A simple mound in the Hiroshima Peace Park covers the remains of unknown victims of the bomb.

*Below:* American B-29 Superfortresses drop incendiary bombs on a Japanese target. One of the severest incendiary attacks occurred in Tokyo March 9, 1945, when 2,000 tons of such bombs burned out 15.8 square miles in the center of the city.

The victims of the atomic blast buried, the hope remains that it was the only such attack the world will ever see. *Above left:* Nagasaki's sole official monument to the blast is this somewhat grotesque statue. *Above right:* Japanese students toll the Memorial Peace Bell in Hiroshima. *Below:* a cylindrical memorial in Hiroshima's Peace Park to a fourteen-year-old victim of the bomb who died of leukemia.

with pretty Chinese girls they have bought for the duration of their leaves, dragging the women, almost as if they were excess baggage, from one shop to another. For voracious Americans, the wares are plentiful: pirated copies of American best sellers marketed for a quarter of the price they sell at in the States; jade, somewhat inferior in quality, but still cheaper than that sold in Hong Kong; lacelike ivory figurines; and fancifully designed tablecloths.

This is the new prosperous Taipei, where everything not nailed down is for sale. But there is another, more poignant aspect of the city. In a park across the street from the Nationalist headquarters, a massive building with a lumberingly dull façade, some of the lesser officers sit at lunchtime under a small pagoda near the dried bed of a man-made stream. There are almost as many lines in their faces as in their soft brown uniforms, and their voices are unobtrusive against the street sounds of midafternoon. They carry a certain dignified stoicism that goes with being a permanent exile, and the park is where they come to escape from repeating the official hope, made more illusive each year by reality, of returning as conquerors to the mainland. Deceptions are not necessary in the park for these weary, aging veterans with no more wars to fight.

There are also in Taipei American Army officers and their wives, brash and slick, produced almost as if by an assembly line. Everything must eventually give way to the arrogance which is theirs, the arrogance of the liberators. One afternoon, the youngish wife of a junior U.S. Army officer rammed her private car into an Army truck in front of one of the main hotels. A military policeman immediately ordered tourists on the sidewalk not to take pictures, threatening to confiscate the camera of one American who had snapped several before the orders were barked. The American woman was not visibly flustered. Everything was being taken care of. She was an American abroad in a country made safe by the American presence on it.

Though down from its high of $100,000,000, the current yearly American military budget for Formosa stands at $40,000,000. There are 8,800 American servicemen stationed on the island, none of them combat troops, or so the American military insists. Most are in the Air Force at Chuan Kang Air Base in central Formosa.

What the American economic and military muscle in Taiwan is defending is hardly a democracy. There is only one effective political party, the Kuomintang, headed by the ancient Chiang. Free speech is curtailed, especially if it comes from the mouths of political leftists. There are political prisoners—some estimates are as high as 6,000. There are only 2,000,000 Chinese mainlanders on Taiwan, compared to 9,000,000 Formosans; but the latter have little or no voice in running the government, though they are drafted into the Nationalist Army to serve the government's aims.

The one outpost where almost every able-bodied man on Taiwan eventually ends up for a tour of military duty is Quemoy, a name vaguely remembered from the 1960 United States Presidential campaign debates between John F. Kennedy and Richard Nixon. This island is in the entrance to Red China's Amoy harbor, a Nationalist Chinese fortress staffed by aging officers who know they will probably never go home again to the mainland that is only a few miles away.

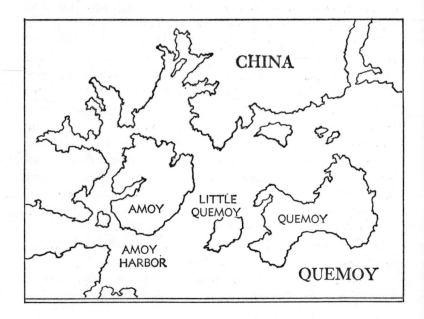

The more celebrated conflict of the past decade in Asia has been in Vietnam, but one continues here between Nationalist and Communist Chinas, and it has tragicomic overtones.

The Chinese Civil War ended in 1949 with the flight of Chiang and his forces to Taiwan, about 150 miles off the mainland in the East China Sea. In their retreat the Nationalists stopped to claim the offshore islands of Quemoy and Matsu, the latter lying farther to the north, and these islands have proved to be an ideological bone stuck in the throat of the Red Chinese.

A state of paper war exists now between Quemoy and Red China. Every odd night the enemies exchange volleys of nuisance shells, which, when they explode, shower propaganda leaflets. It makes no difference that the shells don't carry live ammunition; the sound of their coming through the darkness, leaving a whistling trail in the sky, can be equally terrifying. There hasn't been a serious shelling of Kinmen, the accepted Chinese name for Quemoy, since 1958, and no attempt has been made by the Red Chinese to invade the island since 1949.

That year 20,000 Communist soldiers in wooden boats crossed the few miles of water separating Quemoy and the mainland. They were met by a withering artillery fire and charged by Nationalist soldiers on the beach. In a two-day battle, 8,000 Communists were captured and the rest killed.

The last major shelling of Quemoy was in the late summer and early fall of 1958 when 479,910 rounds fell, killing 400 civilians and destroying 3,000 small farms.

The senior American military adivser on Quemoy in the winter of 1970 believed that the United States was committed, morally if not by a signed treaty, to defend Quemoy against any Communist invasion from the mainland. Colonel Robert Barber of the U.S. Army acknowledged, however, that the 1954 treaty between the United States and Formosa did not include Quemoy and Matsu in the protective shield provided by the United States. When he took over his assignment on Quemoy in June, 1969, Barber said it was his understanding the United States had "tacitly" agreed to defend Quemoy, and he believes this position is justified. One of the reasons, he said, is that the Nationalists hold two tiny islands near Quemoy, and from them a binocular surveillance can be made of the port of Amoy, the third largest on the China coast. If there is any preinvasion build-up of Communist forces there, Nationalist troops on Quemoy and Formosa can be alerted. Besides, the presence of Nationalist soldiers in Quemoy ties down an estimated 250,000 Red Chinese soldiers in neighboring Fukien province.

Barber also insists Quemoy has propaganda value. Though there is a 10 P.M. to 5 A.M. nightly curfew, there is no black-out, and he thinks the night lights from Quemoy are torches of freedom for those on the mainland who might be considering the possibility of defecting. Last year 40 mainland Chinese came over, bringing the total to 4,000 in ten years.

Barber is strongly anti-Communist with an uncluttered faith in simple cold war morality. He believes Formosa and Quemoy should be defended by Americans if for no other reason than that the Nationalist Chinese are pro-American and the Chinese on the mainland are Communists, and thus our enemies.

One of the commitments to the Nationalists is the patrol of Formosa Straits by the U.S. Seventh Fleet. This doesn't mean, however, that ships are permanently stationed in the straits. The fleet roams freely over the waters of the Far East, and in October, 1969, the only U.S. ship in the straits was an 1,850-ton radar picket ship.

There were once several dozen American military advisers on Quemoy, but now there are only seven, including a naval corpsman, and a further reduction is expected in the already-minuscule American garrison. The Americans there live in a compound in the middle of the island. The married men are not permitted to have their families with them during the year's tour of duty, and their hostel here is much like any bachelor officers' quarters in the States. There are individual small rooms off a long, bare corridor, a dining area and a recreation room with bamboo furniture and stacks of popular record albums and best-selling paperback books.

During an evening when Barber was entertaining some Chinese Nationalist officers and an American visitor, the sound track music from the movie *2001: A Space Odyssey* came roaring out of the corpsman's room, drowning out the cold war dialogue between the officers. The corpsman sat with legs folded under him at the head of his bed. The wall over him was decorated with framed pictures of the female nude centerfolds of *Playboy* magazine, and next to them were lists of girls' names with various check marks against them, indicating the degree of sexual success. Under the bulletin board was a set of weights for body building. The twenty-seven-year-old corpsman said he thoroughly enjoyed duty on Quemoy, especially the frequent weekend trips to the fleshpots of Taipei. He planned to ship over for an extra six months on Quemoy, though he considers himself nonpolitical and feels no animosity toward the other Chinese only a few miles away.

If the futuristic music made the cold war recede temporarily, the sentries deployed outside didn't, and after 10 P.M., acting on orders, they lunged out of the darkness to challenge drivers at certain checkpoints. In that evening, between the American compound and the village of Kinmen, a distance of five miles, one car was stopped ten times.

The Chinese Nationalist Army has transformed Quemoy into a maze of underground fortifications of such strength and diversity that the U.S. military advisers believe it could withstand any sea invasion started today by the Red Chinese—if the Nationalist lines hold instead of disintegrating rapidly as they did in the last year of the Civil War. The island is covered with armed sentinels, camouflaged pillboxes, antiaircraft guns, and miles of slit trenches protected by rolls of barbed wire. Spiked poles also are stuck in the water just beyond the beaches, their tips bent toward Red China, which at some places on Quemoy is only a mile and a half away.

Despite all this, Quemoy in the daytime has a semblance of normality. The civilian population of 60,000, most of whom either work for the military or are peasants, go about their business, the farmers heading at dawn to the reddish clay fields to harvest sweet potatoes, corn, wheat, some rice and sorghum, from which a deceptively mild-tasting wine is made. The children also contribute to the appearance of surface calm. Education is compulsory through the first nine years, and there are 37 elementary, 5 junior high, and 1 senior high school.

But this pastoral communal life can be disrupted whenever the alert siren blasts. Then the civilian men of the villages who are between the ages of eighteen and forty-five group into combat units to supplement the Nationalist troops. The government has classified all information about the size of its army on Quemoy, but estimates range up to 40,000 soldiers.

Though most of the Nationalist officers are in late middle age or older, having fought the Japanese in the 1930's and the Red Chinese a decade later, there are many young soldiers on Quemoy because military service is compulsory on Taiwan for every male of nineteen. The military tour of duty is two years for the army and three years for the air force and navy. The Nationalist military establishment now has about 600,000 men.

To get to Quemoy today, a civilian foreigner must be the guest of the Nationalist government and be transported there in a military plane, usually a C-119 cargo plane painted with the brown and green swirls of traditional army camouflage. There are no seats. For the 125-mile flight, passengers are strapped into hammock nets strung along the wall. The center is filled with baggage piled into a bin of metal bars. C-119's are not made for comfort. The slightest turbulence sends them into a prolonged series of bumps and shudders, and on takeoff they sound as if they were being subjected to a rainstorm of pebbles. Most of the passengers are officers with regulation haircuts—skin-close on the side and shaved high on the neck. The haircuts are too youthful for these elderly men, whose faces are creased and lack the tautness of youth. On the flight to Quemoy from Taipei, most of the passengers sleep, except for one who is airsick, and he tries to use the brown bag without being noticeable, attempting to contain the sound of his wretching within the bag.

The flight is down the western coast of Taiwan and then across the straits in a narrow prescribed air corridor, its path monitored in air by Red Chinese planes flying next to it in close quarters. Halfway over the straits the cargo plane is met by two Nationalist fighters and they escort it to Quemoy.

The airfield is very small and dug out of the clay bluffs on the eastern shore of the island—the farthest from Red China. Because there are officers on the plane, young recruits have been ordered to the airstrip to greet the distinguished visitors, and they form two ragged lines at the steps of the plane, snapping dutifully to attention when the doors at the rear are pushed open.

The terrain of Quemoy is at first sight deceptive. Once devoid of any vegetation, the island is now covered with 55,000,-000 trees, most of them Australian pines planted by the Nationalists since 1949. But among the tree trunks are trenches, at first not noticed, and rising through the branches are shiny gun barrels. On closer inspection what appear to be harmless mounds of dirt turn out to be pillboxes with ventilation pipes sticking through the domes. And at each major traffic intersection there are tall cylindrical pillboxes with machine guns on top of them and barbed-wire barricades at the sides.

New visitors are taken first to the Quemoy Museum on a bluff facing Amoy harbor. On the ground floor is a small auditorium and a map in the center identifying the nonmilitary installations: schools, reservoirs, hospitals, and stores. But most of the exhibits in the museum are from the war going on between the two Chinas.

There are examples of the propaganda leaflets and consumer goods sent over to the mainland by balloons or shells or on water by buoys. There are pictures of fishermen from the mainland who have escaped to Quemoy, and of the food and hospitality awaiting those who defect. There are also examples of the propaganda sent to Quemoy by the Red Chinese. Quemoy peasants are forbidden to read any of the Communist pamphlets dropped on them in the barrage of propaganda shells.

There are no hotels on Quemoy, and visitors are put up in a pleasant simple stone hostel next to the civilian police station. While sleeping quarters for most of the soldiers are underground, visiting civilians sleep in rooms above ground. There is nothing to worry about, the Nationalist officer insists, because a bomb shelter is nearby.

The military hosts are exceedingly polite, and the food is served in typically Chinese fashion from bowls on a wheel tray in the center of the table with everyone digging into the same bowls with their chopsticks. The food is delicious, not at all like the pasty Chinese food sold in American restaurants, and the toasts with the strong white wine are many, each getting more eloquent as the wine glasses are continuously refilled.

Invariably the conversation gets back to the mainland and the homes, parents, wives and children these men probably will never see again, having left them behind in their flight. There is a terrible sadness about the lives these men, serving what is now almost certainly a lost cause, are living. Standing against their return is a massive Red Chinese army, and nobody seriously believes it can be defeated by the Nationalists alone.

Chinese life is centered on home and family, and a religious reverence is given to ancestors and birthplaces. This compounds the loneliness and sorrow of these men. One of the officers said his family lives only a few miles into Fukien province, and that he has not seen his wife and daughter, who was then three years old, since he left in 1949; nor has he been able to contact them by letter. These stories of enforced separations are told by almost every man at the table. While none of them really believes the Nationalists can militarily defeat the Communists on the mainland, they can still hope for a popular uprising agaist the Red regime. Meanwhile, they tell their children born of new wives on Taiwan about their ancestral homes and how important it is for them to return there one day.

After the meal the officers and their guests walk through Kinmen, a charming collection of shops on squares and gently sloping side streets. The movie house near the hostel is jammed with soldiers and civilians who roar appreciation at the clumsy humor of the film. Outside the theater one of the officers politely asked the American if he wanted to use the Happy House, one of the brothels he said is maintained on Quemoy for the soldiers, each man being alotted a certain amount of time in it a month. It sounded very clinical, and the American politely declined.

On the point of land closest to Red China there is a radio station from which a daily bombardment of propaganda and music is directed across the channel from a loud speaker sunk in the side of a cement wall. From this embankment through binoculars an armed Red Chinese guard is seen walking stiffly on the beach of the neighboring coast. The broadcast that morning was conducted by an extremely attractive girl in un-flattering army pants and boots. After each prerecorded speech, music was played and on the program were "The Notre Dame Fight Song" and "The Battle Hymn of the Republic."

All the major military weapons on Quemoy are underground in an enormously complex network of tunnels where most soldiers live and work. An officer said a man can walk in these tunnels for three hours without reaching the end. Also underground is a 1,000-seat auditorium carved in the side of a cave, which can be converted into a hospital. The soldiers sleep in double-decker bunks in partitioned compartments of six to ten men. The main entrance to the tunnel is protected by four separate metal doors which, when closed, provide a formidable barricade against the shells of most conventional weapons.

On one of his frequent visits to Quemoy, Chiang told the story about a Chinese state called Tsi which was overrun by its enemies in 284 B.C. and lost all its cities except Chu. Because Chu remained free, all the cities of Tsi were eventually liberated. "Don't forget what happened to Chu," Chiang said, and his words are painted in red script on the side of a mountain facing the Chinese mainland.

# Okinawa

In every war there has to be one last land battle, and the one in the Pacific was on Okinawa. Probably the bloodiest of them all, it began on Easter morning, April 1, 1945, and ended three months later when the Japanese, pushed to the cliffs of the southern tip of the island, began hurling themselves to the rocks far below. More than 36,000 Americans were killed, but the Japanese losses were even more staggering, about 100,000 dead.

Relics of this titanic struggle are preserved in glass cases and on the walls of a two-room war museum on the Army base at Kadena, in the center of the island. There are pieces of piano sheet music of American pop tunes, left behind by GI musicians, the pages now yellowing and curling at the edges. There are insignias from battle dress aligned in rows on a felt-covered board. There are mess gear, side arms, and first-aid packs displayed in geometric designs on the bottoms of the cases. There are stark black and white photographs of the fight arrayed on the walls. And in the center of the room there is a scale model in relief of Okinawa with the various battle lines illuminated by lights switched on and off by an attractive Okinawan woman guide, who gives the important facts of the battle with the aloofness of one detached emotionally from the thing of which one speaks. It is supposed to be a museum of Okinawan culture, but from the exhibits, history there must have begun the morning the American armada arrived off the coast of the central part of the island.

Maintained by the Americans as one of the largest military installations outside their country, Okinawa will shortly be returned to Japan, the modern rulers of the Ryukyu Islands, of which Okinawa is the largest. American influence will be difficult to erase. No part of the southern half of Okinawa, which has 75 percent of the island's 900,000 population, has been left untouched by American culture. The dollar is the official currency on the island, the symbol of the accepted way of life. The roadways are tributes to American commercialism. There are all-night drive-in restaurants; one of them, built along the lines of a do-it-yourself car wash, is on a bluff over the beach where the Americans came ashore during the war. There are also pawnshops, all with expensive stereo sets and precision watches in their windows; used car yards—one of the less flambuoyant is called Uncle Sam's Used Car Lot; and Army and Navy surplus stores advertising twenty-four-hour service on tailor-made uniforms. Tawdry and transient, these commercial operations are plugged into the times. Hotel names are changed to keep up with the day's headlines, and there are several Apollo motels on the road between Naha, the capital, and Koza, which is outside the gates of the huge American air base at Kadena. This is the commercial America that has been grafted onto Okinawa, and it is doubtful the Japanese will be able to change it, even if they want to.

But there is also another America here: meticulous housing with spacious well-kept lawns behind the fences on the military reservations. Life goes on in these oases much as it does in hometown America. Mothers line up patiently with noisy children outside a movie house showing Walt Disney's *The Love Bug*. Bronzed teen-agers go off to their piano, tennis and golf lessons, given at reasonably low rates on Army bases. Husbands mow lawns and putt golf balls, and at night, there is the organized social hour at the clubhouse with cut-rate cocktails between 4 and 7 P.M. This life is run efficiently and according to the script of the good life, and nothing is allowed to disrupt its essential orderliness; even the damaged Army trucks from Vietnam are parked in neat rows inside a compound—like wounded soldiers trying to stand in a correct military posture.

There are about 90,000 Americans on Okinawa, including civilians and dependents of servicemen, and, away from home for a minimum of two years, they have brought America with them, transforming an alien culture into their own. When pieces of it resist, they are covered so that old stone houses of peasants are hidden behind highway billboards.

Everything off base that is touched by the military begins to look run-down even when it is new, and this is what has happened to the supposedly first-class hotels in the towns near the major camps on Okinawa. More attention is paid to the selection of girls in the bars off the lobby than to the condition of the rooms, since those regularly using them are more interested in the resiliency of the mattress springs than in the room's decor or housecleaning. These are the places for young American servicemen on Saturday nights with a weekend pass in their pockets, ready to make the rounds in search of friendly and not-too-expensive girls before returning to rooms of cigarette-burned furniture and stained sheets. If the search for women is futile—and it would be only if the soldier didn't really try—the rooms are used for men to conduct marathon drinking bouts, ending with the youths falling asleep on the floor. Girls are very easy to find on Okinawa. The commercial social life is the same as in Japan, revolving around bar hostesses. To drink with these girls is almost costlier than sleeping with them.

These young soldiers with their modified GI crew cuts and traditional Post Exchange clothing are extremely adaptable to local customs, most of them picking up the knack of eating with chopsticks in native restaurants and bargaining to get the price reduced for a night with a bar hostess. Even when they are being unconsciously rude to the natives, they are eager to be liked. The Army television and radio stations, reflecting this concern about getting along while abroad, offer numerous programs in Japanese language instruction. There are also spot radio announcements about how Americans are usually good neighbors in foreign countries that are friendly to them. But the Americans are not greatly appreciated on the island, a fact substantiated by the willingness of the Okinawans to live again in a province of Japan. "There is a silent majority among the Oki-nawans," an important American civilian official said, "and it is for realignment with the Japanese." Agitation for the return of the Ryukyus to Japan increased in the 1960's, and President Nixon agreed in principle that Okinawa should revert to Japanese civilian administration in the early 1970's. "But don't worry," an American military officer said, "you can bet the United States will still have her bases here even though Japan will run the place."

The United States believes Okinawa has an important role in global defense, a position stated bluntly in a tourist guide available to civilians. "Poised here are Army, Marine, Air Force and Navy units trained and ready to fulfill any defensive or offensive mission required of them to protect the interest of not only America but also to fulfill what America regards as her duty to other free nations in the Far East and Southeast Asia." One such mission was sending B-52 bombers on raids to Vietnam.

After World War II, the United States set up the civil administration in the Ryukyus with the top job of high commissioner going to a military man. Underneath the military hierarchy there is a civilian Ryukyus government which can enforce or modify the rules imposed by the Americans, but it can never enact its own laws unless they are first approved by the Americans. When Japan takes over, Okinawa, by becoming a prefecture of Japan, will have merely substituted the Japanese for Americans as administrators of their civil government.

The prosperity of Okinawa has been dependent almost entirely on the U.S. military bases and, to a lesser degree, upon financial aid from Washington and Tokyo. The per capita income is $497, much higher than in most independent nations in the Far East, and the gross national product is well over half a billion dollars. But 69 percent of the national income is derived from military employment, and this is what the Okinawans resent. "Everyone works for the American military on Okinawa," a young native male said disgustedly, though the prosperity of his taxi business was directly linked to the American residents. The local native enterprises are mostly agricultural. The principal crops are sugarcane and pineapple and the only major manufacturing is the processing of these crops.

The Okinawan landscape is not particularly attractive, dominated as it is by rugged hills and marshy coastal plains. The major cities have the tired, washed-out appearance of the faded stucco buildings in the shabbier sections of Miami Beach, and the junk shops along their main streets are hardly alluring. Only 125,000 tourists came to the island in 1969, 81 percent of them from Japan.

The Japanese language forms a natural barrier between Americans and Okinawans, but an even stronger barrier is the feeling among Okinawans that years after the war they are still a conquered people. In conversation, the Japanese are referred to as "us" while the Americans are "them." Still, young Okinawans quickly adopt the imported American culture, and the best customers at the pinball machines in the Koza hotels are Okinawan boys fascinated by the shiny silver handles and the metal balls weaving among the maze of colored obstacles.

Instead of being abrasive, this American culture hypnotically dispels aggressive hostility. Even the taxi driver modifies his dislike of Americans. "We do like individual Americans, but not those in the military. Okinawans don't get the same pay for the same job held by both Okinawans and the Americans on these military bases. We ask the military for more money and it says no. I have a friend who is a radio technician, a very skilled job, and he gets a hundred and eighty dollars a month, while an American doing the same job gets twelve hundred dollars. It just isn't fair."

The truth of his story is irrelevant since it is spread among the Okinawans as truth, and they are eager to accept it. Because of such attitudes, there was no big official celebration of the 25th anniversary of the American invasion in the spring of 1970. "We play down old battles around here," the American civilian official said. "We don't want to open old sores."

But the island is not entirely free of memorials to its brief bloody moments at the end of the conflict in the Pacific. There is a green cliff, its side on the sea rubbed naked by waves and wind and projected by an eruption centuries ago out from the

southern end of the island. On its peak, leveled by man, are dozens of odd-shaped commemorative stones placed in an irregular pattern by Japanese visitors in honor of their countrymen
who died on Okinawa. A few feet from where the ground drops
away to the swirling foam made by the sea slashing against
rocks, a tall, plain stone stands, and on it is told the story of the
last hours of the thousands of Japanese soldiers on Okinawa,
who, rather than be captured by the Americans, leaped to their
death from the cliff onto the jagged rocks below.

On the evening of June 21, 1945, the two commanding gen-
erals of the Japanese forces put on their ceremonial white robes
and, almost within sight of American troops scaling the walls
of the cliff, committed suicide by plunging knives into their
stomachs. Below, where their bodies lay, the carnage continued.
Americans aimed their flamethrowers into the entrances of the
many caves dug into the side of the cliff, incinerating hundreds
of Japanese. In a large one near the base of the cliff, the Americans, not seeing their faces, only their outlines in the darkness,
killed eighty-five student nurses who had retreated with the
soldiers to the southern end of the island. Today at the entrance there is a simple statue of three naked, vulnerable humans clutching each other's hands, not in terror but in the
aching human need to touch someone at the moment of extinc-
tion.

The cliff, now one of the major tourist attractions on Okinawa, can be reached only by car or bus over a road winding
through the limestone plateaus in the foothills at its base. On
Sundays the parking lot is filled with tour buses, letting out
Americans and Japanese, mostly middle-aged and memory-
haunted, who wander among the memorials, leaving behind a
trail of candy wrappers.

"The Japanese come down here, take a look, order another
memorial put up, and go home," a young Okinawan said.

The graveyard maintains a carnival atmosphere. Old Okinawan ladies walk among the tourists hawking seashells strung
into colorful necklaces. A professional photographer and his
pretty female assistant set up a camera on a tripod on the grass
by the parking lot and begin searching out the tourists with-

out cameras around their necks. The cliff is nominally a Japanese shrine, but now that the United States and Japan are allies, the real war which these stones commemorate is played down and the stones are said to be an expression of the universal search for peace.

But there was a war on Okinawa for three months, beginning on March 23, 1945, when ships off the coast began a constant bombardment of the central and southern ends of the island, forcing the peasants to abandon their small stone houses and flee to the more uninhabited northern part which the Americans left alone in their preinvasion air and sea assault. Planes from American aircraft carriers flew 3,095 sorties against the island before the invasion, and the Navy fired 5,162 tons of ammunition on it; the duration and intensity of the shells directed on Okinawa made up the greatest concentration of naval gunfire in history.

The object of this ferocious attack was an island 60 miles long and from 2 to 18 miles wide, inhabited by a population of under a million, most of them peasants engaged in farming on the 20 percent of the land not covered by dense growth and arid plateaus. As the objective of a centuries-old struggle between Japan and China, Okinawans had absorbed cultural traits from both nations, making them members of neither nationality but similar to both. Settled by Chinese, attractive to the French in the early nineteenth century, and annexed finally by the Japanese in 1875, Okinawa was of interest to the Americans as far back as the middle of the nineteenth century, when Commodore Matthew C. Perry raised the flag near Shuri in the south central part of the island and forced the regency then running the island to pledge that American shipping would receive friendly treatment.

The Americans selected the beaches on the central coast of the island for invasion because they were near the best airfields, and on the morning of April 1 the Americans sent 1,300 ships carrying 180,000 men to the coast of Okinawa. The men, standing on the decks waiting to be crammed into the landing barges, expected the worst on land. They knew the Japanese had about 100,000 troops there.

One of those waiting to come ashore was the famed war correspondent Ernie Pyle, and he remembered climbing into a landing craft before dawn and then sailing aimlessly around in the confusion of a thousand bobbing boats waiting for the lead control vessels to bring order to this navigational chaos. When he was finally brought to shore, Pyle was surprised, as were most Americans, that there were no Japanese on the beaches. Sixty thousand men waded ashore without a shot being fired.

The Japanese had now perfected the battle strategy they had so effectively put to use on Peleliu and Iwo Jima, awarding the beaches to the Americans and meeting them inland from underground fortifications. The place where this strategy would be put to the test on Okinawa was around Shuri Castle on a hill near the city of Naha. By nightfall on the first day, with amazing ease, the Americans had secured a beachhead 15,000 yards long and 5,000 yards deep in some places. Three days later the Americans had crossed a wedge 15 miles long and 3 to 10 miles wide.

Before the U.S. Army units began their push south toward Shuri Castle, the Japanese began a last desperate kamikaze attack from the air. Planning at one time to defend Okinawa with 4,500 aircraft, the Japanese had only 699 available planes, and on April 6 and 7 they sent them in waves toward the picket line of American ships off the coast, approaching at heights of 10 to 35 feet above the water, and then plunging suddenly into the ships. From April until late June there were ten organized kamikaze attacks, 1,900 suicide sorties, and before it was over, twenty-eight American ships had been sunk.

Unlike other landing beach sites in the Pacific today, those at Okinawa have no rusting barges or gun emplacements. There is only a small Japanese memorial on a rise overlooking the small sandy mounds strung along the beach. This obelisk memorial is unattended, and the ground around it outside a wire fence is littered with trash. At the base of the bluff is a makeshift wooden pen filled with rotting car tires, and farther down the beach, rows of housing for American enlisted men— dingy, unpainted cement blocks with new American cars parked in front of them.

The road south toward Shuri and Naha is called Route 1, and alongside of it for most of its length is a horrendous clutter of gas stations, junkyards, garish roadside stands, surplus clothing stores, used car lots and unkempt third-rate lodgings. In Naha the traffic is often stalled because the road is too narrow to handle the daily volume.

As the Americans encircled Shuri Castle for the major confrontation in the battle for Okinawa, Naha was completely leveled in air and artillery raids. In this area and north of the city, the Japanese in early May conducted their massive counteroffensive of 15,000 men with instructions that each soldier was to kill at least one American. For two days the fight was waged, with the Japanese trying to infiltrate American lines, firing mortars almost point-blank at the enemy, charging with bayonets fixed. Yet when it was over, the Americans still advanced, slowly, painfully, up the grassy slopes of another plateau, and another 5,000 Japanese soldiers lay dead.

After the failure of the counteroffensive there was nothing for the Japanese to do but go to their death defending the heights of Shuri Castle or withdraw farther south. For a while it seemed they wanted to die in Shuri. Through the middle of May the Japanese repelled charge after charge of Americans climbing up the hill. Two thousand rounds of artillery and naval gunfire were dropped on Shuri, and the castle, built in 1544, was reduced to rubble. The fighting took on the quality of a nightmare as the torrential spring rains churned the soil to boot-sucking mud, and men trudged through it, as if in the slow motion of a dream. Not only buildings but vegetation was cleared from the heights; leaves were ripped off trees by bullets and grass torn up by mortars, so there was nothing on the slopes but bruised, barren earth and shattered tree trunks. The battle was fought with everything: flamethrowers, tanks, machine guns, rifles, pistols, bayonets and mortars, and then suddenly the Japanese decided to withdraw south.

The postwar growth of Naha has been haphazard. The streets in the center of the city are too winding and narrow, and there has been no attempt to zone residential or business areas. The result is such scenic incongruities as having a *Peyton Place* car-hop standing in front of a peasant's cottage with a classic pagoda-shaped roof.

All that is left today of Shuri Castle are a small shrine a few feet beyond the original and an archway of a tiled roof bridging two cement columns. On weekends many Okinawans come up the hill to bow deeply before this shrine, some stopping to place flowers in a glass bottle in a recess in the wall. Over the ruins of Shuri Castle was built the University of Ryukyus, opened in 1950.

South of Naha, on a road that follows the coastline through swampy rice fields until it enters the plateau land, are two impressive war memorials. One is the Cave of the Virgins, where 158 students and teachers, acting as nurses and aides for the Japanese Army Hospital, were killed by the Americans when they refused to come out of their small but extremely deep cave dug straight down into the earth. A memorial stone marks the entrance to the hole, and to the right the statue of an angel. It is in a glass case, but the windows are dirty and the angel is almost obliterated from view behind the chalk streaks on the panes. The shrine has not escaped commercialism. Both sides of the street nearby have roadside stands, and old ladies drift among the parked cars selling photographs of battle scenes, most of them of men shooting each other or of corpses sprawled in the bizarre positions of broken bodies.

The other memorial is on a slight rise outside the fishing village of Itoman. Here General Simon Bolivar Buckner, commanding officer of the American forces on Okinawa, was killed on June 18. His death was a freak accident. He had gone to the rise to watch American mopping-up operations in the southern region when a Japanese shell exploded over his head and a piece of shrapnel dislodged a sliver of coral rock which pierced his chest. He died within ten minutes of being struck. The location is marked by a round stone surrounded by a white fence, and from here there is an unhindered view of the sea behind Suicide Cliff. Okinawan children come to this memorial to play in the bushes and make dart guns from the strong, hollowed-out weeds.

An American official said the only two World War II memorials the U.S. government is really concerned about on Okinawa are Buckner's and the one for Ernie Pyle, probably the most famous casualty of the battle. Pyle was riding in a jeep with a regimental commander on the tiny island of Ie-Shima, off the northern coast of Okinawa, when a Japanese machine gun nest opened fire and the two men dived to safety in a ditch on the side of the road. Pyle, who had survived some of the worst fighting in Italy, was instantly killed when he peeked over the side of the ditch and a bullet struck his temple just below the rim of his helmet. He was buried by the soldiers in a cemetery on Ie, and on the marker at the head of the freshly turned earth was written, "At this spot the 77th Infantry Division lost a buddy, Ernie Pyle, 18th April 1945." The body was later removed but a monument was erected near where he was slain.

In addition to the human casualties, the Americans paid their price in hardware: 368 ships sunk, 763 aircraft shot down, while the Japanese lost thousands of airplanes, leaving them only slightly more than 5,000 kamikaze planes for the defense of the mainland.

The battle for Okinawa was declared finished on July 2, 1945, and the dead became faceless inert bodies, except to those who remembered them, now piled into stacks for burial in common graves or shipment home. This is what war eventually does to men, renders them anonymous, and the suffering and pain that accompanies their death is gone, with nothing of the humanity of all men under fire remaining. And then the survivors begin to erect the memorials on top of the ground—cold, plain, oddly shaped stones that replace the guns and wreckage—and the story of the battle becomes letters chipped into stone.

# Japan: Final Victory

## TOKYO

A leaflet fluttered down on the ruins of Tokyo in May, 1945, one of the thousands dropped by American bombers. It read: "You have no way of escaping the bombs. You have no place to hide. Continued resistance means only a horrible death. Demand an end to such hopeless resistance. It is the only way to save your homeland." But still the Japanese resisted the death from the sky that began to fall in November, 1944.

The high-altitude bombing raids on selected industrial targets outside the major cities of Japan were begun in the fall of 1944. Launched from the recently captured Marianas Islands, they had not been entirely successful. The first major raid was against the aircraft manufacturing Musashino plant ten miles north of the Emperor's Palace in Tokyo. It was conducted by 111 B-29 bombers, carrying more than 270 tons of bombs, coming in at altitudes up to 27,000 feet. The weather was foggy and bumpy, and the results were unimpressive. Only forty-eight bombs hit the factory, damaging only 2 percent of the machinery. Subsequent air attacks on Japanese heavy industry from bombers at high altitudes were equally unspectacular, and the blame was put on the daily bad weather. There had to be a better way to bring a more comprehensive destruction to Japan, and a study finished in October, 1944, indicated that way.

The report, prepared by the U.S. Army Air Force, suggested that Japan, because of the nature of its building construction and housing congestion, was more vulnerable to incendiary bomb attacks. Since it had been a victim of so many natural disasters, most notably earthquakes, Tokyo was rebuilt after each catastrophe with the expectation that it would inevitably be destroyed again. Most of the private homes and the small hotels, called *ryokans,* were made of wood. If a quake pushed them over, as a violent upheaval did in 1923, they could be quickly rebuilt; thus, when the fire-bomb raids began, Tokyo was a collection of thousands of highly inflamable structures.

Incendiary raids don't require precision. For this specialized kind of assault, the bombers can come in at much lower altitudes, from 5,000 to 6,000 feet, permitting them to carry heavier bomb loads. And because fire-bomb raids don't require the sighting of specific targets, they can be conducted at night when the weather tends to clear over Japan.

The incendiary bomb war was devised by U.S. Army Air Force General Curtis LeMay, and before it was over in May, 1945, it had offended humanitarians around the world.

The attacks began in early 1945, but the most ferocious one took place on the night of March 9-10 over a densely populated 4-mile radius of Tokyo, where there were about 103,000 inhabitants per square mile. Over this area 334 B-29's dropped 2,000 tons of incendiary bombs, and the fires started by them could be seen by the tail gunners on B-29's 150 miles away on their return to the Marianas.

The fires raged beyond the planned radius of the attack. Within thirty minutes flames were out of control, and before morning 15.8 square miles of the center of Tokyo had been burned out. Metropolitan police records show 267,171 buildings were destroyed, one-fourth of Tokyo's total number; 83,793 people were killed; 40,918 wounded; and 1,000,000 made homeless.

Next to undergo an incendiary attack was Osaka, and on March 13, 8.1 square miles of that city were destroyed by fires started from 1,732 tons of incendiary bombs. The result of this single attack: 3,988 dead, 678 missing, 8,463 injured, 134,-744 homes and 119 major factories destroyed. Of the 274 U.S. bombers to participate in this raid, only 2 were lost.

Without any adequate Japanese air defense, the U.S. bombers

were able to come night after night throughout the spring of 1945, knocking out the country's six largest industrial cities and then going after the medium-sized cities, fifty-eight of them, until 178 square miles of Japan were in ashes. In Tokyo alone, six separate incendiary bomb raids gutted 56.3 square miles, or almost half the city. The average size of these attacks consisted of from 300 to 500 planes. When the fire raids were over, Japan had suffered 806,000 civilian casualties, of whom more than 300,000 were killed.

But American military historians now believe it was the naval blockade, rather than the air attacks, that actually began to weaken the Japanese will to resist; for without food coming in, starvation began to stalk their cities. Yet even hunger didn't stop them, and the Japanese continued to refuse to surrender, resisting through April and May while their forces were being crushed on Okinawa.

For one who was a child during the war in the Pacific, and whose memories consist mainly of the hideously ugly face of a Japanese soldier painted on a stuffed, weighted pillow to be knocked off a rack by baseballs at a concession stand, it is still difficult not to think of the Japanese as enemies when arriving for the first time in their homeland. If there are any grievances by the Japanese against the Americans for a war in which half a million of their soldiers lost their lives, they are concealed. The individual Japanese will go out of his way to perform extraordinarily kind individual acts that often take on the air of overcourteousness.

But man is capable of not only forgiving but forgetting, and the hatreds of war vanish quickly when the victor is told his former enemy is now his ally in the defense of the Far East against a new enemy. So one tries to forget the war, an event of long ago, by trying to get to know the Japanese, and the guidebook suggests one way is to take a bath with them. What the guidebook failed to do was make the distinction between the different kinds of public baths, to note that some are only for tourists, others are integrated, and some are exclusively for the Japanese.

Although this particular public bath with massage was listed in the popular guidebook *Japan on $10 a Day*—it used to be $5 but inflation is even more virulent in Japan than it is in the United States—the cab driver had trouble finding it. The bath was eventually located on the sixth floor of a commercial building in a district of Tokyo comparable to Greenwich Village.

The driver left the American in front of the right building— but at the wrong entrance, which the American discovered when he took the elevator to the sixth floor and stepped into the ticket booth of a seedy theater showing a dirty old foreign movie. The correct entrance was around the corner on another street. Standing at the elevator was an elderly Japanese man in a frayed, starched uniform, its odor and condition boding ill for what lay ahead. He bowed to the American, who returned the bow, which required the Japanese to bow again. This ballet of manners continued through the ride to the sixth floor with the bows rising gradually from the waist to the neck.

The reception room of the bath was in the decor of the waiting room of a dentist with a good address. It featured thick wall-to-wall carpeting, an abundance of plastic flowers and shrubs growing from clay urns, wrought-iron furniture, a coffee table stacked with magazines, and a bosomy woman leaning over the desk, her face set rigidly in a polite smile. The American's licentious dreams of a sexual debauch with a Madame Butterfly expanded. Could this really be what he had hoped for—a coed bath like the one in the movie *The Bridges at Toko-Ri?* Next to her was a rather large Japanese man in a tuxedo, no doubt the bouncer, and his physical presence prevented further exchanges of meaningful glances.

The only words of English the receptionist and bouncer knew were "bath" and "massage," and this reassured the American who thought their use of these words meant they could speak English. He nodded yes to both and was politely steered into the locker room.

It was not to be coed. The locker room was filled with young Japanese men stripping down before a Saturday night on the town, an activity somewhat curtailed in duration because all the public nightclubs and bars close at 11 P.M. Shorn of his clothes and handed a towel by the attendant, the American was pushed into a sauna bath where a dozen Japanese men sat perched on wooden racks, their bodies covered with a film of sweat. The heat was excruciating. The only sounds were sighs, groans and the plops of buttocks being shifted on the wood for maximum comfort. Most Japanese remained inside fifteen minutes. The American lasted five. When the attendant couldn't tell if the rivers of water under his eyes were tears or sweat, the

American was led into the next room, which contained five huge square tubs, each large enough for six or seven men, depending on how the bodies were arranged in the water.

It was obvious the Japanese in this room hadn't seen many naked Western bodies, and the novelty of it stopped their soaping and splashing. By the height of his fellow countrymen, the American wasn't really tall, an inch under 6 feet, but he was huge compared with the Japanese, and, unlike any of them, he was very hairy. Never before had the American felt so naked. Everyone was staring at him. A few pointed. Some giggled. The American clutched his towel to his groin as if it were a security blanket. Slipping on the wet tiles, he went to the least-crowded tub, and rather than first test the temperature with his big toe, he dropped quickly into the steaming green-colored water. He was struck numb by the paralyzing heat. The one leg in the tub turned rapidly from white to pink to scarlet. It seemed to the American every Japanese in the room was laughing at him. Undaunted, he slipped the rest of his body into the water and wondered if he had left his wallet in his pants so the management would know where to ship his body.

A man can reach a state of euphoria in many ways, and one of them is being scalded in a Japanese public bath. Very soon every nerve ending that had been tied in a knot came undone and the lightness of head the American thought was a fainting seizure when he first dropped into the water spread throughout his body. He felt weightlessness and the possibility of floating airborne over his new friends, who showed him what parts of his immersed body could best be protected from the heat by washcloths. The American nodded his thanks; the Japanese responded with graceful bows; ripples of friendship were cast on common bath water.

At the end of the room was a circular tile fountain from which dangled shower hoses. Around it the Japanese squatted on wooden stools, soaping themselves before showering under the hand-held nozzles. The American joined them.

No longer feeling naked, he next walked with his tub mates into the adjoining room, where he saw, positioned over leather tables of the sort used by doctors for examining patients, women in white jackets ready to begin their assault on the male body. One short plump girl with stocky legs and beefy arms demurely handed the American a towel and led him to a table in the middle of the room. He stretched out on it, the towel over his buttocks. She kicked off her slippers, hopped on the table and began to walk up and down his spine. The cracking sounds, he thought, were his fifth and sixth vertebrae going. Turning him over, she giggled, pounding his hairy chest with the palms of her hands. He giggled. She giggled, jerking his leg until his heel touched his back. His giggle turned to a silent wince. Saving face is a national defense mechanism in Japan, and the American adopted it. Not wanting to show he was suffering pain, he refused to cry out when she knelt over him, her knees on each side of his waist, and while sitting on his buttocks, put her arms under his shoulders and yanked his body back. Once the pain was diminished by his self-control, the therapeutic benefits of the massage took over. As had happened to him in the hot water, a light-headed euphoria came over him, akin to a physical nirvana. She was no longer brutalizing his body; she was freeing it from the impurities of urban living. Sinuses cleared up; lungs began functioning; blood went swishing through misused veins.

A tug of his foot by the woman indicated the massage was over, and she assisted him to an upright position, handed him a fluffy terry cloth robe and pointed him in the direction of a post-massage room. Metal lawn chairs ringed a wall decorated with a mural of Finnish country life. An attendant offered cigarettes and a cold fruit drink. No stimulant was needed to increase the American's feeling of bodily well-being; in fact, a cigarette or drink would probably have interrupted the flow of natural sensations that had become nearly sensual. Wrapped in his robe, the sweat forming on his brow over oil rubbed into his skin by the woman, his muscles given back a certain youthful elasticity through the tugging and pulling, he put his head on the pillow, folded the ends of the robe over his knees, closed his eyes, and allowed the images and impressions of his two weeks in Japan to tumble wildly in his mind.

The sensuality beneath the puritanism of Japanese life. The girl in his room at night, not a whore, but a legitimate masseuse, the nails of her fingers making erotic tinglings on the flesh of his thigh. Her complimentary remarks on the width of his shoulders and the muscles in his legs, and the gliding, soft touch of her fingers on the small of his back, and lower. . . .

And there were the sights and smells . . . chunks of raw fish piled in china cups . . . old ladies in kimonos and wooden sandals walking with quiet majesty in streets crowded with Japanese in Western dress . . . Tokyo itself rebuilt almost entirely after the war, now architecturally uninspired and monotonously imitative, the tallest structure being the Tower of Tokyo copied after Paris' Eiffel Tower, and the smog making it look as if the tower were sunk in brown custard pudding . . . and the courteousness . . . taxi drivers refusing tips . . . salesgirls putting paperback books in separate jackets to protect their covers . . . the narrow back streets of Tokyo crammed with traditional small wooden homes and tiny tearooms, where wandering off the main street is to go back several centuries . . . 11,000,000 people in Tokyo . . . the jumble of lights on the Ginza, Tokyo's main shopping and entertainment section . . . the department stores modeled on those along New York's Fifth Avenue . . . the mannequins in the store windows, Caucasian rather than Japanese, with long, blond wigs . . . the television programming heavily borrowed from America, two of the more popular shows based on *This Is Your Life* and *Queen for a Day* . . . still a very cosmopolitan city filled with representatives from many countries wanting to do business with Japan . . . conversations in a bar catering to foreigners dominated by German accents, making it sound like a scene from an old war movie where the enemy gets together to conspire against the Americans . . . the elaborate night life in the city established around the bar hostess system—it can easily cost 40 American dollars to drink with a girl in a cellar club in the Ginza for just an hour . . . the notorious hostesses, the legendary women of Tokyo.

The American had sworn he could go two weeks in Tokyo

without getting involved with a hostess. Every foreigner had been warned about these girls, and he almost made it, but on the next to the last night of his stay in Tokyo, after working most of the day in his hotel room, he decided to take a walk before the cafés closed, possibly to get a massage. He even considered going to one of the parlors where the girls perform special sexual acts with their hands for a few dollars more. He stood just a moment too long in the hotel doorway; the Japanese man stepped out of the shadow and in almost perfect English offered him a ride to the Ginza. Naïveté is an appealing quality in an adult of today's raucously pornographic world, but it can also be a costly one when he's abroad. His suspicions relaxed by too many acts of kindness, the American took up the offer.

The man parked in front of a cellar café and said he was going in to see his girlfriend. He invited the American along and said any drinks bought would be dutch treat. Fair! Okay! The American sat down in the booth and was joined by a lovely hostess, her ample bosom rising unchallenged from the front of her plain black dress. He knew he could resist her, and to show his determination to prevail over her obvious sexuality, he set his lips in a Humphrey Bogart sneer—it had helped Bogart when he had to send Mary Astor to jail at the end of *The Maltese Falcon.* Then she placed her hand on the inside of his thigh and said he was different from all the other Americans she had ever met. Without shifting once in his seat, he spent all the money he had with him, 20 American dollars, in less than an hour. He had one drink. She had five. His was a bottle of beer. Hers were colored water. The girl, toying with the American, announced she was a transvestite. The American squeezed her breasts through the outside of her dress and said it was a lie. "Did you ever hear of the operations in Copenhagen?" she shrieked. All the girls in the bar became hysterical. Suddenly most of them did look like men in drag, their hairlines unnatural, the bosoms on some suspiciously small. He was almost convinced until the girl, still laughing, placed his hand on a spot of her anatomy where he could be reassured. "You come tomorrow?" she asked. "Where do you stay? I like you better than most. You're cute." The hand never left his thigh. When the club closed, she was considerate enough to have set aside a few coins for his taxi fare, and while propelling him to the stairs, whispered in his ear that it was illegal for her to do this but she would call his hotel room the next day. Out in the street he discovered the car and his Japanese friend gone. It had begun to rain and the lights of the Ginza were smeared. She never did call.

There is also the historical Japan, the one culled from books and learned magazine articles. This Japan did lose World War II and is still the only country to have been subjected to atomic bomb attacks. Considered completely devastated in 1945, it is today one of the most prosperous nations in the world and has the highest standard of living of any Asian country. It also has the third-largest gross national product in the world, after the United States and Russia. Some economists predict that by the twenty-first century it will be number one. To combat Japan's economic resurgence, tariff walls are being erected around the world.

But this economic prosperity does not tell all. Ichiro Kawasaki, a distinguished Japanese diplomat, wrote a best seller, *Japan Unmasked*. Its theme is that the Japanese think of themselves as physically unattractive, especially when compared with what the West believes is beauty, and that this has created a national inferiority complex that is constantly being compensated for by aggressiveness in business. For writing this publicly, Kawasaki was sacked from his job in the Japanese foreign office.

Thus, the contrast in Japan is highlighted . . . the rudeness of the Japanese when they are part of a faceless crowd, pushing in line with no regard for those next to them . . . an old woman on a train slamming into the arm of an American at least eight times without once excusing herself . . . but then the unbelievable politeness of individual Japanese . . . a woman closing down her booth in a subway station to take the American a block away and put him on the right train. Such contradictions make a visit to Japan a source of perplexity, anger and exhilaration about the possibilities and the limitations of reforming public manners in an overcrowded world.

And in the euphoria of the post-massage room, there are

other lasting impressions: The Japanese are smaller than most Americans. It is almost impossible to buy a suit off the rack in any clothing store if one is 6 feet tall . . . Japan is the best country in the world for cameras which sell for less than half what they cost in the United States . . . Whatever happened to the idea that all Japanese goods were junk? . . . Japanese women have stumpy legs, but, then, so does Elizabeth Taylor . . . Considering Japan was occupied by Americans for almost eight years, it is surprising so few Japanese speak fluent English. Most of them have learned to read and write it, so communication is possible if the words are written . . . the Japanese love American Western movies: *Butch Cassidy and the Sundance Kid* went through the roof, as they say in Hollywood trade papers, breaking box office records around the country. American war movies are also very popular, and the bloodier and more violent, the better they are received . . . Mass transportation in Japan is a half century ahead of the United States. The traveler's dream is the monorail connecting downtown Tokyo with the International Airport. The rapid train between Tokyo and Osaka is also astonishing, and when it runs a few minutes late, a conductor goes down the aisle apologizing . . . Japanese food is excellent, but it would take most Americans forever to get used to eating raw fish . . . Japanese shrines, as do churches in Europe, get to be a bore when seen too often . . . Japanese traffic makes that in Rome look like an orderly driver education class . . . The Japanese still have not emotionally recovered from losing the war. It was the first time their country had been occupied by a foreign power.

The reverie over, and his clothes once more on, the American took the elevator to the main floor. The woman at the reception desk was gone and the lights behind the desk turned off. There was a new, younger elevator operator, and he didn't go through the ritual of bowing. The American crossed the square and stopped at a fruit stand to buy two apples. The clerk, smiling and reverently holding the fruit, walked to the back of the stand and carefully washed each before handing them to the American.

Back in his hotel room, he undressed quickly and pulled back the thin blanket and clean sheet from the bed. He was supine, his body covered by a kimono, when the familiar masseuse came through the unlocked door and, without speaking, began slowly to caress his flesh, helping him off with his robe until it was only a fold of cloth over his middle. Trying to concentrate on the death and destruction dealt the city so many years ago, and the moral questions raised by it, he could feel only her hands and he became sexually aroused as the conflicting images of dead bodies and a woman's sensual touch occupied his mind.

# HIROSHIMA

We are all survivors of August 6, 1945, when at 8:15 A.M. the U.S. Army Air Force B-29 *Enola Gay* dropped a black and orange five-ton atomic bomb on the 255,000 residents of Hiroshima in southwest Japan. The bomb was responsible not only for the official casualty figure of 78,000 dead—Hiroshima claims 200,000 were killed—but for making the world aware there was now a weapon that could bring an end to life as known on earth.

The jet prop passenger plane, having left a cold Tokyo two hours earlier, broke through a layer of stringy, brown-tinged clouds and descended in a wide circle to the city of Hiroshima, wedged between the mountains and the sea on a brown delta dissected by seven rivers. Several passengers still suffering from late winter colds had considerately placed gauze masks over their mouths to protect others from contamination. After the plane had landed, these masked men gave the lobby of the small airport the sterile appearance of a hospital waiting room. The airport is a half-hour drive from the center of the city, and the only fast way to get to there is by taxi. On the way, the driver, fairly fluent in English though most Japanese have an extremely difficult time speaking any foreign language, repeats a litany of welcome whose warmth and sincerity have been removed by repetition.

Hiroshima, rebuilt almost completely after its destruction, is a collection of one- and two-story structures spaced evenly in square blocks. The few tall office buildings and department stores are contained in the center of the city. The cab made a turn into the wide main boulevard, and though the driver was eager to talk about many things, especially the impressions Japan made on the first-time visitor, he was quiet as he passed a huge park, empty except for what appeared to be several monuments. At the side of the park nearest the boulevard, a bunker-shaped building extended across two concrete necks.

It was the Peace Park built at the hypocenter of the atomic bomb blast, and it gives the city its distinction. In its center is an unusual curved-roofed memorial at one end of a reflecting pool. There is a long walk to it from the boulevard, up a plain sidewalk through a bare field. The memorial is called the Cenotaph, and buried under it are the names of the 78,000 known dead from the atomic bomb explosion. The Cenotaph contains the controversial inscription: "Rest in peace. The mistake shall not be repeated." Many Japanese take offense at this, claiming it places the responsibility for dropping the atomic bomb on the victims rather than on those who dropped it.

The site of the memorial is in the vicinity of the old National Industrial Exposition Hall, whose beautifully designed dome and façade had made it one of the most popular buildings in prewar Hiroshima. The remains of it, several hundred yards away, are three crumbling walls and the twisted, exposed steel frame of the dome. The only ruin that was permitted to remain standing in the new Hiroshima, it is already being dwarfed on the skyline by a baseball park and a high-rise office building.

In the middle of the reflecting pool is a slab of stone with a crack in the center, through which burns a single flame.

During the afternoon, groups of schoolchildren arrive at the Peace Park in buses. They file out and walk under the bunker building, which is the Atomic Bomb Museum. Then, moving along the sidewalk behind teachers who continually wave flags so that their charges won't become separated from the group, they stop at the Cenotaph, arrange themselves in orderly lines, and on the command of the teacher, make the ritual bow, repeating it three times, before walking in the same orderly ranks back to their bus.

During these stylized demonstrations of Japan's enforced reverence for its tragic day, an old man sits alone on a bench to the right of the Cenotaph. His hands are resting on a cane, and under a cap his eyes follow the children. He is a survivor of the atomic blast, and there is nothing more for him to do but watch these children, aware that they can feel nothing of the horror that took place in their city one day in August: the blinding, paralyzing flash of light, and the rolling layers of heat and flame, balls of fire incinerating everything in their path. Buildings were leveled and men reduced to shadows imprinted into concrete bridge abutments. Some survivors lived only a few days. At first they seemed to be unhurt, but then their hair began to fall out, discolored blotches rose on their skin, and their red blood cell counts dropped alarmingly. Death came swiftly thereafter. But there were others, some 200,000 of them, who were exposed to the atomic explosions at Hiroshima and three days later at Nagasaki, many of them branded now by keloids, bunches of burnt, twisted skin on their bodies.

The man on the bench had survived the explosion without his body being marked. He is now old and alone, waiting for natural death, and he shifts his cane and redirects the glance of his eye to another memorial, probably the most popular one in the park. It is cylindrical-shaped and resembles a hollowed-out bomb shell. On its top is a statue of a naked child in the position of the crucifixion. The memorial is dedicated to a fourteen-year-old girl who died from leukemia after being exposed to the bomb's radiation. Inside the shell dangle hundreds of wreaths made of paper birds. There is a legend that if one completes a wreath of one thousand paper birds, one gets one's wish. But this girl, trying to compete with time, died before hers was completed, and her classmates, having collected money to build the memorial, then filled it with their own wreaths, a tribute schoolchildren continue to make every day.

There are two other prominent memorials in the Peace Park: a rather cumbersome, umbrella-shaped dome under which hangs a bell that is rung by swinging a log into it, and a mound of earth under which are buried thousands of unidentified victims of the atomic explosion. In front of the mound stands a Buddhist altar, and to it the devout bring fresh flowers daily to fill the vases.

Among the survivors, the Reverend Kiyoshi Tanimoto of the Hiroshima Methodist Church is one of the more famous. He was one of the six written about in John Hersey's *Hiroshima.* Unlike many of the others, who are wary about speaking of their unique experience to foreigners, Mr. Tanimoto talks freely in fluent English learned at Emory University, Georgia, from which he was graduated in 1940. Though he gives the impression of having adapted quite comfortably to postwar Hiroshima, he finds the world is too much with him and his congregation, and he is preparing to follow the route of many other urban Christian churches around the world: He is taking his congregation into the suburbs.

"The church was rebuilt after the war," he said, pointing to a photograph taken the day of the atom bombing, which shows only the concrete walls standing. "This skeleton was left, and it still has cracks in the frame. But the church here has been swallowed by the developing city. We're too near the center." Shopping arcades and wide, crowded streets now cluster around the small church, and its location on a narrow side street makes it almost hidden by the back sides of office buildings and a department store.

Mr. Tanimoto's church office is sparsely furnished. There are several straight-backed chairs, a bench, and a small altar on which are two stem vases of fresh carnations. There are also a map of the ancient Holy Land on the wall and a kerosene stove in the center of the room, the latter for warmth against the damp walls that keep in the coldness of late winter.

Mr. Tanimoto speaks quickly and rather blandly about his war experiences, almost as if by rote, thus raising the suspicion that he secretly enjoys being a public celebrity who is sought out by visiting foreigners. Now in his early sixties, Mr. Tanimoto has a full head of gray hair parted in the middle, and, though short, he is still compactly built without any evidence of middle-aged heaviness around his waist. His clothes also reflect a youthful determination: a sports jacket, a plaid shirt, and a string tie around his neck secured by a metal clasp on which is printed, "Methodist Men."

He said Hiroshima was the center of Protestant Christianity in Japan before the war and his congregation then numbered 500, a size reduced considerably during the war when many moved to villages outside the city to escape the bombings expected any day.

On the morning of August 6, 1945, Mr. Tanimoto was in a suburb, a mile and a half from the hypocenter of the explosion. Hiroshima had not yet been bombed during the war, and, like many others, Mr. Tanimoto suspected it would eventually be subjected to an air attack. He had gone, therefore, to the house of a friend in the suburbs with the personal belongings of his wife and daughter, who were soon to move there.

His family survived the blast, and his daughter later went to college in the United States, graduating from Centenary College for Women in Hackettstown, New Jersey. Others of his congregation did not survive. Of his 150 members on that morning, 70 were killed outright.

"I started to rebuild my congregation right after the bombing. I preached in front of the railroad station to people who were homeless and suffering from radiation sickness. They were not necessarily Christian but were struggling to survive, and the words of the sermon were like seeds to the wind because these people needed the word of God to survive."

The effect of the atom bomb on the survivors in his congregation was to convert them from ultranationalism "to the oneness of humanity" and a faith in pacifism. "Emotionally," he said, "the Japanese are now against all types of war. After the atomic bomb was used on them, they realized the absolute nothingness of war and they stood in deep solidarity in their awareness of their hopelessness.

"They also felt a true sense of dependence on the past and that they had to repent. They became pacifists but were distrustful of the organized peace movement because it had become infected with left-wing political bias."

Mr. Tanimoto said his idea of pacifism was developed by his exposure to the atomic bomb. "I believe now there is no justification for any kind of war." Asked what he would do if a man invaded his sanctuary with a loaded gun, Mr. Tanimoto said, "It is a difficult question, but I would try to protect myself," and added, "Nuclear war is not meaningful or relevant to the question.

"Nuclear weapons should be banned because they make no distinction between children and soldiers." His pacifism, however, didn't preclude limited wars. "A limited war can be stopped, but once nuclear weapons are used, nothing can be stopped."

Mr. Tanimoto's conversion to quasi-pacifism came after World War II. "I couldn't say anything about the war in my sermons. There were always one or two spies from the police in the church. I had to deal only with Biblical studies. I never preached out against militarism even before the war. Because I had studied in America and had many American friends, I was suspected of being an enemy of Japan, even though I was born here."

He still doesn't speak of war or peace in his sermons, and he has transformed the lesson of Hiroshima into an exclusively Christian symbol of the suffering that sinners must undergo. "After the bombing we realized how sinful man is because of his inherent selfishness. We asked God for forgiveness of our selfishness. It was natural for the Japanese to repent, and after repenting, to embrace the idea of a brotherhood of mankind."

His congregation has never regained its prewar size. It now has three hundred baptized members. Christianity is the faith of only 2 percent of the Japanese population, and Mr. Tanimoto concedes religion has little appeal, particularly to the young of Hiroshima. "Young people marry, get good jobs and promotions, and lose interest in church work when they get caught up in the secular life of business, drinking and sex."

Mr. Tanimoto said the lasting impression to him of the

morning of August 6 is of wandering through an island park in the middle of the river near the hypocenter and of passing a cup of water among persons whose eyes and lips were burnt closed. "In these destroyed bodies fought human spirits, and however dreadfully a body is destroyed, the spirit of man can't be conquered, not even by a nuclear weapon."

The effect time has had on the emotions aroused by the dropping of the bomb can be measured in the distance separating the attitudes of the aging survivors in the A-Bomb Hospital of Hiroshima and the young students across the street in the University of Hiroshima. The injured cannot forget what happened to them on one sunny, warm morning, but the young, mesmerized by the extraordinary material prosperity of Japan, don't want to remember.

The A-Bomb Hospital is a dingy, gray stone, four-story structure attached to the Red Cross Hospital, which was one of the few buildings to remain standing in the center of the city after the explosion. Opened in 1955, it has the depressing appearance of a ward for the impoverished, where care and comfort are compromised by skimpy budgets and staff shortages.

There are about one hundred fifty patients in the hospital, most of them distinguished by burn scars on their faces and hands. These survivors are crowded three each to very small rooms, and those who are ambulatory must use strollers unaccompanied by hospital personnel to go down the long corridor to the bathroom.

Because the fear of being contaminated by the atom bomb survivors persisted, as if radiation sickness could be passed on, the survivors found it difficult to marry or to obtain good jobs, and today they are mostly in the lower third of the economy. And they are daily getting older. More than 60 percent of the patients admitted annually to the A-Bomb Hospital are at least sixty years of age, and most of them are suffering from eye cataracts or various forms of cancer, the disease most dreaded by the survivors because of the large incidence of leukemia among those exposed directly to the radiaton from the bomb.

An estimated 160,000 Japanese who had been exposed to atom bomb explosions at Hiroshima and Nagasaki are still alive.

Ninety thousand of them are in Hiroshima and they make up a fifth of the city's current population. If they share a common psychological trait, it is their feeling of being outcasts after having experienced personally one of the greatest man-made holocausts of the twentieth century. This feeling of uniqueness has been strengthened over the years by the attention given them by doctors and journalists, so much so that the survivors are now fairly reticent about talking of the bombing to strangers.

Their obsession with the A-bomb doesn't carry over to other generations. A young female university-trained hospital worker said, "I don't feel anything about the bomb. I'm indifferent to it." A friend of hers, a male university student, said, "Most of the people my age are indifferent to the atomic bomb. You can't sustain an emotion of hatred for this long."

A most articulate spokesman for the survivors is Dr. Fumio Shigeto, the pleasantly gregarious director of the A-Bomb Hospital. He was at the Hiroshima railroad station when the bomb exploded. Because he was standing in the protective shelter of a concrete wall, his life was saved.

"I saw a white flash and heard the blast, and the building crumbled and something hit my back. I fell on my face and put my hands over my eyes. When I looked up, the city was at first dark, and after the cloud lifted, I saw all the buildings were gone in the center of the city. Many people near me were dead, and the others were burned and crying."

He stayed on the platform for hours, administering, until it ran out, an emergency supply of pain-killing drugs he kept with him in a satchel. He didn't get to the hospital until the next day, and though its walls had withstood the explosion, the inside had been gutted by fire and thousands of survivors, many of them dying, were outside seeking help. "I knew then that Japan was defeated and the war had to end to stop the suffering. I had no special bitterness toward America. I only wanted the war over."

Dr. Shigeto said it is imperative the children of Japan be told what happened to Hiroshima. "It is our duty to see that an atomic bomb is never dropped again." Quoting from the inscription on the Cenotaph, he said the meaning is universal. "Everyone in the world must oppose atomic wars.

"There is still some bitterness among a few of the survivors, but there is very little anger. The Japanese have an important proverb. It is: The enemy of yesterday is the friend of today. Some Japanese still argue about whether the United States was justified in dropping the bomb on a civilian population. Many think the bomb should have been dropped where nobody lived, to show its power, and then, if the country didn't surrender, dropped on a city."

One thing Dr. Shigeto remembers is that after the war Americans came to help out in the Red Cross Hospital. Many medical men stayed on to work in the Atomic Bomb Commission, whose job it was to classify and study the survivors, charting their medical histories. The work of these Americans on the commission was resented by many Japanese, who contended they were using their countrymen as guinea pigs.

The A-Bomb Hospital, operating with an annual budget of under $700,000, treated 2,000 outpatients and 350 new patients in 1969. Almost any sickness of a survivor will be treated at the hospital, even those not remotely connected with exposure to radiation, so long as it is a natural disease and not something man-derived, such as a car accident or a self-inflicted wound. "Many patients continue to connect anything wrong with them today with the effects of the bomb, including diseases of the heart and liver, even when there is really no connecting evidence," Dr. Shigeto stated. He said statistics collected among the survivors showed there was a dramatic increase in leukemia and eye cataracts among those exposed directly to the bomb, but that these increases leveled off about 1952. But, he added, there has recently been another notable increase of cancer among the survivors, and at a higher rate than the national average.

The charts and statistics about the havoc created in the human body by the atomic bomb are of little moment to the students of the University of Hiroshima except for the small left-wing minority that uses them to justify a wide variety of assaults on the university administration. Most of the students appear to be materially sated and not very interested in world politics. Theirs is a self-centered contentment. "The greatest happiness is in doing anything I want," one student said. But these young Japanese are activists, if not for any clearly defined cause. "Several years ago we had demonstrations that shut down our university for a few weeks. They were against all authority, not against anything in particular."

These opinions were given in a round table discussion with a dozen students during a luncheon break, and they seemed to be fairly representative of those expressed among students in other parts of Japan:

"The students used to talk about the morality of the bomb, but not too much anymore. The only people who do are those in the left-wing peace movement who use the bomb for their own political purposes."

"Most students don't have any special feelings about the A-bomb. When they do talk about it, most qualify their opinions about whether it should have been used. They know any country who had it in the war would have probably used it. What if the Germans had invented it first?"

"When we hear the word 'U.S.A.' we don't think of atomic bombs but of joyous, gay people and of Vietnam. The U.S.A. is too big with too much money and weapons. It thinks of itself as the first race of the world and tries to protect all other countries. This idea got them into Vietnam."

"We love to travel but we're not interested in visiting America. The U.S. and Japan are too much alike today."

"The young are against Japan rearming. They believe if you are allowed to have small weapons, they become bigger and bigger."

At this time of their life, death is a distant abstraction to these young. So they never discuss death in connection with their post-atomic bomb life in Hiroshima, though death is the city's most marketable commodity, attracting thousands of tourists who come to the Peace Park to feel its overwhelming presence. Death is not a visitor to Hiroshima; it is a permanent resident, and it came to the city as death does to many in the modern world: absurdly, gratuitously, unexpectedly.

Hiroshima was selected to die because it met the requirements of those men planning to use the bomb on humans: It was a city which had not been previously attacked and the destructive force of the atomic bomb could be better studied, and it had a military installation, an army base in the center of the city which had been a collecting place for soldiers being shipped to conquered territories overseas. Having escaped death so long in the war, Hiroshima had to die quickly, as if it had to pay for living so long with what proved to be a false sense of security. A few voices in American military planning circles were raised about the wisdom of using the bomb on civilian populations, but the overriding consideration was with ending the war with as few American casualties as possible. Some contended the Japanese might be impressed by the horror of the bomb and surrender if it were dropped at sea, but this suggestion was not really explored because those who had invented the bomb, even after it was tested at New Mexico, didn't know what its actual destructive potential would be on a real target. The military feared the consequences, especially on the Japanese will to continue the war, if they did this and the bomb failed to explode, or if its destructiveness was found to be less than anticipated.

Although sirens were sounded when two American bombers were seen moving slowly against the blueness of a summer sky, the people didn't take refuge in air raid shelters. Instead, they went about their private business, riding in buses, walking along the banks of one of the seven rivers, or waiting at stations for trains to take them to work. Almost immediately after the bomb went off, in their new roles as the deceased they became statistics, and any personal feeling of horror was drained from their slaughter because they had become a cold impersonal set of numbers.

Today death in Hiroshima is on display in the chamber of horrors known as the Atomic Bomb Museum. At the entrance to the museum, a pleasant woman hands the visitor a machine with a taped lecture in English that describes what is in the specific glass-cased exhibits. The first ones are the least unnerving. On a table is a relief map of the city showing in scale the radius of destruction, and on the walls around it are photographs of the destroyed buildings. Arranged in glass cases are pieces of broken dishes and articles of burnt clothing.

But then the subjects of the photographs change from buildings to burnt humans, many of them children with layers of skin peeling from charred backs and arms. Glass jars contain parts of human bodies deformed by tumors produced by atomic radiation. In the yellowish liquid of the bottles, ruptured vital organs float, and the voice on the tape fails to express the unsettling sense of dread one gets from seeing these pieces of human bodies. Finally, the only recourse is to flee from the museum through a side door flanked on its side by a concession stand at which are sold pictures of the burnt victims and the ruins of buildings.

Relief is sought in the new and functional Hiroshima, riding in escalators through department stores overflowing with a variety of consumer goods, sipping tea with other customers in a restaurant, and seeing an American Western in a crowded theater. The canned American music in the hotel elevator and the skilled hands of the masseuse in the hotel room temporarily rid the visitor of the oppressive sense of death generated by this city. But the female hands and the music are not enough. Not even the children help, smiling and giggling in their yellow school caps as they climb over Hiroshima Castle, rebuilt completely after the explosion. Their laughter can't dispel this panic, and it is imperative to escape quickly from Hiroshima.

But one can't leave without returning for a last visit to the Peace Park to walk among the memorials. Parents are placing their children in front of the Cenotaph and taking pictures of them framed against the skeletal dome of the exposition building. The old man still sits there, recording the human traffic in his lifeless eyes. There is nothing left to experience in Hiroshima because everything has become overshadowed by the death that thrives there. What is Hiroshima? It is the twentieth century, and one cannot escape the city or the time. They are with us, the survivors, always. Hiroshima and death. They put us in restless flight from our destiny.

# NAGASAKI

While Hiroshima lives, almost exults in its atomic bomb encounter, Nagasaki, the second and last city to be subjected to nuclear attack, goes about trying to forget its experience. Everything about Nagasaki—the pace of life in its streets, the customers crowding the shopping arcades, the men day and night climbing up the scaffolding of new buildings or working the heavy machinery that is changing the skyline—presents a façade that tries to hide the city's part in an atomic holocaust. Because of this, Nagasaki is much more representative of modern Japan than is Hiroshima.

Its only reminders are a statue on a hill up the valley from the port and a museum with a collection of torn clothing, pieces of broken dishes, smashed clocks, and photographs of burnt corpses. The museum is on the second of the six floors of the International Cultural Hall. Displayed inconspicuously in a case near the main elevator is one of the leaflets dropped by Americans, warning residents of the atomic bomb and urging them to evacuate the city. Many of the survivors claimed they never saw the leaflets.

Nagasaki was destroyed on August 9, 1945, because bad weather over the primary target, Kokura, prevented visual bomb sighting. The B-29 named *Bock's Car* turned to its secondary target, the port city made famous in Puccini's opera, *Madame Butterfly*. Nagasaki, too, was almost saved by the same cloud covering, but just when the pilot of *Bock's Car* decided to head back to the Marianas, there was a break that allowed the plane to make its bomb run. A plutonium bomb, three times more powerful than the uranium variety exploded over Hiroshima, was detonated at 1,540 feet over the Urakami Valley above a Roman Catholic cathedral filled with late-morning worshipers. The time of the explosion, 11:02 A.M., is verified in the museum on the faces of broken and bent clocks, and at that moment the war in the Pacific was over, though the official Japanese surrender didn't come until August 15.

After the Americans dropped their second atomic bomb, Emperor Hirohito, who by tradition could not reverse a decision made by the country's political leaders, intervened and ordered the war stopped. His decision reflected the reality of his country's desperation. Most of its ports were blocked. Even though airplane production continued at an amazingly high rate, there were not enough pilots to man them, and Americans roamed the skies over Japan at will, reducing city after city to rubble. Food was rationed, and each person's daily meal was limited to 1,200 calories. When the emperor learned that in the two atomic explosions over his country 100,000 Japanese had been killed, he knew, better than did the militarist minority in his cabinet, that, even if the Japanese continued the fight, resisting an American invasion was futile.

Nagasaki's sole official monument to the bomb is in a park on a hill at the end of the Urakami Valley several miles up from the docks on Nagasaki Bay. It is incredibly ugly, portraying a huge green Buddha with one arm lifted toward the sky and the other outstretched parallel to the ground. A sign printed with many misspelled English words explains the meaning of the statue, which was erected by the city in 1955. The right hand is pointing to the sky to warn of the atomic bomb and the left is leveled to represent tranquil peace. The statue's eyes are closed in respect for the bomb's victims. But the statue is so grotesque that it is an object of mockery among the young who stand in front of it imitating the pose.

At the other end of the park is an oval-shaped reflecting pool with fountains of various heights. Although the park is popular with tourists, without a guide it is difficult for a foreigner to find his way since few signs are in English. The Cultural Hall is at the bottom of the hill from this park, but it might as well be in another city. Unmarked and without any signs pointing to it, it resembles every high-rise apartment going up in the valley, slowly blocking the splendid view of the bay from the park.

This memorial is treated less than reverently by the owners

of the refreshment stands across the street. Atop their establishments they have erected loudspeakers which alternate commercials for an American soft drink company with recordings of Dixieland jazz.

The Japanese, especially the young, want to be liked, and a boy in his early teens approached an American, identified by the expensive camera equipment around his neck, and asked him if he were new to Nagasaki. When he answered yes, the boy quickly interjected: "Of course, you like Nagasaki, don't you?"

Just beyond the park is the new Urakami Cathedral built over the ruins of the one destroyed by the bomb. No effort is made to connect it with the atomic attack, except for post cards and booklets sold at souvenir stands outside its main door and a few chipped, beheaded religious statues in a cluster of shrubs to the right of the entrance.

How has Nagasaki so disassociated herself from what should be the reason for her immortality? To begin with, it suffered fewer casualties than did Hiroshima. Again depending on whether the Japanese or American figures are used, either 35,-000 or 75,000 Japanese were killed. The Americans list 35,000 dead, 5,000 missing, and 60,000 injured. The Japanese say 73,884 were killed and 74,999 injured. There was also less devastation to Nagasaki's buildings. Although the bomb was exploded over an industrial complex located in the city's suburbs some miles from the downtown center, the line of mountains on each side of the valley tended to hold the effects of the bomb within a contained radius.

Nagasaki was a major port before the atom bomb, a role in the economy it has reassumed. It now possesses one of the largest piers in the world, and ships from all over come into its harbor, their passengers making their way up the hill to the house which was supposedly the inspiration for Puccini's opera.

There is daily air service with Tokyo, but none between Hiroshima and Nagasaki, the only available transporation being the train, and it is a long day's trip between the two. The cosmopolitan attitudes of Tokyo have not reached many of the provincial travelers on these trains. They eat from box lunches and small sacks of fresh fruit bought at the station and litter the aisles with the debris of their meals. The men also think nothing of changing their trousers on the train. They stand and drop them, exposing their legs in long underwear, and, trying to gain their balance in the swaying coaches, hop on one leg while jamming the other into a new, cleaner pair of pants. Nagasaki is still the center of Catholicism in Japan, and two passengers on the train, an American nun and her brother, a priest, seemed unfazed by the public disrobing.

Nagasaki is a city better entered at night when the lights from the ships in the harbor and the houses on the sides of the mountains form a corridor of light down which the train comes through the valley to the terminal a few blocks from the pier. The hotel catering to foreigners is near the station, and most of the guests are there after 11 P.M., by which time all the nightclubs have closed. A middle-aged American woman and her mother, resigned to watching alone the television set in the lobby, sip drinks from the hotel bar; two sailors off a Scandinavian ship, drunk and loud, shout obscenities at their Japanese whores while squeezing their breasts; two American businessmen go over a graph plotting their company's economic fortunes; and a homosexual Japanese salesman from Tokyo coyly flirts with a young employee.

"There is really nothing to do in Nagasaki," the middle-aged woman said. "We've been here too long already."

After she went to bed, the young Japanese hotel clerk said, "We don't think much about the atom bomb these days. But we remember it was dropped on Japan."

Though it is basically an uninteresting city, Nagasaki distracts her citizens from their past with enough material comforts to give them an illusion of security and well-being. The Nagasaki of today is not back up the hill in the shadow of the Buddha statue; it is in the shopping arcade near the hotel with all the things modern man is told makes his life worth living: cameras, stereos, jewels, electrical appliances, transistor radios. The moment is there in the windows, the rows of marvelously shiny gadgets, the today for which wars are forgotten, and

the crowd swirls by these windows and around an old man standing in the way, a sign in both Japanese and English printed on
a piece of cardboard hung around his neck. He is an old veteran,
and he denounces the crowd for forgetting man is born to die
by the sword. His shrieks can't rise above the noise of the shoppers, and his face, in the midst of a cry, is frozen into an agoniz-
ing expression of aloneness.

# Postlude

In war men die for things they might not believe in or personally experience, but they have been told by their country they must fight for these things because every war is fought for a just cause. When the shooting stops, new lives take the places of those who made the ultimate sacrifice, new buildings rise on the ruins, and a hillside shorn of its covering by bullets and grenades is reclaimed by weeds. The prints made by man and his weapons on the beach are washed away by the waves, and the graves settle into the earth.

Hawaii is a good place to remember the war in the Pacific, for the disorder of humans, surf boards, and discarded suntan lotion bottles on Waikiki Beach can make the past seem more attractive than the present. No longer is Honolulu a city of the past, a place remembered from the early days of the war; it is very much a city of the present, transformed by the demands of the tourists and a consumer society. The new hotels are awesome in their unfeeling heaviness—glass cubicles strung up a shaft of steel with balconies attached, large enough to hold two elderly persons playing gin rummy in the late afternoon shadows.

Because Hawaii's present economy is based on tourists spending a great deal of money there, it is necessary to provide more places of entertainment and living quarters. And this has taken precedence over saving the land and the institutions of the past. Hotels rise indiscriminately in front of Diamond Head, the one remarkable natural site in Waikiki, and when the residents of Honolulu are asked of what in the city they are proudest, they invariably say the mammoth two-tiered shopping center that extends over several city blocks. It is a mechanically efficient structure with escalators swiftly taking customers between levels of cement, while soothing canned music drifts innocuously over wide stone terraces with fountains and chairs. The stores are many and the goods varied, but there is something foreboding about them, a statement of values in the new Honolulu. The choice locations in front of the stores have been reserved for not shoppers, but cars, and all that can be seen from the main street are parked cars.

Some things have survived on Waikiki, and one of them is the Royal Hawaiian Hotel. Once the elite hotel on the beach, it is set back from the main street and kept in semiseclusion by a long rolling lawn covered with palm trees. But since the war a line of stores has gone up on the edge of the lawn between the hotel and the street, and its pink stucco architectural beauty is being ruined by two new ugly wings. Now it is a friendly, familiar hotel in a booming middle-class playground, patronized often by those who were young during the war returning to where it began.

On the beach are girls pinched into bikinis, followed by long-haired males denouncing the establishment, some of them stopping to smoke pot. These are the children of the American middle class which gained its affluence after fighting the war in the Pacific. Moving among the young are the parents, those who fought the war, many coming here for the first time since the early 1940's, having worked all these years to make the money to take a vacation at the spot where they were first exposed to the world. These men from the past seem oddly out of time and place, walking by themselves apart from the young in Bermuda shorts, loud-print aloha shirts outside their pants to hide their expanding stomachs.

Some of the young on the beach are temporary exiles from the current Asian war, here with their wives and girlfriends for a six-day leave, staying close to their women, building a protective intimacy against the moment in the future when they must return to Asia.

Then it is night, and the torches are lit on the patios of the seafront hotels, and the orange glows are splashed in streaks over the water. The young remain on the beach, sitting in tight circles to sing folk songs and debate politics. Some of the couples drift off to the darker recesses to make love. The middle-aged retreat to the tables on the terraces to eat and drink. But everything begins to close in on the memories—buildings, music, people—setting up distractions to those things one wants to remember a little longer.

Of them all the most vivid is the native father on Tarawa, carrying his son to the grave, meeting the worst in life with grace, being responsible to himself and his actions, an uncompromising obligation to manhood in a time when duty and self-restraint are mocked. He moves, as did the soldiers who preceded him on the islands, with the lyrical grace of those who do what they have to and then do more. And he and his kind will remain alive until night comes to all those who fought and still remember the war in the Pacific.

# Index

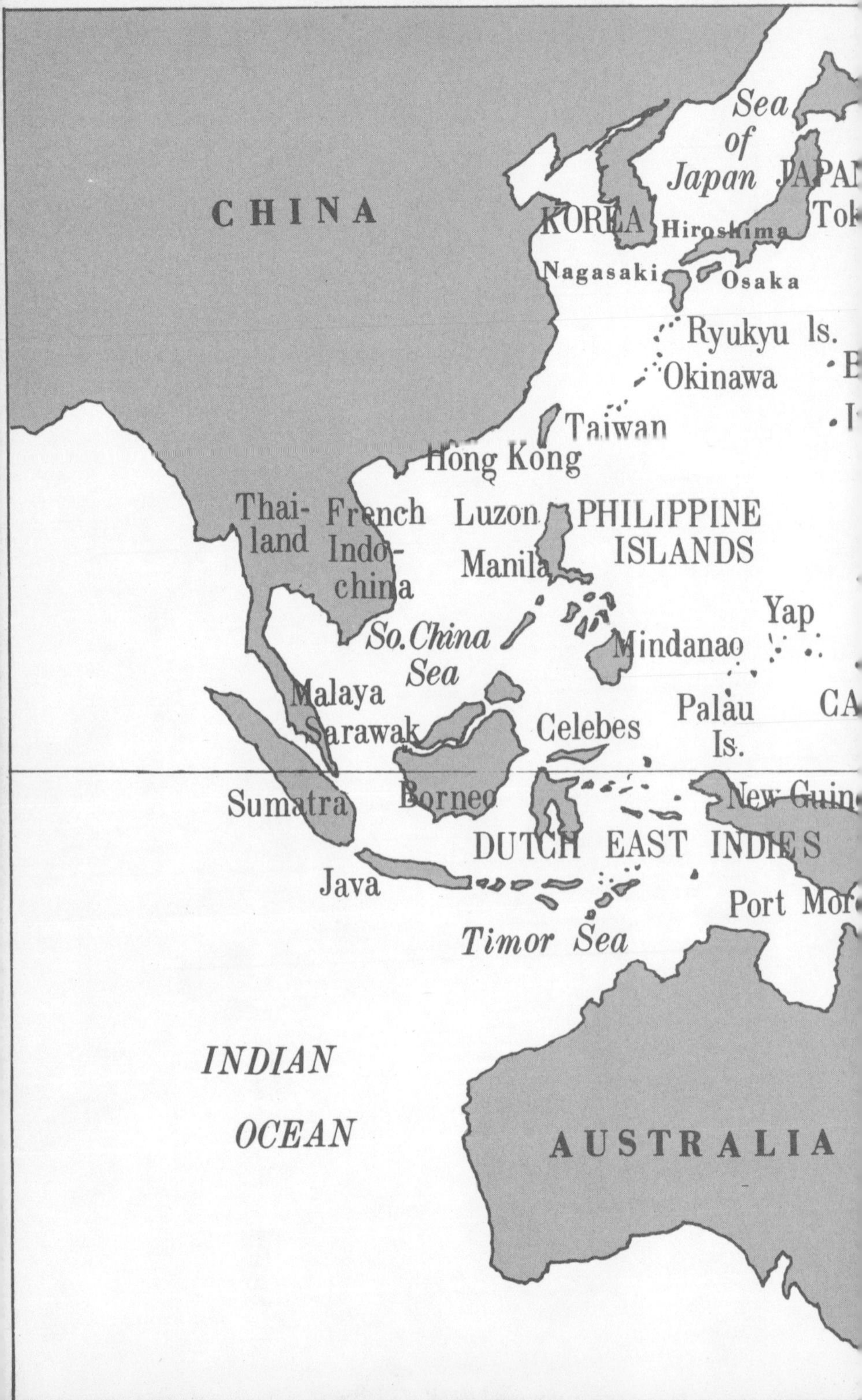
CHINA
KOREA
Sea of Japan
JAPAN
Hiroshima
Nagasaki
Osaka
Ryukyu Is.
Okinawa
Taiwan
Hong Kong
Thai-land
French Indo-china
Luzon
PHILIPPINE ISLANDS
Manila
So. China Sea
Mindanao
Yap
Malaya
Sarawak
Celebes
Palau Is.
Sumatra
Borneo
New Guin
DUTCH EAST INDIES
Java
Timor Sea
Port Mor
INDIAN OCEAN
AUSTRALIA